THE SCREAM SISTERS

A TROUBLED SPIRITS NOVEL

J.R. ERICKSON

COPYRIGHT

AUTHOR'S NOTE

The Scream Sisters is inspired by a true story. To avoid spoilers, that story is briefly retold at the end of this book.

PROLOGUE

With a yawn, she waited for the big hand on her Minnie Mouse watch to hit the twelve, signaling the end of her shift. She clocked out of her job at the Husher Student Store and left the Den.

Sometime in the hours she'd sat selling candy bars and energy drinks to fellow Husher students, night had fallen swift and black. No moon lit the dark sky and even the stars were obscured by heavy cloud cover.

She hitched her backpack higher, tightening the straps, and set off for her dorm, sandals clapping on the cement path.

Exhaustion tugged at the corners of her eyes. Her first week at Husher had started out perfectly. She'd made new friends, had a blast doing rush activities, met a boy. But in the previous forty-eight hours, her experience had turned, revealing the darker side of college life, and she suddenly longed for home.

She turned onto the dimly lit path that ran along a rarely travelled road on the north side of campus. She wasn't a fan of the isolated walkway, but it offered the fastest route back to Pine Hall.

Behind her, another set of footsteps joined her own, nearly

in sync. She started to glance back, but a trickle of unease crept between her shoulder blades and stirred the fine hairs at the base of her neck.

There was no reason for such paranoia, but it wasn't an easy emotion to rationalize. At night the mind was on full alert, ready to ward off an attack from a nocturnal predator, an instinct hard-wired from thousands of years of evolution, but hardly applicable to modern times.

She knew all those things, but picked up her pace just the same.

Behind her, the steps sped up as well.

She forced the corners of her lips into a smile and glanced back, intending to dispel the fear by getting a look at her night-time walking companion. The sight that greeted her nearly stopped her cold, but some survival instinct kept her legs moving even as her thoughts ground to a halt.

A masked and hooded person walked behind her. They wore all black, the only color the ugly burlap mask with slits for eyeholes and a crude black stitched mouth.

1

T wo Years Later

"IT'S REALLY HAPPENING. We're here. This is our school now," Harley marveled as they walked down the wide cement pathway flanked by trees thick with dark glossy leaves.

Ivy clung to the red-brick exterior of their dorm. The sun shone down, reflected off the dark windows, made Teagan shield her eyes as they approached the building.

"Yep," Teagan agreed, less enthused than her friend, but doing her best to hide it.

She was looking forward to their freshman year at Husher University, but didn't eye it with Harley's optimism. It was still school, after all, and only an hour north of their hometown of Baldwin-not exactly a new world. Not to mention classes, exams, rules, and then there was the cost. They'd both leave college with debt in the five figures, even with grant money and part-time jobs.

They wove through groups of girls in the lobby of Willow Hall, their home for the upcoming year, and trudged up the staircase to the second floor. Harley unlocked the door, and Teagan followed her into their dorm room.

With the help of Teagan's grandmother, they'd moved into the dorm the day before, but much of their stuff had yet to be unpacked. At least much of Teagan's stuff. Harley, the organized one in their duo, had not only hung all her clothes, arranged her desk, and plastered the walls with calendars and dry-erase boards, she'd coordinated her bookcase according to her class schedule.

"*Crush the Rush*?" Teagan read the large black and pink calligraphy on a booklet Harley had left on her desk.

"It's a guide to sorority recruitment."

Teagan flipped it open. "'Aim for extraordinary conversations! Nothing will kill your chances of getting into your ideal sorority quicker than yes and no responses! Elaborate!' There are a lot of exclamation marks in this book," Teagan mused.

Harley snatched it from her hand. "I happen to like exclamation marks."

"Oh, I know." Teagan pointed at the dry-erase board above Harley's computer with a bullet list of to-dos, each punctuated with an exclamation mark, the dot replaced with a heart.

"I've got to get changed. The All-Greek Meeting starts in forty minutes," Harley said, opening the closet door.

Teagan eyed Harley's shorts and t-shirt. "You put that on fresh this morning. Why do you have to change?"

"Because this"—Harley gestured at her outfit—"is not sorority-ready. Are you coming with me?"

"To a meeting about Greek life? No."

"Why not? It'll be fun. It's a great chance to make some friends."

"It's not my jam."

"Oh, come on. It's our freshman year. Step out of your comfort zone."

"I'm not going because if I witness one more public display of infection between two girls who 'can't believe we didn't see each other all summer!' I'll barf. Is that a suitable answer for you?"

"Affection, not infection," Harley corrected.

"I think I had it right the first time."

Harley gave her best friend a peeved look, pulling off her shorts and folding them in her drawer. "Seriously, T, you're going to miss all the good stuff with that attitude."

"The good stuff? Neanderthals and Barbie dolls talking over each other? No, thanks. Plus, it's better if you go without me so I can make a dent in all this chaos." Teagan pushed a cardboard box with the corner of her toe. "I know you're going to break out in hives if you have to live in this squalor for another day."

Harley laughed. "I would have died years ago if that were the case. You've seen my mom's cleaning skills."

Teagan sat on the edge of her bed, staring at her friend as she fussed with her hair in front of the mirror. "Why are you going? There have to be better ways to make connections than joining a sorority."

Harley braided her long hair and turned, her eyes serious. "Because this is my new start. The Harley Rand I want to be. I'm sick of being the rebel, the girl who gets driven to school on the back of her mom's motorcycle. She named me after her bike, for God's sake. I just want"—she dropped her voice—"a different life. Someday I want my kids to have a different life." Tears sparkled in her eyes.

"Hey." Teagan jumped off her little bed to a shout of rusted springs. She grabbed Harley and hugged her, patting her friend's glossy golden hair. "I take it back. Go to your meeting. Have fun. Rub elbows with the Chi Beta Kappa Omegas or whatever they're called. I'm sorry I judged you." Teagan rested her chin on Harley's head.

Harley sighed and leaned into her. "It's okay. You're judgey. It's one of the things I love about you."

"Hey." Teagan pulled away. "I'm not judgey."

"You so are. I watched you scanning the faces in the cafeteria this morning. You looked like you'd just eaten a wormy peach."

Teagan grinned. "I was merely scrunching my nose at the tidal wave of cotton candy- and peony-scented body sprays leaking out of every girl in the room."

Harley scowled and plucked a bottle from her nightstand. The body spray fragrance read 'Grapefruit Cotton Candy.'

"For real? Grapefruit cotton candy? In what universe is that a thing?"

"At Bath Girls," Harley insisted. "It's their hottest scent of the season." Harley directed the nozzle toward Teagan and released a sickly-sweet spray.

Teagan screamed and dove out of the way, landing on Harley's bed.

"Knock, knock!" someone yelled, pounding on the door.

Harley hurried over and answered it.

Two guys stood in the hall. They wore white t-shirts with blue jeans. "Hey, I'm Corbin, this is Mark. We build lofts during welcome week. Do you guys want lofts?"

Harley turned and looked at Teagan, puzzled. "Do we want lofts?"

"We don't even know what that is," Teagan said.

"Let me explain. May we come in?" Corbin flashed a smile so white and straight his teeth reminded Teagan of the plastic vampire teeth sold at Halloween.

Harley stepped back to allow the two boys inside, but Teagan walked over and blocked their entrance. "Hold up.

We're not letting random guys in our room. Do you have some I.D.?"

Corbin and Mark exchanged a grin. "Unfortunately, there's no laminated loft builder identification card, but"—he pulled a wallet from his back pocket and flipped it open—"here's my student I.D., driver's license, our business card and, if you have more faith in the Greeks, we're both members of Alpha Lambda. See?" He showed a card with his name, photo and several Greek symbols that Teagan didn't understand.

"You are?" Harley asked, gently pushing Teagan back into the room. "I'm rushing too. I've heard of Alpha Lambda."

Corbin gazed at Harley. "Very cool. Which sororities are you rushing?"

"My top picks without having met anyone are Rho Upsilon Nu, Delta Gamma, and Chi Omega, but I'm trying to stay open-minded."

"As well you should. We Lambdas are pretty tight with the Rhos. I'll make sure to put a good word in for you."

"Wow. Thanks. I would so appreciate that, and come in, please. Tell us about the lofts."

Teagan scowled at the two guys, who made the dorm room feel about as big as a matchbox. She backed to the far wall, mildly irritated that they'd invaded their space.

"Basically," Corbin said, "we build loft frames and boost your bed up to about this height." He held his hand at forehead height. "Frees up space beneath to put your dressers, maybe a couple of bean bags. Some people put their desks under there, but I always hit my head if I do that."

"How much does it cost?" Teagan asked.

Corbin glanced over, but Mark spoke first. "Fifty bucks apiece, fully installed."

"And we'll take your bed frames to the hall storage," Corbin added.

"It would be nice to have more room." Harley gave Teagan a hopeful look.

Neither Teagan nor Harley had an extra fifty dollars lying around, but begrudgingly Teagan nodded. They could come up with the money and she could see the glint of desperation in Harley's eyes, not only to have more space in the cramped room, but to potentially make a connection with the fraternity.

"Fine. What do we need to do?" Teagan asked.

Harley smiled and gave a little hop. Corbin grinned at her.

"We just need an hour when the room will be empty, and anything under your beds right now should get moved out of the way. When do we have an opening?" Corbin asked Mark.

Mark looked at a clipboard. "We can come back this afternoon? Around three?"

"That's great," Harley said.

"It works," Teagan agreed.

"You're on the schedule," Corbin told them as he and Mark moved toward the door. Halfway out, Corbin turned back. "One more thing, we're throwing a party at the Alpha Lambda house tonight. The two of you should come. It'll be great. It's nice to let off a little steam before the chaos of rush week."

Harley nodded. "Absolutely. We'll be there."

"We will?" Teagan asked after Harley closed the door.

Harley put on her droopy lip puppy face. "Please?"

Teagan sighed and flopped down on her bed, reached beneath and searched through her tote. "Fine, but I'm bringing this." She held up her pellet gun that could easily have passed for a real handgun.

"You did not bring that to school! Teagan, if someone sees that you'll get kicked out."

"It's a pellet gun."

"Put it away, and no, you are absolutely not bringing it to the party."

Teagan scowled and dropped the gun back into the tote. "We're not bonging any beers."

Harley laughed. "Eew, no. I once read that beer bongs are loaded with bacteria."

"Where exactly did you pick up that bit of trivia? One of your ten zillion magazine subscriptions?"

"I only have four. And yes, actually I think it was *Scientific American.*" Harley slipped on a pair of sandals. "Last chance to change your mind and go with me. You know, being in a sorority could probably help with getting into medical school."

"How is that?" Teagan propped her feet up on her pillows.

"Sororities are all about making connections. You might have sorority sisters whose dads work in big hospitals, some who are deans of colleges. It can open a lot of doors."

Teagan scowled. "If I can't get in by my own blood, sweat and tears, then I don't deserve to be there."

"It's not the worst thing in the world to have a little help."

"It is if that help requires pedicures and slumber parties with matching pajamas."

Harley laughed and bumped against Teagan. "You're such a toad."

"And you're such a frog. Frogs fit into sororities. Toads prefer one single very best friend and that's you. Come on, you've read the stories. Frog is Frog, Toad is Toad. You can't change 'em."

"No," Harley agreed. "And I wouldn't want to. You're going to bring me back down to earth when I start to float away on a frothy pink sorority cloud. And speaking of Frog and Toad"— Harley plucked her framed photo of the cover of the book *Frog and Toad are Friends* from the wall and set it near her desk—"I'll have to hang this above my desk now that the beds are going up."

2

Blair stared around the little dorm room with the two single beds shoved against the cinderblock walls that had been painted an off-putting beige color. Creeper vines strangled the view from the single window that looked out on the quad below.

"Oh..." Her mother pushed into the room and rested a hand, fingernails freshly painted pink on her chest. "It's just how I remember it. My goodness, so many memories are enclosed in these walls."

Blair considered the walls again, the lumps of uneven concrete beneath the waxy-looking paint.

"You should choose this bed," her mother said, lifting the heavy floral-print suitcase onto the mattress. "It's closer to the window."

Her dad struggled into the room carrying a massive blue tote. He set it down, wincing and rubbing his lower back. "Good grief, Blair. Did you pack bricks for your first year at college?"

"No," her mother said sharply. "She packed books because

Blair is our smart girl. Aren't you? And soon to be a Rho Upsilon Nu."

"Mom, you don't just get to be in the sorority. You have to rush."

Her mother plastered on a simpering smile. "You'll get in. You're Margo Davenport's daughter."

"Lunch reservations at one sharp," her dad interjected, tapping his Rolex. "Blair, are you joining us?"

Blair opened her mouth to say no. They'd had lunch at the country club when they'd visited Husher for her orientation. It had been stuffy, reeking of expensive cologne and filled with the drawl of men talking about their golf game and sports cars. "I think I'll stay and get unpacked."

Her mother pouted. "But today is meant to be our day. We're leaving you at school and—"

"Mom..."

As if remembering who had the power, her mother stood up straighter. "Genevieve and Fiona will be there with their own daughters. You have to go. It's not open for debate."

AN AGONIZING TWO HOURS LATER, after her mother paraded her to half the tables at the country club, Blair and her mother returned to her room in Willow Hall.

Blair was exhausted and overwhelmed. She wanted to be alone, to sink her hands into some clay or take her sketchpad to the quad.

"These are your outfits for rush week," her mother said, pointing to the rack in the tiny closet. "I didn't want to ruin them with labels, but I marked each in your planner."

"Great, thanks," Blair murmured. "I think I'll take a walk around campus and just get a feel for things."

"You can't. We're scheduled for manicures at five."

"What? Why? We just got my nails done three days ago." Blair waved her hand as evidence of the recent manicure.

Her mother grabbed her hand and pursed her lips. "And then you spent yesterday ruining them with your Play-Doh. Look!" Blair's mother thrust her fingers closer, pointing out the barely discernible gray blotches edging her cuticles.

"It's clay, Mom. Not Play-Doh. And my nails look fine."

"Fine? Is that what you think Rho Upsilon Nu wants—fine? And while we're on the subject of rush week, remember during your interviews, no 'umms,' no 'you knows,' no fidgeting." Her mother's eyes sharpened. "And none of this!" She plucked Blair's pale hair from between her fingers. "I told you before and I'll say it again, sororities want girls with long blonde hair, but if we have to chop this all off to stop you playing with it like some insolent child, that's what we'll do. Don't look at me like that. It's not a threat. You'd be divine with short hair. People could finally see those enormous green eyes and your lovely cheekbones." She pressed a thumb into one of Blair's prominent cheekbones.

Blair winced, but said nothing.

"Emergency!" Her mother spun away from Blair and returned with a pair of tweezers. "Hold still, you have a runaway brow hair."

The door opened and a girl wearing a Mackinaw City Comets ball cap, wrinkled t-shirt, and cut-off shorts stood in the doorway.

"Hi," she said, smiling. She held out her hand as she walked into the room. "I'm Colette. You must be Blair."

Blair stepped away from her mom and extended her own hand to Colette.

"This is my mom, Alley," Colette said, gesturing at a woman who dragged in a green tote on wheels.

"Great to meet you, Blair," Alley said, hoisting the tote onto the bed Blair hadn't claimed. Alley's hair was tucked beneath a bandana.

"This is my mom, Margo," Blair offered.

Margo grabbed Blair's hand and pulled her toward the door. "Lovely to meet you both," Margo said. "Blair and I are late for our manicures. We'll give you a little time to settle in." Blair's mother dragged her into the hallway.

"Where are we going?" Blair asked as they moved toward the stairs. "You said the manicures were at five."

Margo blew out a breath and wrung her hands. "Colette is unfortunate, but maybe it's not too late to request a new roommate, or even a solo room."

"What? Why?"

Margo pushed through the door to the stairway, then shot her daughter a sharp look. "Why? She's clearly not a future Rho Upsilon Nu. I specifically requested a girl who intended to join a sorority, preferably a Rho. And did you see her mother? My God, she was wearing a men's flannel, for Christ's sake. This is a disaster. A complete disaster."

Blair said nothing as she followed her mom down the stairs, through the front hall bustling with girls, to the administration office. Margo rapped her knuckles on the door and a moment later, a tall, thin woman wearing jeans and a Husher University t-shirt opened the door.

"Hi there. How can I help you?" she asked, smiling first at Margo, then Blair.

"I'd like to speak with you about my daughter's room situation," Margo said.

It was after seven when Blair finally returned to her dorm room to find Colette stuffing the last of her clothes into her dresser.

"I hate unpacking," she told Blair.

"Yeah, me too," Blair murmured, though she hadn't actually unpacked. Her mother had put away all of her things, arranging skirts and dresses based on the events scheduled during rush week.

"Do you like the show *The Crown*?" Colette asked. "My mom and I have been totally obsessed with it." She turned on the television that hung in the corner of the room.

"I've never seen it." Blair eyed a book Colette had set on her bedside table. On the cover it showed a pretty stone cottage with a silhouette of a person standing in an attic window. "*The Babysitter*," she read out loud. "*The Disturbing Disappearance of Laurel Shannon*. Is this any good?"

Colette, who'd been adding login information to a streaming channel, glanced at the book. "My mom actually wrote it. It came out this year. It's about a true crime that happened in the Upper Peninsula."

"Wow, really? Your mom wrote it?"

Colette nodded. "Yeah. It's a totally crazy story that she ended up in the middle of. She actually found out what happened to Laurel after the case had been cold for years. You can read it if you want."

"Maybe. I haven't read a book for pleasure in ages."

"What books have you been reading then? Just stuff for school?"

"Yeah, and..." Blair thought of the stack of books her mother had insisted she read over the summer to prepare for rushing. Titles like *How to Be Interesting* and *Traits of the Irresistible Woman*. "Books to help prepare for Greek life."

"Greek life? As in sororities and fraternities?"

"Yeah. I'm rushing. Are you?"

Colette made a face. "No, probably not. I hadn't really thought about it, but..." She shook her head. "I don't think I'd fit in with a sorority."

Blair wanted to say 'me neither,' but the words stayed lodged in her brain. Uttering them would have felt like a betrayal of her mother, who'd been preparing her for joining a sorority since she was a child. "I'm a legacy at Rho Upsilon Nu, so that's my first choice."

"What's a legacy?"

"My mom was a member. It's a big deal to her, so I'm trying to get in there."

"That's neat. I'll be curious to hear how it goes. Hopefully there's none of that crazy stuff that happens in movies like getting spanked with a paddle. Have you seen *Animal House*?"

Blair shook her head. "Spanked with a paddle? I sure hope not."

Colette laughed. "I bet it's all made up. Want to watch this with me?" She gestured at the opening credits of the show.

"Maybe another night. I'm going to head to the fitness center. I'll see you later."

Before she left, Blair grabbed her sketchpad with plans to do a bit of drawing in one of the quieter community rooms before heading to bed.

3

"So, wait," Teagan said, as she and Harley walked across Husher Campus toward Greek Row. "Showing up at this frat that is buddied up with the Rho Upsilon Nu girls will somehow get you into their good graces? That's why instead of staying in our room to watch *Grey's Anatomy*, we're trekking half a mile to a house full of dudes drinking foamy beer and wearing tight t-shirts?"

Harley slipped her arm behind Teagan's back and squeezed her closer. "Exactly! I talked to Heather, one of the Rho girls, today, and she said the sisters want to see the potential new members being social. When the girls are social, the sorority ranking goes up because the frat rates them higher and—"

"Wait, their ranking? What's a ranking?"

"Well... it's like how they're perceived as a sorority. A higher ranking means they're more desirable." Harley waved off the comment. "It doesn't matter. The point is Heather said she knows for a fact she got invited to pledge Rho Upsilon Nu because she went to a couple of frat parties during rush week and the guys put in a good word for her and the Rho girls saw how fun she was, so..."

"How many blow jobs did she have to give?"

"Shut up." Harley laughed, knocking her hip against Teagan's. "Gosh, you're so crude."

"Just keepin' it real. You know those frat guys aren't putting in a good word thanks to Heather's stimulating conversations."

They turned on the street that held the fraternities and sororities. It was not yet full dark, but all the houses were ablaze with lights.

"Aren't these houses amazing?" Harley asked. "I'll show you Rho Upsilon Nu. We walk right by it to get to the Alpha Lambda fraternity."

Teagan gazed at the huge brick houses flanked by flowering bushes and perfectly trimmed lawns. Most of them seemed to be hosting parties. Students herded into the front yards, drinking, throwing frisbees, or playing beer pong.

"That's it," Harley said, nodding toward a house. She watched it from the corner of her eye as if she didn't want to be seen gawking at it.

Rho Upsilon Nu occupied a large Tudor-style red-brick mansion. Green leafy bushes, neatly trimmed, covered the face of the house beneath the first-floor windows. Twinkle lights hung from the trees, and girls dressed in Greek t-shirts clustered on the lawn.

"Huh," Teagan muttered. "It's all right, I guess, but can you imagine the electric bill?"

Harley giggled. "Or the water bill in a house with like twenty girls?" Half a block down, Harley pointed at a three-story white colonial with enormous pillars flanking the front door. "Alpha Lambda," she murmured, slowing as if suddenly unsure about attending the party.

"Last chance to turn back," Teagan offered. "Popcorn and *Grey's Anatomy* could be yours."

Harley took a deep breath and shook her head. "Nope. Carpe diem. We're going in."

"I'm much fonder of the saying 'JOMO.'"

"JOMO? What's that?" Harley asked.

"'Joy of missing out,'" Teagan told her.

Harley grinned, looped her arm through Teagan's and dragged her toward the front door.

"TEAGAN, this is Brody. He's an Alpha Lambda."

Teagan eyed the tall, broad guy who wore a scorchingly bright red button-down shirt, open at the collar to reveal a necklace with a Greek symbol. He smiled, white teeth glowing, and draped an arm casually around Harley.

"Ooh! Salt-N-Pepa!" he said. "Get it?" He pointed first at Harley then Teagan. "Blonde hair, black hair. Salt and pepper?"

Harley offered an unconvincing laugh.

"Harley tells me you're not rushing." He pouted, eyeing Teagan. "Don't you want to make new friends? The Rho Upsilon Nu girls are besties with the Alpha Lambda guys. Think about all you'll be missing."

Teagan didn't bother hiding her repulsion at the suggestion, not to mention at Brody himself. Everything about him struck her as false and potentially dangerous, a wolf in sheep's clothing.

"Darn," she said dryly. "I'm really going to be missing out."

Brody's eyes narrowed, but he kept his smile plastered on. He leaned close to Harley and whispered in her ear. She blushed.

"Looks like that drink's running low," he said, peering into Harley's plastic cup. "Let me refill you. And you too, Teagan." He snatched the red plastic cup from Teagan's hand, though it was more than half full, as was Harley's.

"Whatever he brings back, we're not drinking it," Teagan said.

Harley frowned, watching him weave through people at the party. "What? Why not?"

"Because he's a clodpole who's probably slipping us both roofies as we speak."

Harley's eyes widened. "No. Teagan, come on. He wouldn't do that."

"Bullshit. You're not drinking it. Here." Teagan walked to a box of beer someone had set near the couch. She pulled out two cans, lukewarm, and popped the top for Harley.

Harley wrinkled her nose. "It's beer, and did you just call him a clodpole?"

"It's better than jungle juice with a roofie kicker. If you want to look social, drink this, but seriously, Harley, steer clear of that guy. He's oozing bad intentions. And yes, I said clodpole."

Harley leaned into Teagan. "You're so suspicious of everyone."

"Not everyone. That guy looks fine." Teagan pointed at a tall, thin guy perched on a couch reading a book with one hand, a beer that he'd likely not touched in the other.

"Who comes to a party like this and reads?" Harley asked. "He's the most suspicious one of all."

"Maybe," Teagan agreed, "but we could both take him, so that makes me feel better."

"Oh, jeez, that's her," Harley whispered, nodding toward a tall, slender girl with blonde hair that hung to her waist. "Sloan, the president of Rho Upsilon Nu."

"Huh. She doesn't look that intimidating. Go talk to her."

Harley bit her lip and nodded. "Okay. You're right. I'm going. Wish me luck."

"Break a leg," Teagan said. "Hers, not yours."

Harley stuck her tongue out at Teagan and then strode toward the girl, feigning confidence.

Color crept into Harley's face and she nervously chewed her bottom lip. Teagan forced her eyes elsewhere and wandered to another part of the room, not wanting to make Harley even more uncomfortable.

"Having fun?" a voice asked.

Teagan looked up to see the guy she'd noticed on the couch with the book standing beside her.

"How could I not be? What's more exhilarating than keg stands?" She gestured at a guy flipped upside down, his friends holding his legs as he slurped beer from the keg spout.

He grinned. "Want to walk outside? There's a great back patio here and tonight there's an alleged meteor shower."

"Umm... no. I'm not big on traipsing through the woods with random frat guys at night."

He laughed. "It's a backyard, not a forest."

A guy with a tray of red and blue shots stopped in front of them. "Red for the ladies, blue for the boys," he told them.

"None for me tonight, Ray," the guy beside her said.

"I'm good," Teagan added.

"Probably a wise choice," he told Teagan. "A study last year showed girls at fraternity parties are three times more likely to be given the date rape drug than at a regular campus party."

Teagan stared at him, incredulous. "Shouldn't you be guarding that secret with your life? You're in a frat and you're handing out that fact like it's a solo cup of Pabst Blue Ribbon."

He laughed, gray eyes sparkling. "You think I'm in this frat? I'm flattered, or maybe I'm offended. I'm not in a fraternity. I'm a T.A. for one of Corbin's poli sci classes and he invites me to all their parties. He's trying to butter me up for a good grade because he's applying to grad schools."

"Oh... jeez. Now the book makes sense." Teagan gestured at the book in his hand. "And here I was thinking they had a kid in this frat who could read."

"Oh, don't underestimate these guys. Not only can they read, but a lot of these fraternities will produce the top achievers of their generations. They're smart, they're clever, and some of them are totally decent human beings—most of them, even. I think of fraternities like the law enforcement and military. A lot of really great people are attracted to those organizations because there's a brotherhood, a call to service, but there's another segment that's attracted to the power that comes with those roles. Same with fraternities. And sororities, for that matter."

He winked at Teagan and she stared at him, appalled. "I'm not rushing a sorority."

"Oh, believe me, I know. You could have worn a t-shirt that shouted your disdain for sororities and it wouldn't have conveyed your feelings better than the look on your face when you were staring down those Rho Upsilon Nu girls over there."

"You were watching me?"

He shrugged. "I watch everyone. That's why I like parties. I'm a people-watcher. I mean that in an entirely uncreepy way."

She wrinkled her nose. "Maybe don't say it out loud then."

"You're what? A freshman? Sophomore?"

"Freshman."

"I thought so."

Teagan rolled her eyes. It was true, but his comment bothered her anyway, as if pointing out how obvious it was that she was new and out of place. "And what are you, then?"

"A senior."

"A legit senior or one of those guys who takes seven years to complete college so he can keep going to frat parties?"

His eyes lit up at the suggestion. Rather than being annoyed by her abrasive comments, he seemed to delight in them. "Believe it or not, I am managing to graduate in four years. Though I strongly considered adding a minor in German, which would have tacked on another semester or two."

"And then what?"

"I'll head to Wayne State next year to start my master's in public administration. I'm Lex, by the way," he told her.

"Teagan," she offered, jumping back as the guy doing the keg stand spurted beer halfway across the room. "All right, let's go out back. That guy's going to puke and I don't want to be in the line of fire."

"Good choice," he said. "This way."

Teagan followed Lex down a hall and through the enormous kitchen crowded with students to double glass patio doors. The backyard was an extension of the party. Students stood on the brick patio that surrounded an in-ground pool. Teagan stared at a guy in the pool pretending to make out with an inflatable unicorn. "What were you saying about frats turning out top achievers?"

Lex looked at the guy in the pool and chuckled. "Everybody's gotta let loose somehow. So, tell me about you, Teagan. What's your major?"

"Pre-med."

"You're pre-med?" He raised an eyebrow.

"What's with the tone?" she snapped.

He shrugged. "I'd imagine most future doctors have a slightly more pleasant bedside manner."

"I'm not at your bedside. I'm talking to you at a frat party on a campus I've lived in for less than forty-eight hours. I know you're used to those girls"—she pointed to the side of the house where two girls swayed drunkenly—"but I'd like to make it home without getting groped or worse."

"At the rate you're going, I suspect you'll be successful."

"Good," she said dryly.

Lex tilted his head up and studied the sky. "I'm afraid Greek Row is a bit too lit, no pun intended, to see the meteor shower tonight."

Teagan looked up as well, but the lights from the house blotted even the stars out.

"Lex, you out here?" a guy wearing a t-shirt that said *This Guy Needs a Beer* called from the back door.

"Yep. Over here." Lex waved a hand.

"I need you to settle a debate about whether the voting system is democratic."

Lex chuckled and nodded at Teagan. "It was interesting, Teagan. I'll see ya around."

Teagan said nothing as he disappeared back into the house. She checked her phone. They'd been at the party for nearly an hour. Maybe Harley would have put in enough face time to call it quits.

4

Teagan wove back through the throngs of students in the house and found Harley standing alone. Teagan stopped and watched her.

Somewhere in the previous years, Harley had lost her gangly awkwardness and turned into a knockout. It wasn't that Teagan had never noticed, but she'd always been up close—heard her friend grow breathless and hiccup when she laughed too hard, witnessed her trip as she grew into her too-long legs. They'd gone through their funky pre-teen years together battling acne, and the dawning realization of PMS, bras, armpit hair.

Now Harley looked like some iconic actress in her long black skirt and white blouse, her wheat hair flowing over her shoulders, her cheeks pricked pink by a summer in the sun. Teagan pulled in a hitching breath, simultaneously proud of her friend and terrified of the way the girls and guys at the party watched her—either with jealousy or unconcealed lust.

"What are you looking at?" Teagan asked, pausing beside her friend and leaning her head on Harley's shoulder.

"The graduating classes of Alpha Lambdas through the years," she said.

Teagan stared at the wall of photographs. Harley was studying the graduating class of 1996. In each of the group photos, the brothers wore dark suits, their hair neatly combed, handkerchiefs poking from the pockets of their jackets. "Are these the same guys I just saw dry-humping an inflatable unicorn in the pool?"

Harley made a face. "No?"

"Yes, I assure you it's happening as we speak. Are you ready to get out of here?"

"Affirmative," Harley said.

They left the party and started back for the dorm.

"Who was the cute bookworm you snuck outside with?" Harley asked as they walked the dark streets.

"Cute? I'd hardly call him cute."

Harley shot her a look. "You're kidding, right? I'd call him hot if I didn't loathe that word, unless I'm referring to curry, at which point 'hot' is an appropriate adjective. You know who he reminds me of? Robert Pattinson."

"Oh, God, not the vampire obsession again. I thought you'd moved on from *Twilight*."

Harley giggled. "I'll never move on from *Twilight*, but enough about fictional vampires. Tell me about the guy."

"His name is Lex. He's a senior, a T.A. for some political science professor. Blah, blah, blah. You tell me about the girls. Did you find out the secret in-code for surviving rush week and getting picked as the princess of Rho Upsilon Nu?"

Harley laughed. "Unfortunately, no. Sloan said hi, but otherwise barely acknowledged me, which makes me feel super nervous about the start of interviews tomorrow."

"You'll kill it during the interviews. She was probably drunk tonight. Every other person in that house was."

Harley held up her fingers and Teagan wound her own

through Harley's, which created an awkward four-fingers-crossed mash-up they'd been doing since childhood.

"Fingers crossed," Harley murmured.

Teagan pushed open the dorm door after class the next day to find Harley standing in the center of the room, face creased with worry. Colorful flowery skirts and dresses covered their beds and hung from every available surface. Shoes lined one wall. Earrings and necklaces populated their desks.

"Ah, I see. You wanted these lofts so you could turn them into a giant clothes rack," Teagan said, eyeing Harley's clothes.

Harley didn't smile. She picked up a yellow dress. "What do you think of this one? Too bright?"

"If you're attending a funeral, definitely."

Harley glowered at her. "It's rush week and today is the first round of interviews. Hello? Weren't you listening to me last night?"

"When you were droning on after midnight? No. I was sleeping, which is what you obviously should have been doing."

Harley's eyes went wide, and she hurried to the mirror, leaning close. "Why, do I look tired? Are there bags under my eyes?"

"Harley, you look ready to be on the cover of *Cosmo*. Stop freaking out. Here." Teagan picked up a black dress. "This is my favorite."

Harley winced and shook her head. "I can't wear black on the first day."

"I thought this was about sisterhood and philanthropy. Does the color of your dress really matter?"

"You just don't get it, Teagan. You've never cared about this stuff, but for me..." Her voice cracked and tears spilled down her face.

Teagan stepped to her friend and hugged her. "Okay, okay, I hear you. I'm sorry. Don't cry and get your face all blotchy. Tell me how I can help."

"I need something fun, not too formal, that shows my personality."

Teagan nodded, surveyed the outfits. "All right. I'm looking for the quintessential Harley ensemble. I vote for the light orange dress, the white shoes, the dangling white hoop earrings and, umm"—Teagan bit her lip—"no necklace. The color is fancy enough."

Harley, who'd collected the items as Teagan spoke, held the dress against her body in front of the full-length mirror. "You're sure? You think this one?"

"Yep. That's the one. Definitely."

"When I bought this dress, you said I looked like a ruffly peach."

Teagan grinned. "I've changed my disparaging ways. I think it's perfect."

It was after six when Teagan heard Harley's key in the lock. A moment later, the door opened and Harley walked into the dorm room.

"All right, spill. Did Rho Upsilon Nu immediately invite you to join and offer you a room in the sorority house? You better say no to that last question."

Harley sat in her chair, face troubled. "I don't think I did well."

"What? Come on. There's no way you didn't do well. What makes you say that?"

Harley smoothed the hem of the orange dress, spotted a

piece of lint and plucked it off. "The president of Rho Upsilon Nu, Sloan, asked about my family. She didn't just ask, she grilled me, and... I had to answer. How could I not, right? If I get in, they'll find out anyway, but when I said my dad was in prison, she just"—Harley waved at her face, tears welling in her eyes—"went blank, like the interview was over. She still asked me a few more questions, but I could tell she'd written me off, which made me talk faster and stumble over myself."

"Fuck her then."

Harley pressed her lips tight and tears rolled over her cheeks. "They're all going to feel that way. No one wants a sorority sister whose dad is in prison and whose mom is... is..."

Teagan waited, watched her friend warring with how to describe her mother, who could hardly be defined as mother of the year. "Human," Teagan finished. "Your mom is human. She's flawed, sure, but show me one of those Upsilon girls who isn't."

"You should have seen the house, T. The floors were all covered in white rugs, like perfectly white. Pink and white and gold furniture. It smelled like fresh flowers and they had them everywhere in these big glass vases."

"White carpets? That's just poor decorating. It's full of college girls, for God's sakes. They probably stuffed all the grimy brown rugs in the closet and pulled out the white ones to scare the new rushes. I don't buy it. Isn't the entire purpose of a rug to wipe your dirty feet on?"

"Not these ones," Harley said wistfully.

"So, tell me about the other interviews. Did any of them feel like maybes?"

"I think so. I mean, the sister at Chi Omega didn't ask anything at all about my family. She asked about my high school curriculars, jobs, my plans while I'm here at Husher."

"And you liked her?"

"Yeah, she seemed really down-to-earth."

"Then that's great."

"Except they probably talk. The president at Rho Upsilon Nu will tell Chi Omega and all the other sororities that my dad's in prison. By the end of the week the whole Greek community will know and I'll be canceled."

"Canceled? When did your show air?"

Harley didn't smile.

"Harley, seriously, if these girls are shallow enough to disregard you because of your dad's shitty choices then they don't deserve you. Hello? If anything, they should be fighting to get you. Look at all you've accomplished despite having a dad in prison. You're a diamond in the rough. They've all had it handed to them. You're the one who's special, not them."

Harley's face brightened, but only slightly. It didn't matter what Teagan said, Harley had wanted to join a sorority for years. It was one of the primary goals of her young life, a goal that Teagan absolutely could not relate to, and it made her furious that the Rho Upsilon Nu girl had left her feeling inadequate.

5

The first days of school had both dragged and flown. Blair had attended classes, her favorite being Intro to Sculpture, gone to rush events, and fallen into bed each night exhausted.

Amid her busy schedule, her mother called incessantly, demanding they video-chat so she could approve Blair's rush outfits, check her hair and nails and lecture her on how to make a good first impression with the sisters at Rho Upsilon Nu.

Now Blair stood in line for breakfast in the cafeteria, eyes gritty, wishing instead of rush events she could go back to bed.

She watched two girls who sat at a table, their heads close together, dark hair and blonde hair merging to create a shield of solidarity as they murmured above their bowls of cereal.

They were an odd pair. The dark-haired girl wore ripped jean cut-offs and a t-shirt that said *Tacos are Life*. The blonde wore a sleeveless white blouse paired with a yellow skirt. They were both pretty, the blonde in a more traditional way, while the dark-haired one had an edgy, stay-back sort of energy. Blair had seen the blonde at rush activities and suspected she too was hoping to pledge Rho Upsilon Nu.

They had that elusive 'best friend' energy that Blair had always coveted, but never experienced. She'd had friends, sure, but no one she confided her deepest secrets to. Her journal held those, her art, her head, but as she looked at the two girls whispering over their breakfast, likely sharing the overwhelm of their first week at college, she longed for such a friend.

The dark-haired girl looked up as if she sensed someone watching her. Their eyes locked, and Blair turned, walked her tray of fruit and cottage cheese into the back of a guy who'd just emerged from the food line. He jumped when the cold cottage cheese splattered down his legs.

"Oh, shoot, I'm sorry," she mumbled.

He turned, glanced down at the spilled food, and shrugged. "Not a big deal. Here, let me help."

Together, they mopped up the spilled cottage cheese.

Blair didn't bother returning to the food line. She dumped her tray in the trash and hurried from the cafeteria.

BLAIR'S PALMS sweated as she followed several other potential new members, including the blonde girl from the cafeteria, up to the house and to the front door of Rho Upsilon Nu.

The girl turned and smiled at her. "I'm Harley," she said.

"Blair," Blair offered, hoping the girl didn't try to shake her hand and discover how sweaty it was.

"You're living in Willow Hall too?" Harley asked.

Blair nodded, but before she could say more the front door to Rho Upsilon Nu opened and the girls were ushered inside.

Heather, who Blair had met the previous day, intercepted her in the foyer as another sister led the rest of the potential members into a sitting room where several Rho Upsilon Nu sisters waited for them with clipboards balanced on their knees.

"As a legacy, you're going to come with me for a quick tour, Blair. Okay?"

"Sure." Blair watched the other pledges disappear into the sitting room. Harley shot her a nervous, but hopeful look.

Heather started down the hall, glancing back at her and smiling. "We are so excited to have you here. You still have to rush, technically, but"—she lowered her voice—"your mom and Sloan's mom go way back. And your mom is kind of a legend around here." Heather led Blair to a second living room arranged with pink and white loveseats and club chairs. An enormous framed photo hung above the fireplace with Blair's mom front and center. "The year she was president, Rho Upsilon Nu had its highest ranking."

"Wow," Blair murmured, staring at the picture of her mother with her long blonde hair tossed over her shoulders. Her pink and gold strapless dress hugged her perfect figure. All of the girls in the photo were pretty, but Margo Davenport was stunning.

"So anyway," Heather went on, "this is the more formal living room where we do meetings and whatnot. This rocking chair is an antique. It's been here since the very first chapter of Rho Upsilon Nu at Husher University. We also have a memento from every class. That fox on the mantel is bone china from a super-old Rho class. This year we're adding a crystal fox—that's our mascot. See?" Heather lifted her hair to reveal a dangling plastic fox earring with a jeweled eye.

"That's really cute," Blair said, following Heather out of the room and into an enormous kitchen with marble countertops and stainless-steel appliances. It reminded her of her kitchen at home and Blair wondered if her mother had modeled it after her former sorority.

"Bathroom, coat closet, laundry room." Heather pointed through doorways as they walked. They backtracked to the front of the house and walked upstairs. Many of the doors in the long second hallway were closed. Little decorative signs hung on the doors with names. "These are the bedrooms. A few of the girls are in there studying, but I've left my room open for tours, so here it is."

Blair stepped into the brightly lit room, awash in pink and gold.

"Obviously pink and gold are our colors at Rho, so I totally decked out my room in pink and gold, which you don't have to do. Mindy and Kate are in the room across the hall from me and they stick with white. White bedspread, white curtains, white dressers. Everything is white.

"Full bathrooms at either end of the hall and then a handful of rooms share baths. Sloan and I each have single rooms and we share a bathroom." Heather looked at her cell phone. "Time for you to see Sloan. Let's walk back downstairs."

Blair cast a final glance at the room and tried to calm her nerves. She wished she'd gotten back in line in the cafeteria and eaten something. Her stomach growled and she felt light-headed.

"You don't need to worry too much about the talking points," Heather said. "I mean, look at you. You're even prettier than your mom. God. It's like... you could totally be an actress or something, which, not to disparage one of my sisters, will drive Sloan wild. She's the prettiest girl at Rho right now, but all that's about to change."

Heather walked Blair back to the living room where the photo of her mother hung.

"Blair!" Sloan beamed, pulling her in for a hug. "I cannot believe how much you look like your mother." She gestured at the picture above the fireplace. "Come in and have a chat with me. This is all just a formality, of course," she whispered in Blair's ear, guiding her toward the two white club chairs.

Blair sat across from Sloan, smoothing her hands over the skirt of her pink dress.

"Beautiful and perfect for Rho at every level," Sloan said, waving a sheet of paper with Blair's name at the top. "You had a 4.0 GPA, very good. And I see in your extracurriculars you played tennis and ran track, lovely. Tell me about your major here at Husher."

Blair considered her major: business administration. She didn't even know what it meant exactly, but the two words conjured visions of quiet cubicles and glaring white walls.

"Business administration," Blair said, attempting a zeal she didn't feel.

"And what do you hope to achieve with that area of study?"

"Umm..." She heard her mother's voice, 'no umms!' and blushed. "I'd love to run a finance company."

It was a lie. Her father owned a finance company and the few times she'd visited his office had been akin to a dentist appointment without the drilling. The office always felt tense, the people inside it verging on nervous breakdowns as the stock market followed its usual roller coaster of chaos.

"Finance." Sloan made a note. "Very good. Now, I want to clear up a few quick things. Let's see." Sloan slid her index finger down the page. "Ahh, yes, right here. I don't see any titles for homecoming queen or prom queen?"

Blair tucked a strand of hand behind her ear, trying to imagine what her mother's response would be to such a question. "I was, umm... sorry, I was runner-up for homecoming queen, but it went to my best friend."

This was also a lie. She'd not been a runner-up or friends with anyone on the court. In high school, Blair had been considered part of the in-crowd, but only on the fringes. But when her mother had coached her for the interviews, she'd more than once told Blair to exaggerate, lie if she had to, to gain the favor of the girls.

Sloan made a face. "That's the worst, isn't it? I was homecoming queen at my high school, but I had a friend on the court and if she'd have won, I'd have crawled into bed and died." She returned her gaze to her clipboard. "Tell me why you want to be in Rho Upsilon Nu. What does joining our sorority mean to you?"

Blair's pulse quickened. It was a standard question, one her and her mother had gone over, and yet the answers eluded her. She flicked her eyes from Sloan's face, gaze skipping over the pristine white furniture, the photos of former members glowing in the afternoon light through the window, her own mother gazing down at her.

She sucked in a breath and squeezed the chair beneath her, searched for the answer as Sloan watched her intently.

"Friendship is probably the primary reason I want to join," Blair breathed.

Sloan's lips thinned, but she smiled and clasped her hands on her knees. "Friendship is very important, yes, but we're more than that here. We're about sisterhood, an unbreakable bond, relationships that endure. If you pledge Rho Upsilon Nu, we're together forever. That's the commitment we make to each other."

"Together forever?" Blair echoed, sweat beading between her shoulder blades.

Sloan laughed, her eyes sparkling. "Not in a gross way." She leaned forward and patted Blair's knee. "In the way that families are. We can call on each other. In fact, I know Heather's mom called on your mom last year when Heather's dad got into a pickle over some investments. And your mom called on my mom this year to make sure I, the president of Rho Upsilon Nu, knew you were coming in. Which is why..."

She picked up Blair's resume and ripped it in half. "This is unnecessary. Our connections here at Rho Upsilon Nu are bound by something much stronger than flimsy pieces of paper. You still have to rush and pledge because the experiences in the weeks ahead are your opportunity to prove your commitment. And as you're the daughter of Margo Davenport, I have no doubt you will."

6

"How was Curly's last night?" Teagan asked as she and Harley got dressed for breakfast.

"It was good. It's a typical fast-food job, but it's kind of fun serving other Husher students. I chatted with a bunch of people who are rushing and a few kids from my classes and the time just flew. How was the library?"

"Perfect. I checked in books and only two people talked to me all afternoon."

Harley laughed. "It's your dream job then."

"Pretty much," Teagan agreed.

"WHAT'S YOUR SCHEDULE TODAY?" Teagan asked Harley after they'd finished eating breakfast in the cafeteria.

"I'm meeting with the rush counselor first thing to see who invited me back for round three. Fingers crossed they haven't all cut me."

"What's round three again?"

"Philanthropy round. So they'll want to know about my

volunteer work in high school and I'll find out about theirs, assuming anyone even invited me back."

"They did," Teagan assured her.

Harley put on a brave face and nodded. "You're right. This is all going to work out exactly as it's meant to. I have faith that everything is falling into place."

"There you go," Teagan said. "There's the nauseatingly optimistic Harley I know and love."

They parted ways outside Willow Hall with a plan to meet in the cafeteria at lunch.

WHEN LUNCH ROLLED AROUND, Teagan watched the door for Harley, her stomach squirming at the thought of what Harley might have learned during her rush counselor meeting that morning.

When her friend walked in, she was beaming and Teagan knew instantly she'd been invited back to her top sorority choices.

Harley grabbed a sandwich and bottle of water and joined Teagan at the table.

"So?" Teagan asked, raising an eyebrow.

"I got invited back!" she squealed. "To Rho Upsilon Nu, Chi Omega and Delta Gamma. All of my top three! Can you even believe that? It's like unheard of."

Teagan grinned. "How did the talks go?"

"Really good. They all seemed impressed by my work with the special needs school, and it just totally flowed today. No mention at all of my dad. It was like it never even happened."

"That's so good, Harley. I'm really happy for you." Teagan hugged her friend and ignored the niggling unease at the thought of how their lives might change when she joined a sorority.

"Promise?" Harley asked.

"Of course I promise. I've been sick to my stomach worrying about how the morning went. You could have texted to let me know."

Harley smiled. "I almost did, but then I got this weird idea in my head I'd jinx it. Enough about me. How did your classes go today?"

Teagan finished chewing her bite of ham sandwich and nodded. "Decent. My biology teacher has the most monotone voice I've ever heard, but there's shelves with jars full of preserved animal brains, fetal pigs, birds. I even saw a bat, so that should keep my mind occupied when I start to doze off."

"Gross, but I'm glad you were entertained."

They finished their lunches, emptied their trays and walked up to their room.

"I'm off to math," Harley said, making a face, "then work at Curly's until nine, so I'll see you tonight."

"Sounds good. I might walk over to the student theatre and catch *Kill Bill*."

"I don't know why you like going to the movies alone."

"No one talks to me that way. Plus, I want to check out the campus theatre and see if the popcorn is any good."

"If it's good, bring me some."

"Will do. Are you coming back to the dorm after work?"

"I'm planning on it, though a couple of girls during the philanthropy round were talking about some Greek stuff going on tonight, so if I get a message from one of the sororities, I might walk over and check that out."

"All right. Don't accept beers from any of the dudes."

"No beer for me. Gotta be bright-eyed and bushy-tailed for Public Speaking 101 tomorrow."

∾

TEAGAN ROLLED over and shrieked as her center of gravity shifted and she nearly toppled from the loft bed. She clung to the wood frame, teetering, then managed to edge herself back from the drop.

"Jesus, Harley. Why did I let you talk me into these death traps?" Teagan sat up and swung her legs over the bed, expected to see Harley still tucked into her own bed or up and getting ready, but her friend wasn't there.

Harley's bed was made, the purple comforter tucked snugly beneath the mattress in the style fashioned by mothers who seemed intent on forcing their kids to sleep in straitjackets. Where Harley had picked up the inclination was beyond Teagan, who'd never seen Harley's mom make a bed in her life.

Teagan dug through her tangled bedding and found her cell phone, which she'd forgotten to plug in the night before. She half expected the phone to be dead. Why else hadn't she heard Harley's call about not coming home? She found the phone wedged near the foot of the bed and gazed at the screen. The battery was at fifty percent. No missed calls or texts. It was just after eight a.m. and, though Harley had a nine o'clock class, there was no way she'd have left without waking Teagan to say goodbye.

Frowning, Teagan clicked Harley's name and sent her a text.

Teagan: *Where are you?*

7

While Teagan waited for a response, she opened her email and scrolled past several messages from her new classes with upcoming assignments.

No text from Harley came in. After another minute, Teagan returned to her home screen, opened her recent calls and clicked Harley's name. The phone went straight to voicemail.

"What the heck," Teagan murmured. Unlike Teagan, Harley religiously charged her phone.

She always plugged it in at night so she'd have a full battery the following day, but she hadn't come home the night before, so maybe she hadn't been able to charge her phone. Still, if she'd stayed in any other dorm on campus the other girls would surely have had a phone charger.

Teagan left her a voice mail. "Harley, it's me. Where are you? You seriously didn't come back last night or even call me? Not cool. Call me ASAP."

Teagan ended the call and stared at her phone for another minute, hoping it would ring or a text would come through, an innocent explanation, a few words to quell the anxiety creeping into her chest. Her phone remained silent.

Teagan hopped off the loft bed, landing with a thud. She pulled off her ratty shorts and t-shirt and slipped into a black tank top, jean shorts, and her Converse sneakers. She yanked her hair into a ponytail, grabbed her bag, and left.

After a quick stop in the bathroom that reeked of hair spray and a zillion different floral- or tropical-scented lotions, she stopped into the cafeteria. Two girls she and Harley had met during orientation sat at a table eating cereal.

"Hey," Teagan said, pausing beside them. "You guys haven't seen Harley this morning, have you? Or last night maybe?"

Both girls said they hadn't. Teagan asked a few more vaguely familiar students, but no one had seen Harley in the dorms or cafeteria that morning.

At nine, Teagan still hadn't heard from Harley and a nervous buzz vibrated beneath her ribs as she walked to her psych class.

She found a seat in the stadium-style rows near the back and watched students file in. There were more than one hundred kids in the class. They wore yoga pants and terry cloth shorts, carried paper cups of coffee and talked amongst themselves. Harley wasn't in Teagan's class, but Teagan found herself scanning faces anyway, searching for her friend.

The hour-long session felt more like three, and when the professor finally dismissed them, Teagan sprang from her seat and speed-walked back to the dorm. She still hadn't received a message from Harley, who must have lost her phone or dropped it in a toilet. She took the steps two at a time to the second floor, bounded down the hall and unlocked the dorm door, pushing it open.

Harley did not sit in one of the bean bags or at her desk. Her bed remained smooth and untouched. Everything in the dorm room was exactly as it had been an hour and a half earlier.

Teagan called Harley again—voicemail. Sent her another text.

Teagan: *WHERE ARE YOU! CALL ME THE SECOND YOU SEE THIS!!!*

Harley had printed her schedule in her planner. She had Public Speaking from nine to ten and a writing class from ten-thirty to eleven-thirty.

Teagan arrived at Harley's writing course just as class ended. The double doors swung open and students poured into the hall. She searched the faces for her best friend, for the tell-tale bun or messy ponytail she'd likely be wearing after not having come home the night before. Dozens of faces flitted by, none of them Harley's.

The pit in her stomach grew larger as Teagan pushed into the room, hindered by the students rushing out, all focused on their next class or some other destination, barely aware of her as she shoved against them.

The professor stood at his desk gathering papers into a cracked leather briefcase. He glanced up when she stopped in front of him. "Yes?"

"Was Harley Rand in class today?"

"Excuse me?"

"Harley Rand. She's in this class. Was she here today?"

He frowned, appeared annoyed at the question. "I'm not at liberty to discuss student attendance, Miss—?"

She waved off the request for her name. "Just tell me if she was here or not. She's my roommate and she didn't come home last night. I'm not stalking her. I'm trying to make sure she's okay."

He narrowed his eyes at Teagan. "Your intentions are not my concern. As I said, I'm not at liberty—"

But Teagan had already spotted the attendance sheet stuck to a clipboard on top of the desk. She snatched it and turned.

"Hey. Stop. You can't take that. I'll report you to student services!"

Teagan ignored him, marching away, eyes following the alphabetical list to Harley's last name. Two squares sat beside each name. 'Attended. Absent.' The box next to 'Absent' was marked.

The professor was still talking to her, but she barely heard him. She ran a couple steps back and he recoiled as she tossed the clipboard onto his desk. It hit the surface and slid, stopping before it plunged off the edge.

Teagan turned and ran from the classroom.

Her next stop was the student center known around campus as the Den. Teagan pushed through the heavy door and strode up the stairs to the food court, stopping in front of Curly's Sandwich Shop.

"Hey." She slapped a hand on the counter to get the attention of the two guys chatting next to the fryer.

The taller one with spiky dark hair turned to look at her. He loped over. "What can I get ya?"

"Nothing. I need to know if Harley Rand worked last night."

"Who?"

"Harley Rand. She just started this week. She had a shift yesterday evening."

"Never heard of her."

The second guy, wearing his Curly's hat slightly askew, walked over. "She worked. I came in to get food at seven and she was here."

"You didn't work with her though?"

"Nope. I work the ten-to-two. She worked with Paul."

"Who's Paul?"

"Umm... he's a sophomore, I think. Lives in Kramer Hall."

"When's his next shift?"

The guy walked to a wall where a clipboard hung, leaned close. "Not until the day after tomorrow at noon."

"And when is Harley's next shift?"

The spiky-haired guy glanced at his co-worker as if suddenly unsure about the information they were sharing. "She's on tomorrow at four."

"Okay." Teagan bounded from the Den and sprinted across campus back to their dorm. When she burst through the door, the bubble of hope that Harley would have returned, that it all had been a big misunderstanding, disintegrated. The room remained empty.

8

Blair woke hot, her sheets sticky with sweat. She pushed them off, sat up and dropped from bed, barely reaching the trashcan in time for vomit to spew from her mouth. She clutched the little plastic can, sucking in sour breath, her hair sticking to her wet cheeks.

"Can I get you anything?" Colette asked. Blair's roommate sat at her desk, hair tucked beneath a bandana, a tinge of repulsion in her worried face.

Blair shook her head, cheeks growing hot, and wiped her mouth on her t-shirt.

"Are you okay?" Colette asked.

Blair took hold of a bed post and stood shakily. "Yeah. I think so."

"You were having a nightmare, I think," Colette said. "You kept thrashing and talking. I said your name a few times, but you were out."

"Hmmm..." Blair blinked at her bed, the covers crumpled and damp. She didn't remember the nightmare, though the remnant of something dark and disturbing hovered in the periphery of her mind.

"Did you drink last night?" Colette asked.

Blair bent and picked up the trashcan. "No, I didn't drink. It must have been the stroganoff in the cafeteria. I'm going to go clean this out and take a shower."

Colette gave her a thumbs-up, put in her headphones and turned back to face her laptop.

Blair grabbed her shower bag, stuck a towel under one arm and walked, legs weak, to the shared bathroom at the end of the hall. Several girls stood in front of mirrors applying makeup, straightening their hair. Blair dumped her trashcan in the toilet, grimacing at the spill of yellow-brown vomit that trickled into the toilet bowl.

In the shower stalls, she hurried into the first open shower, pulling the curtain closed behind her. She turned the water hot, stripped off her clothes and stepped beneath the spray. Head tilted back, Blair let the water pour hot over her face.

When she looked up, a shadow moved in front of her curtain. Blair stared at the silhouette of a woman, her heart thumping against her breastbone. The previous night's dreams pulsed in her head, barely there—a dark path, the pounding of shoes on a sidewalk, headlights fading into the dark night.

The shape didn't move and a chill ran down Blair's spine as she studied it, suspected it was the shadow from her dream. It was not alive. It had followed her from whatever dark realm the psyche slipped into during sleep.

Gritting her teeth, Blair ripped the curtain back, expected to see the shadow dissolve or to find nothing there at all.

Instead, a girl from her floor wearing a terry cloth robe turned in surprise. She'd been staring down at her phone and she looked up, eyes widening at Blair's nakedness, perhaps unnerved by the ferocity in Blair's face.

"Sorry," Blair mumbled, whipping the curtain closed.

When Blair returned to the hall, the dorm was quiet. Most

of the students had gone to their morning classes. Blair opened her door.

A girl stood in the center of her room. Long blonde hair rippled with strands of dark like mud, but no... It was blood, dried blood.

Blair stood frozen, robe cinched at her waist, shower caddy tight in her right fist.

The girl turned slowly, bits of her face coming into view, cheek sagging, one eye drooping and sightless.

Blair's own mouth opened, but no sound emerged. She stood, transfixed, and watched the girl dematerialize. Gone in an instant. In her place stood the thin carpet, the jumble of Blair's and Colette's furniture, emptiness.

It's happening again.

The words cut through her head like a tiny crack formed in a mirror. *Crick-crack,* it muttered as it skittered spider-fast across her mind, leaving a web in the formerly pristine glass.

She shook her head. "No, it's not." Her own voice, spoken aloud in the room, sounded tinny and unsure.

"Blair?"

Blair jumped and spun to find Colette in the hallway. She held a ginger ale, her expression hesitant.

"I grabbed this from the cafeteria. For your stomach."

Blair took it, the can cool and wet in her hand, and forced a smile.

9

H
arley had no other activities for the day scheduled in her planner. Teagan took out her cellphone and dialed Harley's mom.

"Hi, Lisa, it's Teagan. Have you heard from Harley?"

"Teagan! Buzz, it's Teagan! Oh, my gosh. I'm so excited you called. I was just telling Buzz that I wanted to drive the bikes up and see you two. Maybe next weekend? Hmmm...?"

"Maybe, yeah, but listen. Have you talked to Harley?"

"Talked to her? Like on the phone? Uh... let's see. She called what? Yesterday... No, the day before yesterday. I remember because I had an interview at the Mattress Warehouse and the manager was a complete shithead. Looked at me like I was scum of the earth, and there I was applying for a cleaning job, doing him a favor. 'Fuck him,' I said, and got up and walked right out of the interview."

"Okay. So you haven't talked to her today?"

"Nope, but you know Harley. Not exactly calling to check in with her mom every day." Lisa laughed. "Why are you asking, Teagan? Isn't she with you?"

Teagan held her phone, palm sweating. She didn't want to

alarm Lisa because the woman was erratic, compulsive. If nothing was wrong, Harley would be upset that Teagan had sounded the alarm. "She's probably in class. I've gotta go. I'll talk to you later."

In the background Teagan heard the flick of a lighter, the sound of Lisa taking a pull on either a cigarette or a joint. "Okay, doll. You tell her to give me and Buzz a call so we can hear all about that sorority hazing stuff."

"Rushing, you mean?"

"Sure, yeah. Just tell her to call us."

Teagan tucked her phone in her back pocket and returned again to Harley's planner. She'd noted her interviews with the sororities, but nothing was marked for evening events. Still, Harley had mentioned the previous day that the sororities might have night activities going on. It was still possible Harley was there. Maybe they had some bullshit initiation that prevented rushes from using their cell phones.

"Only one way to find out," Teagan muttered, grabbing Harley's highlighted map of the sorority houses on Greek Row.

TEAGAN RANG the doorbell at the huge brick house that was home to the Rho Upsilon Nu sorority.

After a moment, a girl, vaguely familiar, wearing white shorts and a yellow sleeveless top, pulled the door open.

"Hi," she said brightly. "How can I help you?"

Teagan swallowed, tried to steady her voice. "I'm looking for my friend. Her name is Harley Rand and she's rushing your"— Teagan gestured at the interior of the house—"sorority. She never came home last night and I thought she might have stayed here."

The girl screwed up her eyes and shook her head. "Definitely not. We don't allow PNMs to stay here at the house."

"PNMs?"

"Potential new members."

"Well, I know she came here yesterday and... maybe she told someone where she was going last night." Teagan took out her phone. The home screen was a photo of her and Harley sitting side by side on the sand dunes during a trip Teagan's grandma had taken them on the previous summer.

The girl leaned closer, pursed her lips and then shook her head. "I don't remember seeing her."

"I know she was here. Who met with the rushes yesterday?"

The girl sighed and glanced back into the house. "That'd be Sloan, Heather or Ginger, but I'm sure they're all busy."

"This is important. You need to ask them." Teagan wasn't going to take no for an answer. If this girl wouldn't help her, she'd barge into the house and find the girls herself.

"Fine. Hold on." The girl started away, then paused and glanced back at the door as if Teagan might follow her inside. "I better close this. Don't want all the cool air to escape."

Teagan was tempted to insert her toe in the opening and prevent the door from closing. She feared the girl would walk away and not return, but she gritted her teeth and stepped back. "Sure. Whatever you need to do."

Students trickled down the sidewalk in front of the house and across the street. The usual hum of college life droned on, but it all sounded muted and far away.

When the door opened again, Teagan recognized Sloan from the frat party she'd attended with Harley several nights before. She wore a white romper covered in red polka dots, the type of outfit Teagan associated more with toddlers than twenty-something-year-old women.

"You're looking for me?" she asked.

"No. I'm looking for my friend Harley Rand. She's rushing this sorority and she never came home last night."

"Harley..." the girl murmured, drawing out Harley's name.

"Oh, sure, I remember—like the motorcycle." A ripple of distaste flitted across her expression. "Hmm... well, she did come for a talk yesterday, but then she left with all the other PNMs. I'm sure she was headed off for interviews at more sororities. That's how rush works, after all. We're one of several places she would have visited."

"Were there any Greek events happening last night? Anything she would have gone to?"

Sloan shook her head. "Nope."

"She wasn't here then?"

"Not last night. Sorry I can't help you. Best of luck finding her." Sloan slipped back into the house and closed the door in Teagan's face.

Two voices fought for control in Teagan's head. The voice of reason insisted Harley was fine and a logical explanation for her absence would soon surface. But the other voice was louder, desperate. *Something is wrong*, it said. *Search! Find her!*

Teagan left Greek Row and boarded a bus, fixing her gaze on the middle-aged man in the driver's seat. "Can you tell me which stop is for the hospital?"

"Yep, Nine Mile and Clam Road. We'll be there in about five minutes."

"Thanks." Teagan dropped money in the slot and took a seat near the back. Only two other passengers filled the rows. A man slouched in the middle, mouth lolling open to reveal a maw largely empty of teeth, and an older woman read a paperback. Teagan's knees bounced as she rode.

When they reached the stop for the hospital, Teagan jumped off and hurried down the wide concrete path and through the glass front doors. The reception desk was large and half-moon-shaped. Two women sat behind it, both speaking on the telephone.

After a moment one woman's call ended and she gazed up at Teagan. "How can I help you?"

"I'm trying to find out if any female students were admitted last night. Maybe an accident or illness?"

The woman nodded. "There are students who come in nearly every night. What's her name?"

"Harley Rand, but... well, she hasn't called me and she didn't come home, so I'm afraid she either got injured or knocked out, or I guess she could have lost her phone, or... I don't know."

The woman typed something on her computer then shook her head. "I don't have a record of anyone under that name."

"But what if she had no name because she was unconscious?"

"I have names for three girls admitted last night. No Harleys, and no one we don't have a record for. I'm sorry I can't help you."

TEAGAN'S FEET HURT. She'd walked for hours, crisscrossed the campus, trekked in and out of buildings, diners, shops. She'd called Harley a hundred times, maybe more, and listened with growing apprehension to her friend's voicemail. She'd twice returned to the Rho Upsilon Nu house, not knocking, but merely watching from afar as girls moved in and out through the front door. Some paused on the lawn to chat. Sometimes an attractive guy in a shiny car pulled up to the curb and took one of the girls away. None of them were Harley.

When Teagan returned to her dorm room well after dark, she paused and whispered a silent prayer that Harley would be inside with some insane story. Teagan slid the key into the lock, twisted the knob and pushed the door open.

Silence. The same stale air greeted her. Without even stepping inside, she knew Harley wasn't there. Teagan swallowed the thickness in her throat, walked in and flipped on the light.

It was nearly ten o'clock and she couldn't remember a single time in the previous decade when she'd gone twenty-four hours without speaking to her best friend.

Anxiety like a trapped wasp buzzed behind her ribs as she moved through the room, full of future potential days before—now empty, dreadfully empty.

Teagan's gaze fell on the corner of a pearl-pink hard plastic suitcase poking from beneath Harley's desk. It had been a graduation gift from Teagan's grandmother, brand new to Harley. Harley, who'd grown up with plastic bags and cardboard boxes, had cried when she'd opened the gift.

As Teagan moved through the room, evidence of Harley peered from every surface. Six shot glasses lined the windowsill, and Teagan's fingers trembled when she picked up the glass that read 'Hell, Michigan' in flame colors. Between the two girls they'd collected at least fifty of the little glasses, a hobby that had begun in girlhood when they started sneaking Lisa's shot glasses out of the kitchen to use for their dolls.

As Teagan and Harley grew older it had become their tradition. Any time they took a trip or even stopped into a truck stop, they purchased one. Both of their bedrooms at home had shelves lined with the little glasses. Harley was everywhere in the room. Teagan couldn't look at a pencil case without memories surfacing. Harley was everywhere and she was nowhere.

Teagan was not an alarmist, but every passing minute ratcheted up the tension in her body. She moved through the room slowly at first and then frantically, dropping to her knees to search the floor of the closet, then standing to reach into the pockets of Harley's skirt and pants. She opened her drawers, sifted through the totes stacked in the corner beneath the loft beds, made a mess of Harley's formerly organized life.

Teagan picked up her phone and called her grandma. "Gran?"

"Hi, TT, I've been thinking about you all day. How's the first week going?"

"Harley didn't come home last night."

"She didn't? Where did she go?"

"She had rush stuff going on and then work in a sandwich shop at the Den. This morning I thought maybe... I don't know, she crashed in the dorm of one of the Greek girls, but she didn't go to her class either. I checked. The professor marked her absent. I know something's wrong. I can feel it and—"

"Okay, slow down, Teagan. Did you call Lisa?"

"Yes, but I didn't tell her I can't find Harley. I just asked if she'd talked to her. She hasn't."

"Okay. Where have you checked?"

"Everywhere. The class she was supposed to be in this morning, she missed it, and I asked at her work, but she's not due for another shift until tomorrow. I checked the sororities she was rushing, every building on campus, and even the hospital."

"That's not like Harley. I have home visits with patients all day tomorrow, so I can't come to Husher until the day after, but I think I'd better call Lisa and let her know. If you still haven't heard from Harley by tomorrow morning, go report her missing to the campus police."

"Okay." The thought of reporting Harley missing, of putting that official stamp on this sudden nightmare, made the room, the floor, the very air too close, suffocating.

"I'm sure she'll be back," Teagan's grandma said, but there was something in her voice—fear.

10

B lair yawned, exhausted, but covered her mouth so her mother didn't hear the sound through her cell phone. "Everything went good at Rho today."

"That's it? Good?" her mother demanded.

"Great. It went great."

"And what did you eat for dinner?"

"A chicken salad in the cafeteria." She stifled another yawn.

"Not with a cream-based dressing, I hope. Those dressings are filled with fat."

Blair frowned. She'd used ranch and even splurged and eaten croutons. "No, umm... oil and vinegar. Mostly vinegar."

"Don't say 'umm.' Have you worked out today? We're going to do weight and measurements the next time I stop by."

Blair rested her chin on her fist. She was exhausted, wanted to crawl into bed and be done with the day. "I'm going to the gym tonight." Blair had not been planning to visit the fitness center, but the thought of her mother's reaction if she'd gained an inch around her hips was enough motivation to put off bed for another hour.

"Good girl," Margo said. "I'll call you tomorrow to check in."

Blair changed into a spandex shirt and running shorts. She sat on the edge of her bed, lacing up her tennis shoes, when Colette walked in.

"Going out?" Colette asked.

"To the fitness center."

"When you were sick this morning? Maybe you should rest instead." Colette held up a brown paper bag. "My plans for the evening include Oreos, Doritos and *The Crown*. Sure, you don't want to skip the workout and join me in a veg session?"

Blair smiled. She did want to, doubted she'd ever in her life had a veg session with a girlfriend, but shook her head. "I better not. See you in a bit."

As she walked through the lobby of the building, the resident advisor from her floor stopped her. "Blair. Can you take a quick peek at this picture?"

Blair looked at the photo, hesitated. A wave of unease shuddered through her.

"She's a freshman on the second floor," the R.A. explained, "and her roommate can't find her. We're asking everyone in the building if they've seen her."

"Harley," Blair murmured. "I met her at a rush thing couple of days ago."

"You definitely haven't seen her in the last twenty-four hours?"

Blair shook her head.

"Okay, thanks." The R.A. marked a note beside Blair's name on a clipboard and walked to another girl who'd entered the lobby.

THE EAST CAMPUS fitness center was deserted. Still, Blair opted for a treadmill at the far end of the row nestled in the corner beneath a mounted television. She propped her water bottle on the stand, plugged her headphones into her ears and stepped on the track, hit the button for a pre-programmed workout, which including running and hill-climbing. Techno blasted through her headphones and she focused through the glass window that looked out on the dark campus.

The workout began with a warmup, an easy three-mile-an-hour pace. Blair bobbed her head to the music, encouraged her legs to wake up. Everything felt a little heavy, and she wished she could be a girl who spent evenings eating junk food and watching television.

Her mother had been weighing and measuring her since she was ten and several times a year she was forced into restrictive diets if she'd gained too many inches in her hips, waist or thighs.

The speed on the treadmill quickened, and she started a slow jog and then a steady run. After three minutes of running the track decelerated, but tilted so she speed-walked at a sharp incline.

She watched the campus through the window. In the misty orange halo from a light pole at the edge of the grassy quad, Blair spotted movement. She gripped the handles on the treadmill and squinted, a cool finger brushing down her spine. The darkness shifted just beyond the light and Blair bit her lip, straining to make sense of the image.

A figure drifted into the light for only an instant, not long enough for any clear identification, but Blair thought instantly of the missing girl.

She swallowed and glanced around, suddenly nervous and wishing there were other students working out. Metallic warmth coated her bottom lip, and she realized she'd bitten it. She dabbed at the cut with her index finger, pulled it away and saw a spot of blood.

Despite the screen showing a deceleration, the track moved faster. Blair hit the down arrow on the treadmill's speed, but nothing happened. Blair kept pace, her feet pounding the belt, but the treadmill sped up until her heart hammered in her ears. She pushed the button again to slow it down, but the belt continued to accelerate. Sweat pouring from her hairline, Blair pulled the kill-switch cord—nothing.

Her legs burned. She reached for the handles, intended to brace herself and jump her feet wide to get off the track, but movement in the mirror behind her caught her eye. She looked up to see the missing girl—Harley, arms limp at her sides, eyes white and unseeing.

For an instant Blair was frozen, felt the conveyor sliding beneath her feet and then she was airborne, flung backward off the treadmill. She struck an elliptical machine and fell sideways, her head smacking the pedals as she landed, tangled between two machines.

11

A sense of déjà vu coursed through Teagan as she watched students file into the room for English 101—Harley's nine a.m. class. Harley didn't appear. The class held only a couple dozen students, and Teagan scanned all their faces. Harley was not among them.

Teagan opened her phone and searched the map of Husher University for the campus police.

The office was located in the Public Safety building at the top of a little flight of stairs. Teagan pushed through the glass door and hurried to the desk where a young man, not much older than herself, sat with an open textbook in front of him.

"I need to report my friend missing."

The guy at the desk blinked at Teagan. "Missing?"

"Yes. She hasn't come home for two nights. Her phone is going straight to voicemail. Her mother hasn't heard from her. She missed her classes yesterday and today."

"Okay, umm... let's see. I've never actually done this, but... there's a form, I think." He stood, a flop of dark hair falling over one eye. He crouched and pawed through drawers.

"Aren't you the police? You've never taken a missing person's report?" Teagan demanded.

He continued rifling. "Campus police, and I'm new this year. Technically I'm not a sworn officer yet. I'm doing criminal justice classes now and heading to the police academy next year."

Teagan clamped her teeth together as she watched him move from one drawer to another, poking through files, but seemingly unable to find what he needed.

"Huh... like I said, I've never done one of these before so it could take me a little while."

"Jesus Christ!" she snapped. "Get someone else then. This is serious. Okay? You can't just write this on a form and stick it in a file cabinet somewhere. You need to get people out there searching, ping her cell phone. We need security camera footage."

He stared at her, his mouth in a little o. Teagan fought the urge to reach across the desk, grab both his shoulders and shake him. "Everyone's out but me. They're on bicycle patrol, and Officer Key called in sick today."

"Well, call him then, or call the regular police department. I'm not walking out of here without talking to someone who knows what they're doing."

OFFICER KEY WALKED into the office a half hour later. Teagan stood and started to follow him as he trudged toward a closed door, but he held up a hand.

"I need five minutes and then I'll be with you," he said gruffly.

She didn't bother sitting, had already practically worn a hole in the carpet with the tapping of her foot as she'd waited.

Instead, she paced around, drawing wary looks from the guy at the counter.

It took more like eight minutes for Key to reappear. He held a paper cup of something steaming in his hand and his nose looked red as if he'd just blown it.

"Come on then," he told her, waving Teagan into his office.

She walked in and sat across from his cluttered desk, which did not appear cluttered with work so much as sports magazines, newspapers, and Husher University paraphernalia ranging from foam fingers to ball caps.

He sneezed, dabbed his face with a wad of Kleenex and sat heavily in his chair.

"My friend Harley Rand is missing," Teagan blurted.

Key held up a hand to silence her. He cleared a space on his desk, took a notepad and pen from his drawer and then returned her stare. "Name?" he said.

"Mine or my friend's?"

"Let's start with yours."

"Teagan Kelso."

"And what year are you?"

"Freshman."

"And you're here to report someone missing?"

"Yes, my friend Harley Rand. She's also a freshman."

"What dorm is she in?"

"Willow Hall. We share a room there."

"And when did you last see or speak to her?"

"The day before yesterday. I saw her midday."

"So, she's been missing for...?"

"Since she left work at the Den two nights ago. That's the last confirmed sighting of her. Her phone's going straight to voicemail. And let me just say this is totally unlike her. I mean, I can't stress enough how out of character this is for her."

Key took in a quick breath and held his pen poised in midair as if awaiting another sneeze. It didn't come, but he lifted his Kleenex and blew his nose. "Okay. This should be all I need. What's your phone number?"

"Wait. That's all you need? You didn't find out anything at all about her or the last day she was seen."

Key sighed and rubbed his eyes, pressing his fingers hard into the sockets. "This is enough to get us started."

"With what? What are you going to do with that?" Teagan spat, unable to hide her fury at his lack of concern.

"I'm going to make some calls to the resident advisor in your dorm, to her professors and to her parents. That's standard procedure."

"I've already done all of that. You're going to spend the next two days tracking that information down only to find out what I already know. Her mother has not heard from her, she has missed all of her classes and our R.A. hasn't seen her."

Key's eyes closed and she suspected if he sat that way long enough, he'd fall asleep. She cleared her throat loudly.

He blinked and stared at her, not bothering to hide his annoyance. Finally, he leaned forward and took a sip of tea, a strong earthy aroma wafting in the tendrils of steam. "Let's go through the last day you saw her. Start with the morning."

12

Blair opened her eyes, yawned and stretched her arms overhead. She glanced sideways to see Colette sitting up in bed, staring confused toward the opposite side of the room.

Blair followed her gaze and frowned. In front of their closet stood both their computer chairs, stacked with the suitcases and plastic bins previously shoved under their beds.

"Why'd you do that?" Colette asked, turning to stare at Blair.

Blair looked at her, then shook her head. "I didn't. I swear. When I went to bed last night that stuff wasn't there."

Colette frowned. "Well, somebody did it."

Blair sat up, swung her legs over the side of the bed and gazed for a long time at the stuff shoved in front of the door, as if to keep someone or something trapped inside.

Colette stood and walked over, reached for a chair.

"Wait," Blair said, voice rising. The tendril of a dream—a nightmare—niggled at the edges of her consciousness.

She'd been running through a corn maze, chased by some creature whose breath exploded in raggedy bursts. From the row of dense, green stalks, a hand had grabbed Blair's and yanked her from the row. When Blair emerged, she no longer stood in a cornfield. In that way that dreamers slip without thought from one place to the next, Blair had followed the girl down the corridor of Willow Hall to her dorm room. As the girl pushed open the door and slipped inside, her body changed. Clumps of her long blonde hair and scalp fell away. Her skin blackened and peeled.

Horrified, but unable to control her dreaming self, Blair followed the girl into the room. The two beds were occupied. Colette in one and Blair in the other-and Blair had stared at her body in confusion.

The girl, a mess of decay, her eyes two opaque marbles in her nearly skeletal face, had opened the closet door, grabbed Blair's hand and dragged her inside.

As the details of the dream surfaced, an icy shudder rolled down Blair's spine.

Colette turned back, her smile falling away. "What? Is there something in there?" She took a step back.

"I don't know, but... I mean that's what it seems like, right?" Blair couldn't share what she thought crouched in the closet.

"Who could have locked someone in there?" Colette whispered. "We were the only ones here last night."

Blair nodded and stood, crept to the closet and strained to hear. Nothing stirred.

"Oh, my God!" Colette shrilled.

Blair started and spun around, half expected to see the missing girl standing behind her. Colette pointed toward Blair's pillow. The white pillowcase was dark with dried blood.

Blair took a step closer, nerves jumping in her legs.

Colette squinted at her. "It's under your nose too. You must have gotten a bloody nose last night."

Blair touched her face, felt the crusty remnants of a night-time nosebleed. She hadn't had one in months, but the treadmill incident from the night before had likely provoked it.

"Okay," Colette breathed. "You know what? We're freaking

ourselves out." She strode across the room, jerked the chairs away from the closet door and flung it open. No one stood inside.

Colette peered into the space. "Nada. No boogeyman." She bent and picked something up off the floor. "Looks like you left your sketchpad in here though." Colette handed Blair the notebook.

Blair stared at it. She didn't remember sketching the night before, but she also didn't remember barricading a nightmare figure in the closet.

"The bruising looks better," Colette told Blair, gesturing at her face. "Except on your hands. Ouch. Did you hit those too when you flew off the treadmill?"

Blair looked at her hands, smudged from her charcoal pencils. "No. That's charcoal from drawing." She gently pressed two fingers near her temple where she'd noted a purplish-blue bruise the night before.

"If I needed another reason not to work out, you've definitely provided it. A rogue treadmill? No, thank you."

Blair smiled, but the memory of that disturbing moment—Harley in the mirror—and then her sudden ejection from the treadmill had left her rattled.

"I guess I better do some laundry and take a shower," Blair murmured, stripping off her bloody pillowcase.

13

Teagan suspected Officer Key was placating her, taking more information just to get her out of his office. But she'd push until he did something. "Harley had class and sorority meetings the last morning I saw her. We met up for lunch in the cafeteria and from there she was going to Math-"

"She was rushing a sorority?" Key interrupted.

"Yeah. Her top pick is Rho Upsilon Nu, second is Delta Gamma, and third is Chi Omega, and then after that she wasn't too sure. Anyway, after her math class, she had a shift at Curly's Sandwiches in the Den."

"Curly's," he murmured, taking notes. "They've got a great Philly cheesesteak sandwich."

Teagan stared at him. "Really?" She didn't bother concealing her annoyance at the comment.

He ignored her. "And you said she attended that class and worked her shift?"

"Yes, I stopped in and checked with the guys working at Curly's yesterday. One of them saw her working. I didn't see her

that evening because I caught a free movie at the student
theatre and ended up chatting with a girl from my psych class
for like an hour. When I got back to our dorm it was around
eleven. I texted her, but she didn't respond. I went to bed and
woke up and she wasn't in our room."

"Is it possible she came home, slept and left early yesterday
morning and you missed her?"

"No. She's not quiet and I'm not a deep sleeper. There's no
way. Plus, after she wasn't in her bed and I couldn't get hold of
her, I went to all of her classes yesterday. She didn't show for a
single one, and she didn't today either. That's not Harley. She's
a straight-A student. She won't even skip class if she's sick."

Key's eyes narrowed as if the comment were an insult
directed at him. "So, she's a little type A, a little high-strung
maybe."

"No, not at all. She's committed. If she says she's going to do
something, she does it."

"Tell me a little about her life. Is she close with her
parents?"

Teagan clenched her fists tight in her lap, her frustration
with the slowness of this conversation inching her toward an
eruption. "Why does that matter? I mean seriously, why in the
hell are we talking about Harley's parents? This isn't family
therapy." Teagan stood and pointed at the closed door. "She's
out there and something is wrong. Aren't we in the critical
forty-eight hours? Isn't that what you guys are always saying?
You have this two-day window and then the chance of finding
someone okay dwindles to nothing?"

Key tapped his notebook. "The more detail you can give me
now, the more quickly we can rule out dead ends."

"Wow, really? Because ten minutes ago you just needed her
name."

He took another sip of his tea, shuddered as if it tasted as bad as it smelled and returned his steely gaze to Teagan's. "I'm just trying to pinpoint where she might have gone."

"Or been taken!"

"Sure. That's also a possibility, but I can't send a swarm of police into the streets searching behind every tree and down every alley. That would be a waste of everyone's time. Details you don't think are relevant could be crucial. Please sit down and work with me on this."

Jaw clenched, Teagan returned to her seat, bouncing one foot on the carpeted floor, unable to still her thrumming body, which wanted out of that room, out of that building, wanted to be pounding up and down the streets searching for her friend. "Her dad is in prison in Marquette for armed robbery and drugs. She was a newborn when he went away. Her mom lives in Baldwin—that's where we're both from, but I promise you she wouldn't go there even if she did decide to leave for some reason, which she didn't because it's not something she would ever do."

"Her dad is in prison?"

"Yes. She doesn't even know him."

"She never visits him?"

"No."

"And is her mother also involved in... illegal things? Has she ever been to jail?"

Again, Teagan could barely contain her growing rage. He was searching for a reason to write Harley off and Teagan wasn't going to give him one. "Nope. She's great. Good mom, good family. Harley had no reason to run off and she would not do it," Teagan lied, knowing the detective would discover the truth soon enough. Still, once he sounded the alarm, got the word out, it'd be too late for him to back away. At least that was what Teagan hoped. "I know you see cases of college kids taking off, but Harley is not one of those cases. Okay?"

"What if she was overwhelmed? New school? Lots of responsibilities? You said she's rushing a sorority. How was all that going?"

"It was going fine. It was... whatever. She was bound to get into one."

He tilted his head. "But not the one she wanted? I know for some girls that's a very big deal."

"It wasn't that big of a deal," Teagan insisted, which was a lie, but she could already sense this guy getting derailed by that one piece of information, convincing himself Harley took off because she was bummed about not getting her first sorority pick.

TEAGAN LEFT the campus police office cautiously optimistic, but with each footfall on the concrete sidewalk, a bit more of her hope skittered away. If something bad had happened to Harley, an accident or worse... the hours that had lapsed should have been more than enough time for word to have gotten back to Teagan. If a student had been hit by a car, or if she'd gotten hurt somewhere and been admitted to the hospital, news would have spread. There'd been only silence.

"Don't think like that," Teagan murmured aloud, searching desperately for a shred of Harley's optimism.

Key had said he'd send an email with Harley's picture to every staff member on campus, reporting her missing. He'd also promised that after he spoke with the dean a similar email would go out to every student at Husher University, which meant within hours every person who attended the school, hopefully, would be keeping a lookout for Harley. Someone must have seen something.

Teagan had blown off her classes all day, but didn't dare risk losing her work-study job at the library. She arrived at the big gray building five minutes late and received an annoyed glance from the student on shift before her, which she ignored. Teagan clocked in and opened a program on the computer to design a missing person's poster for Harley. She printed three hundred copies.

14

By the following morning, Teagan had heard nothing. No call from Officer Key, no calls or texts from Harley, not a word to give her some relief from the constant turmoil morphing her body into a live wire. She'd tossed and turned the night before, fallen asleep after midnight and woken to the sound of two girls in the hallway running and yelling something indistinct.

Without bothering to push off the covers or sit up, Teagan dialed her grandma.

"Any news?" her grandma asked.

A bubble formed in Teagan's throat and for a moment, she could say nothing. She'd intended to ask that very question.

"Oh, honey, okay," her grandma said, interpreting her silence. "Lord help us, let me think."

"How did Lisa take it?" Teagan murmured.

"I'm sure you can imagine she was upset, but Lisa is a master of denial. I'll call her after we hang up. You reported Harley missing? How did that go?"

"Not great. I don't know. Hold on." Teagan minimized the phone screen and opened her email, expecting to see the school-wide message regarding Harley's disappearance. There was nothing. Her only new messages were from her current classes, two noting her absence the day before. She squeezed the phone tighter, anger, fear, a swirl of madness gathering behind her eyes. "The cop said he'd talk to the dean, and they'd send out a school-wide email, but they didn't. I just checked. It's not there."

"All right. Let me call Lisa. It might be best if she contacts the campus police. Who was the person you spoke with?"

"Officer Key."

"Officer Key," her grandma repeated. "Let me give Lisa a quick call, and I'll call you right back."

"Okay. Bye." Teagan stared at the ceiling. She didn't want to get up, didn't want to see Harley's bed still neatly made, her bookshelf, her lined-up shoes.

Teagan lifted her phone again and scrolled her email, then checked the spam folder. No mention at all of a student missing.

She tried to imagine her grandma's call to Lisa. It wouldn't go well. Lisa was a high-emotion person, irrational, prone to going off the deep end. Teagan had witnessed Harley's mother 'go berserk,' as Harley called it, more than a few times. Often it had been amplified by alcohol, but Lisa had been sober for nearly two years, so that at least might subdue the hysteria bound to come with the news that Harley had still not turned up.

Minutes ticked by. Unable to wait, Teagan dialed the campus police and asked to speak to Officer Key.

"This is Officer Key. How can I help you?"

"This is Teagan Kelso. I talked to you yesterday about my friend, Harley Rand."

"Mm-hmmm..."

"Have you found anything? You said you were going to send out an email, but I didn't receive one."

"I spoke with the dean and he didn't want to unnecessarily alarm the students. The email is being drafted and is scheduled to go out at five p.m. today if there's been no news."

"There hasn't been any news! She didn't come home again last night. Her phone is still going straight to voicemail. No one has seen or heard from her."

"I appreciate your concern, Teagan. I really do, but this is a big school and we have certain protocols we have to follow. The dean has the final say, and he said five o'clock today."

Teagan hung up on him, couldn't stand to listen to the man for another instant. She sat up, jumped down from the loft bed and shoved into her tennis shoes, stormed from the room.

As Teagan left the building, her cell rang. She yanked it from her pocket, the flame of hope that it was Harley extinguishing at the sight of her grandma's name.

"I'm here," Teagan said.

"I spoke with Lisa. It was, as I'm sure you can imagine, very upsetting for her to hear. She's calling the campus police right now."

"Okay. I just called too. The dean isn't sending the email until five today. I don't think the police have done anything. I'm freaking out."

"I understand, TT. I'm scared, but we have to stay calm. I know that's easier said than done, but worry doesn't make things better. I have to go take care of Mrs. Jericho this morning because her daughter is in the hospital and her son is driving from downstate to spend the afternoon with her. The moment he gets there, Lisa and I will come to Husher."

"Okay. Can you bring a staple gun? I printed a bunch of fliers last night."

"I'll put it in my van first thing. See you soon, honey. Stay positive."

∽

WHEN TEAGAN WAS eight or nine, a six-year-old boy had gone missing in their little town. Joey Kimble had left home on foot to walk down the block to his friend's house and never arrived. By dusk, the entire town had turned out in search of him. Teagan remembered walking the suburban streets, flashlight in hand, as her grandmother and her grandmother's friends called his name, checked garden sheds and peered under porches. Cop cars had driven up and down the streets, one blaring Joey's name on a speaker, the others shining enormous spotlights into yards and patches of forest.

Joey had been found the next morning. He'd bypassed his friend's house and decided instead to walk to the Stanley Farm over two miles away because he'd recently learned their sow had given birth to piglets. Bernard Stanley had found Joey asleep among the piglets and delivered him home the following day.

It had been Teagan's only real-life experience of a missing person and she'd naively assumed that when someone disappeared, everyone rallied to find them. But Husher was not her and Harley's town. It was a bigger city with a college and hospital and thousands of people who'd never heard Harley's name. People too busy with their own lives to be bothered with a girl who hadn't come home.

Teagan desperately wanted to believe in a Joey Kimble outcome for Harley, but her best friend had not wandered to the edge of town to curl up in the straw with a litter of piglets. Something had happened, some cataclysmic event that prevented Harley from returning to the dorm.

Teagan had no way to hang the fliers she'd printed, so she walked to the student store and bought a roll of heavy-duty duct tape and a box of push pins. Before she left, she hung the first flier on the bulletin board. She stared at it, at Harley's face beneath the word 'Missing.' Her stomach felt queasy. She'd hang a flier on every bulletin board in every building on campus.

As she headed for a cluster of buildings that housed most of the English classes, Teagan passed the clock tower. It loomed over a large patch of grass that held a small stage and seemed to be a sort of meeting place where students gathered for events and protests.

During orientation, Teagan and Harley had noticed a group of students clustered around the small platform wearing Light the Trails t-shirts. It had apparently been a protest by students vying for more light posts along the dark trails on campus for safety reasons. One student had handed Teagan a flier with a group of administrators she could email to voice her concerns.

Today, the banner at the base of the sign read 'Greek Girls Unite.' Teagan recognized several of the girls she'd seen at the Alpha Lambda frat party.

Without a thought, she pushed through the throng and jumped onto the platform. A wireless mic sat on a little table, and Teagan flipped it on.

"Hey!" she shouted into the mic, her mouth too close, which caused an ear-splitting howl to emanate from the speakers. Teagan tried again. "Listen to me, everyone. Listen! My friend Harley Rand is missing. Here, look." Teagan dug a flier out of her bag and held it up. "She was rushing Rho Upsilon Nu."

The girls had all turned to look at her, some curious, more than a few embarrassed, as if she were standing on the little stage parading about in her underwear.

"She hasn't been back to our dorm for three nights. Something has happened to her. Does anyone recognize her?"

The lack of response was deafening. Crickets. The girls had resumed talking to each other. Only a few still glanced in her direction.

"Fine, whatever," Teagan grumbled. She turned to go, then

moved back to the microphone for a final comment. "Next time, it might be one of you. Think about that." Teagan dropped the mic on the table and stomped across the stage. Her foot caught on a thick black wire and she plunged forward, landing hard on her outstretched palms.

15

Tears pulsed behind her eyes, but Teagan gritted her teeth and refused them. She would not cry in front of these frigid bitches who cared more about their makeup than one of their so-called sisters vanishing from the face of the earth.

As she stormed down the stairs and away from the podium, someone caught her arm. Teagan reeled, lips peeled away from her teeth.

"Whoa there, Cujo. Chill out. I was just going to ask if you're okay." Lex, the guy she'd met at the Alpha Lambda frat party, stared at her.

"I'm fine," she snapped, jerking her arm out of his grip.

"Your friend is missing?"

Beyond Lex, she saw several of the sorority girls watching her. "Yes, but apparently, no one cares."

"Let's walk and talk. I have to teach in an hour, but I've got time to kill until then. Which direction are you headed?"

"Back to my dorm."

"I'll walk you there. Have you reported her missing to the police?"

Teagan nodded as they started across campus. "Yeah, but I don't think they took me seriously. Supposedly the dean is sending out a campus-wide email today about Harley, but it was supposed to happen yesterday and didn't. I'm going crazy and feel like I need to do something, but"—she hooked a thumb over her shoulder at the scene she'd just made—"no one seems to give a shit."

"Is there any chance she just left? Went back to her parents' house or went to stay at a friend's for a few days?"

"No. There isn't." Teagan thought of Harley's dad in prison, her mom who'd been in and out of rehab more times than Teagan could count. Teagan was Harley's safe place. If Harley were running anywhere, it would have been to her.

"Okay, I'm not saying you're wrong, but there are freshmen who freak out and disappear for a couple of days. It's not unheard of."

"I know Harley. *I know her.* I am telling you she didn't take off. She didn't."

"All right, which means you think... what? Something happened to her? She had an accident or—"

"Or someone took her."

Lex rubbed the back of his neck. "That's not a very pleasant thought."

"No. It's terrifying, and I'm seriously struggling not to storm into every building on this campus screaming about it."

"I think you'd be drawing attention to the wrong thing, then."

"What's the right thing?" she demanded. "Sit back and let the police do their thing? AKA nothing?"

"No. You're right to make a stink, because who knows what the police are doing. My dad was a journalist and if he taught me anything, it's that every organization is run by a bunch of faulty humans bogged down by bureaucracy and reputation and issues with funding. The difficulty the school has with getting loud about Harley's disappearance is that it looks bad for Husher University, which affects enrollment, which impacts funding. The police, the school, the politicians don't want negative publicity connected to campus, especially a freshman going missing. They want Harley to have run away. That's easier for everyone. When it's time to investigate a crime, they might step up, but right now every minute matters and the only one who truly gets that is you. Still, you might need to work on your approach—a little less sledgehammer, a little more tuning fork."

"I don't even know what that metaphor means," Teagan muttered. "Where's your dad now? Maybe he could write a story about Harley."

Lex shook his head. "He'd love to if he were still alive. He died of a heart attack three years ago."

"Oh. I'm sorry."

"Thanks. It was a rough year, but we made it through and life keeps happening, so here I am. I might be able to help, though. I have a friend who writes for the *Husher Student Newspaper*. Let me send him an email and see if he could write something up. He'd need to talk to you, get all the details."

"Yes. Definitely. I'm losing my mind over this and I don't know anyone here, so getting the word out feels like screaming into outer space."

"Have you talked to Harley's parents? I mean, obviously you must have checked with them."

"Her dad is in prison, but yes, I've talked to her mom. She hasn't heard from her."

"Her dad is in prison?"

"Yeah," Teagan snapped, instantly defensive.

"Okay. Put the claws away. It was just a question. And you reported her missing with who? The campus police?"

"Yes."

"Let me give you my hypothetical next steps if I were in

your shoes. Once I'd exhausted every person who might know where she is, and I'd reported her missing, then I'd go to social media. It's the fastest and most painless way to reach loads of people in a short amount of time. Do you have Facebook?"

"Yeah. I never use it, but I have it."

"Make a page specifically about Harley's disappearance. Blast it to everyone you know, especially anyone who attends Husher. Make sure there's a very clear picture of her and I'd disclose everything you can about the last day you saw her, where she went, had classes, places she said she was going, et cetera. The page won't share itself. Send it to anyone who has a lot of followers or friends and ask them to share it. Clarify that you're worried Harley is in danger." He glanced at her sidelong. "Is that what you think? That someone hurt her?"

Willow Hall came into view, and Teagan swallowed the lump rising in her throat at the thought of returning to their empty room. "Yes. I do."

"And do you have anyone in mind? Boyfriend she dumped before coming to school?"

"No. There's no one like that in her life."

"Anyone who could be connected to her dad, maybe nabbed her as a favor to him or to get control of Harley's mom?"

"No way. He's been in prison since Harley was a baby. He barely knows she exists."

"Then I'd also do some research into launching your own missing person's investigation and see if there are some resources in the area. Most communities have some kind of volunteer search team."

"Thanks, yeah. That's good. This is what I need right now, something I can do beyond running around campus like a dog with two tails."

"Listen, if you need help on any of this, just say the word."

They paused in front of Teagan's dorm and Lex took out his phone. "What's your phone number and email?"

Teagan frowned. "Why?"

"So I can give your information to my friend at the student newspaper. I'm going to text you so you'll have my number. I'm serious. If you need help, ask for it."

"Sure, okay." Teagan rattled off her number and email address, bid him a final thank you and awkwardly waved before trudging up the stairs to her dorm.

16

Teagan's grandma parked her van at a meter and climbed out. Lisa jumped from the passenger seat, looking wild-eyed and rumpled.

Teagan hugged her grandma, then held up the stack of fliers she'd printed. "Did you bring the staple gun?"

"Yep. Got it right here, and Lisa borrowed another one from Buzz."

"I set up a missing page for Harley on Facebook," Teagan said, "so you both need to go online and share it with everyone you know, okay?"

Another woman Teagan didn't recognize emerged from the backseat.

"Who's that?" Teagan asked, nodding toward the stranger.

Her grandma gave her a tight-lipped smile. "Her name is Ramona, and she's a psychic."

Teagan stared at her grandma, mouth agape. "A psychic? Please tell me you're kidding."

Her grandma patted her shoulder. "Let's just try to keep an open mind, shall we? Lisa met her through an AA meeting last year and she agreed to come today and see if she"—her grandma twiddled her fingers in the air—"senses anything."

"We need some reporters here," Lisa said, turning in a circle and scanning the streets. "We need to call WKTV or *Up North News*."

Teagan frowned, eyes drifting from Lisa to Ramona, who'd closed her eyes and tilted her head up as if searching for a scent in the air.

Teagan's grandma put a hand on Lisa's arm. "I think let's not involve the press in this one. If police get wind we've brought a psychic out here, they're liable to spin things in a negative way. Let's just see what we can find. Hmm...?"

Lisa's face darkened. "I damn sure have more faith in Ramona than those morons too busy stuffing their faces with donuts and passing out parking tickets to be bothered looking for my daughter." Her voice rose and cracked. She had an unhinged look in her eyes, a teetering-on-the-edge look, and Teagan's grandma wrapped an arm around her waist and pulled her close.

"I know, honey. I do, and don't you worry, we'll be screaming from the rooftops, but some hands are best played close to the chest. Right?"

"Yeah, okay." Lisa nodded and picked at her eyebrow, a nervous tic that had left her drawing in the eyebrow for years thanks to having mostly pulled all the hairs free. Her fingers smudged some of the brown pencil across her forehead. "Better to hold some stuff back from the police. I hear you."

"You're smearing a bit there," Teagan's grandma told her, gently nudging her hand away from her face.

Lisa nodded, but barely seemed to hear her as the psychic started down the sidewalk. Lisa hurried behind her.

Ramona, Teagan realized, was carrying a small stuffed cow.

"Moo-cow," Teagan murmured. The weathered stuffed animal had occupied a space on Harley's bed for most of their childhood. Harley had chosen to leave it behind when they'd packed for college. The sight of it now made Teagan's breath hitch.

Ramona paused and studied the face of the dorm building. "That one?" she asked, glancing at Lisa, who turned to Teagan for confirmation.

Teagan, puzzled, stared at the third-floor window. "I don't understand," she said.

"Is that your dorm room? Yours and Harley's?" Ramona asked.

Teagan shook her head. "No. We're on the second floor on that side of the building." Teagan pointed toward the other end of Willow Hall.

Teagan shot her grandmother a significant look, frustrated that Lisa had thought a psychic would somehow point the way to Harley. It felt like a waste of all their time.

"Huh..." Ramona studied the window for another moment and then, holding the stuffed cow close against her chest, spoke. "Can we go to the last place she was seen?"

"Sure," Teagan grumbled.

The four women, Teagan leading, walked to the Den. Teagan took them a roundabout way, traversing a path that Harley would not have taken the night she left to return to the dorm, as it added an extra five minutes to the journey. The psychic walked slowly, stopping every few feet to squint at the sidewalk or tilt her face up like a rabbit sniffing out danger.

Teagan tried to hide her annoyance, but suspected it showed. She focused on stapling fliers to every pole they passed. Her grandma covered one side of the sidewalk and Teagan the opposite.

Inside the Den, Teagan pointed out Curly's Sandwich Shop. Ramona said little. She walked to the counter and picked up a menu, resting a palm on the laminated surface and then scanning the page.

"Do you feel something?" Lisa asked.

Ramona's stomach grumbled, and she smiled. "Hungry. And they have roast beef on rye. I might have to come back here later."

If the mood hadn't been so somber, Teagan would have laughed. Instead, she gave her grandma another incredulous look.

A student Teagan hadn't previously met at Curly's looked at the women. "Can I get you something?"

"Not just yet," Ramona told him, wandering away.

Teagan stepped to the counter. She laid one of Harley's missing fliers on the counter. "Have you seen her?"

He leaned down, nodded. "Sure. It's Harley. She works here. I worked with her the other night."

"You're Paul?"

"Yeah. Is she really missing?" He stared at the poster, his mouth turning down.

"No one has seen her since her shift here on Wednesday night. Did she say where she was going when she left?"

Paul drummed his fingers on the counter, forehead wrinkled as if deep in thought. "Umm... dang... I'm trying to remember. Uh, no, I don't think she mentioned it. I figured back to the dorm, same as me."

"You guys didn't walk together?"

"No. I closed the shop at eleven. She was off at nine."

"Did anything happen during your shift? Did anyone come in?"

Paul nodded. "Yeah, for sure. Umm... somebody from a sorority Harley was rushing. The girl came in and talked to Harley for a few minutes and after she left, Harley was like bouncing around and smiling. I asked her what was up and she said it was the president of a sorority she wanted to get into."

"Did she say which sorority?"

"No. I mean, if she did, I don't remember."

"Did the girl invite her somewhere?"

"I don't really know. They were kind of talking off to the side. A big student meeting for study abroad had just broken up, and the cafeteria got packed and we were slammed for like an hour, so I didn't pay much attention to their conversation."

Teagan glanced across the food court where Ramona was moving from counter to counter, picking up paper menus, Lisa following close behind. "Did she seem all right during her shift? Did she seem happy?"

"I mean, sure. I didn't really know her that well, but she wasn't sad or anything."

"All right. Thanks."

"Sure. I hope you find her. She's really nice."

Teagan turned away from the counter, frustrated that Paul couldn't offer more insight into Harley's last night at Curly's.

Teagan stopped by her grandma. "He said the president of the sorority Harley was rushing stopped in the last night Harley worked. It has to be that girl Sloan from Rho Upsilon Nu, but I went to their house and she acted like she barely knew who Harley was."

Her grandma, who'd been hanging a flier on the cafeteria message board, knitted her eyebrows. "Why would she lie? Could it be the president of a different sorority?"

Teagan chewed her lip. "I mean, it's possible, but I really don't think so. Paul said Harley got all excited. Rho was her first choice. It had to be Sloan."

"She wants to go this way. Hurry," Lisa called to Teagan and her grandmother, scrambling to follow Ramona through an exit at the back of the building, the exit Harley would likely have taken the night of her last shift.

"I feel like an idiot following this lady around," Teagan whispered to her grandma as they walked behind Ramona and Lisa.

Teagan's grandma took her hand and squeezed. "I know, TT,

but Lisa needs this and you never know what form a little divine guidance might take."

On the sidewalk outside, Ramona paused, gazing first in one direction and then the other.

After a moment, Ramona held the cow close to her face, closed her eyes briefly and started toward their dorm. It wasn't a revelation. It was a different route, but the same direction they'd walked to reach the Den.

"I think she came this way," Ramona murmured.

As they came to another fork in the sidewalk, one that ran south through campus to several class buildings, and one to the north that led along a patch of woods on one side and a road on the other, Ramona turned to the wooded path. Again, it didn't take a psychic to surmise which path would mostly likely lead them back to Willow Hall.

Still, as they travelled the path and Teagan fell into step beside her grandma, her grandma leaned over and whispered, "Is this the way she'd have taken?"

Teagan nodded. She'd walked this exact path dozens of times in the previous days, searching the sidewalk, the grass and the woods for any sign of Harley.

Lisa kept her eyes trained on Ramona, though she occasionally looked sidelong at the trees. "This path is so..."

"Isolated," Ramona finished for her.

"Yes," Lisa said. "If she came this way, at night..." She didn't complete the sentence, but they were all thinking the same thing. If something had happened to Harley there, no one would have seen it. No one would have heard her scream.

Halfway down the path, Ramona stopped. She tilted her head, looked back the way they'd come and then turned, walked across the grassy embankment and stepped onto the road. It was deserted. Not a single car had driven by in the previous minutes.

"I wonder if she got into a car with someone," Ramona said, staring down the road.

"She wouldn't do that," Teagan said. "She would never have gotten into a car with a stranger."

Ramona looked to Lisa for confirmation, but Lisa only stared back at her, mildly dazed.

"Teagan's right," her grandma said. "Harley was a very careful girl. She wouldn't have accepted a ride from a stranger."

Lisa nodded finally. "Yeah, no way. She won't even get on the back of Buzz's bike."

Ramona looked in the direction that led away from campus. Further down, the road forked and in one direction lay dense woods and several miles beyond that access to the highway.

If someone had taken Harley that way, she could be anywhere.

17

"Now where?" Lisa asked, staring first at Ramona and then Teagan.

Ramona shook her head, clearly uncertain.

"I want to hang fliers on Greek Row," Teagan announced to the women. "And ask that Sloan girl again if she talked to Harley."

As they walked, Teagan and her grandma crisscrossed the sidewalk, hanging fliers. Lisa too had taken a flier and showed it to every student they passed, asking if they'd seen her daughter. The answers were a resounding no.

"This is it," Teagan said as they turned onto the street lined with brick mansions, signs out front with big Greek letters announcing which house belonged to which sorority or fraternity.

Lisa slowed and her eyes grew big. "She'd fit in here," Lisa said. "Harley deserves a home like this."

Teagan bit back her derisive comments. It bugged her that Lisa looked at these places in awe. The only thing that had come out of Harley's time rushing had been anxiety and terror of rejection.

As they passed the walkway that led to Rho Upsilon Nu, Ramona stopped and gazed at a group of sorority sisters gathered in the front yard. They were hanging decorations, preparing for some kind of party, which caused Teagan's stomach to clench. She wanted to stride across the lawn and rip the twinkle lights from the branches of the flowering trees.

The psychic gazed at one of the girls, and Teagan vaguely recognized her as a girl she'd seen days earlier in the cafeteria at Willow Hall. She had stick-straight white-blonde hair and big green eyes.

The girl noticed the woman watching her and her face grew red, as if embarrassed by the attention. She tucked her hair behind her ears and turned, hurried across the lawn and disappeared into the house.

"What was that all about?" Teagan asked her grandmother.

Her grandmother gave her a perplexed expression as if to say 'beats me.'

It was Lisa who posed the question. "Did you see something?"

The psychic frowned and tilted her head. She nodded. "For a moment, yes. There was... something around that girl, some energy."

"And it had to do with Harley?"

"It's hard to say definitively yes, but... I think maybe it did." The psychic turned to Teagan. "Were Harley and that girl friends?"

Teagan shook her head. "I doubt it. I mean, they were both rushing this sorority."

The psychic turned and stared back at the house, her eyes drifting up to the high window in the third story of the house.

"Was she here?" Lisa asked, pushing close to Ramona.

"Of course she was here," Teagan said. "She rushed this sorority."

The front door opened and Sloan walked out, a jumble of pink and gold balloons in her arms.

Teagan stalked across the lawn and stopped in front of her. "Did you go visit Harley at Curly's Sandwich Shop the night she disappeared?"

Sloan's lips pulled back from her teeth. "Excuse me?" she asked, not hiding her annoyance.

"Harley!" Teagan shoved a flier in front of Sloan's face. "She was rushing your sorority and the guy she worked with at Curly's said the president, as in you, visited Curly's and talked to her the last night she was seen."

Sloan's eyes narrowed on the flier, then slid over to Teagan. "He must have me confused with someone else. I wouldn't be caught dead eating at a place like Curly's."

"He didn't say you ate there, he said you stopped by to talk to Harley."

"Well, I can assure you I didn't." Sloan shifted her attention to another girl. "Heather, can you come take these off my hands? I need to grab something from the house."

Another girl scurried across the lawn and took the balloons.

"We're very busy today. Sorry I can't help you," Sloan said coolly, turning and disappearing into the house.

Teagan glared after her, but her grandma stepped up, took hold of Teagan's hand and guided her away from the sorority.

THEY ENDED their search back at the Den at Curly's. They ordered sandwiches and chips, though no one had much of an appetite save Ramona, who ate her entire sandwich and then half of Lisa's.

"Did you get anything, Ramona? Any sense of where she's at?" Lisa asked.

Ramona nodded, still chewing, and swiped the crumbs from the front of her shirt. "A couple of spots felt quite... heavy with her, the energy of her. That area on the path where I think she left the sidewalk for the road, and the sorority house. I believe that whatever happened to her happened in one of those two places."

"And you can't tell what happened to her?" Teagan demanded, unable to keep the disbelief out of her voice. "Isn't that what a psychic is supposed to be able to do?"

Lisa shot her a peeved look and her grandma patted her hand.

Ramona shook her head. "I don't decide what comes through. I wish I could tell you all more. Really, I do." Ramona looked at Lisa and brushed a bit of hair away from her face. "I'd be going plum out of my mind if Carter disappeared. It's easier having a boy, and he's practically grown, has his own apartment and everything, but I still worry if he goes a few days without answering his phone."

"What do we do now?" Lisa asked, picking up a potato chip and then dropping it back onto her plate.

"Teagan, have they sent the email?" her grandma asked.

Teagan took out her phone and opened her email. A message from the dean had been sent an hour before. The subject read: 'Possible Missing Student.'

"It's here," Teagan said. "I'll read it."

Dear Campus Community,

It has been brought to our attention that a freshman student has not been seen or heard from since Wednesday evening. She is a resident of Willow Hall. If you know where Harley Rand is or have seen or spoken with her in the last 24 hours, please immediately notify campus police.

Kind Regards,

Lawrence Falk, Dean

"Is there a picture?" her grandma asked.

"No. Nothing. Not even details about her appearance."

"What the fuck!" Lisa slammed her fist on the table. "What good does that do? No one knows if they've seen her. She started school last week."

Teagan felt a similar surge of rage at the brief and unhelpful message. She noticed another message on her inbox and opened it. It was from the *Husher Student Newspaper*.

Teagan,

Lex Mercer called me this afternoon and mentioned your friend has gone missing. We'd be happy to help spread the word. Call or text me to schedule a time to meet.

Nate Dryden

Reporter for the Husher Student Newspaper

"Okay, this is good at least." Teagan turned her phone to face the group. "A guy from the student newspaper reached out and he's going to write something about Harley."

She copied his phone number into her contacts and texted him.

Teagan: *Nate, this is Teagan Kelso. I can meet anytime to talk about Harley and give you a missing person's poster. Tell me the time and place.*

His reply was immediate.

Nate: *I'm working on tomorrow's issue right now. A few of us will be here in the newsroom until late. Our office is on the second floor of the media building. If you come tonight, we can get the story in tomorrow's edition.*

"The student paper goes out tomorrow," Teagan said. "I can meet with the guy tonight to get Harley's information added."

Teagan's grandma smiled. "Little by little," she said. "That's what it takes. We have to keep putting one foot in front of the other. TT, can we drive you there?"

"No, I'd rather walk. I'm still figuring out where everything's at and I can hang more fliers on the way."

"Can we take some of those fliers?" Lisa asked.

"Sure." Teagan took a stack out of her bag and handed them to Lisa, who burst into tears at the sight of Harley's picture. Teagan's grandma's eyes watered as she and Ramona comforted Lisa. Teagan looked away, felt her own grief creeping in, but refused to allow it.

18

Blair sat in the living room at Rho Upsilon Nu with several other sisters who were draped across the white furniture.

"That girl is a nightmare," Sloan announced, breezing into the room and collapsing on the sofa. "Those fliers are tacked to every telephone pole on our block and she's clearly targeting us. She's going to ruin the rest of rush week. And who were those ladies with her? I have half a mind to report her to the dean for loitering in front of the sorority house."

"An email from the dean came through," Heather said, waving her phone in the air.

"About the disappearance?" another Rho asked.

"Duh," Heather replied. "There's like no details at all, which makes it pretty plain the school isn't worried about her."

"Her dad is in prison. Her mother is a drunk. She's clearly cut from the same cloth," Sloan said.

"How do you know all that?" Blair asked, sweat beading beneath her dress.

Sloan shot her a sharp look. "Because I asked her point blank during the interviews and she told me herself."

"What's her dad in prison for?" Heather asked.

"Robbery, apparently. That's what we need in our sorority. A thief."

"I bet she just buckled under the pressure and left," Heather said. "I saw her during the philanthropy round and she looked like a deer in headlights, way too high-strung."

"Clearly," Sloan agreed.

"It's a little creepy to me, to be honest. Like what if someone abducted her?" said another of the girls, whose name Blair thought was Ginger.

Sloan sat up and glared at Ginger. "Stop being so dramatic. She probably offed herself because our interview didn't go well."

"Didn't it?" Heather asked. "She was on the list for a potential invite back."

"Hardly," Sloan countered. "Anyway, this is boring." Sloan stood and marched across the room. She picked up a stack of hot pink fliers. "Blair, you and the other PNMs are hanging fliers for the toga party. I know right where you can hang them." She exchanged a mischievous look with Heather. "And after you're done, I want everyone cleaned up and back by five o'clock for the preference round. Okay?"

"Sure." Blair stood and took the fliers from Sloan.

"A party at the Alpha Lambda Fraternity?" Blair asked, studying the flier, her heart thudding quicker behind her ribs.

"Obviously," Sloan said. "Alpha Lambda is our frat. They get preference-always."

"I know who you give preference to, Sloan," Heather laughed, tossing a pillow at her.

Sloan caught the pillow and threw it back.

"I wouldn't be so sure about that, Heather," Ginger cut in. "I heard Brody whispering about a hot date the other night."

Heather's mouth fell open. "Sloan? No! You can't pick Brody over Corbin."

Sloan rolled her eyes. "Who said I have to choose?" She waved a hand at Blair. "What are you waiting for? Get the other PNMs and start hanging fliers."

19

Teagan pushed open the glass door into the student newspaper office.

The high-ceilinged office was large and roomy. Desks and cubicles were arranged throughout, cluttered with newspapers, notepads and laptops. A bulletin board hung just inside the entrance and displayed job postings and announcements by campus organizations. Teagan pulled a flier from her bag and tacked it to the center of the board.

As she walked deeper into the office, she found three people standing at a long table that held two large-screen desktop computers. Only one glanced up at her, a girl around her age wearing a backwards ball cap.

"Help ya?" she asked.

"I'm looking for Nate," Teagan said.

One of the two guys hunched over the table stood up. "Teagan?" he asked.

"Yeah. Hi."

"Make room on the front page, Greg," Nate told the other guy, who didn't look at Teagan, but nodded slowly.

"Sure," Greg murmured. "I can move the article about the new sciences building to page two."

"Or cut the size of the Greek week article," the girl suggested.

"Do that," Nate said. He gestured to Teagan. "Come with me. We've got a break room back here."

Teagan followed him through an open door. He flipped on the lights to reveal a scattering of mismatched but comfortable-looking couches. "We have a Keurig. Coffee, tea, hot cocoa?" he asked.

"No. I'm good."

"All right. Let's get down to it then." He lifted a slender laptop from a desk and opened it, propping it on his lap.

"You're going to take notes on there?"

"Yep. Faster this way. We have to get the paper finalized by ten in order to reach the printer by midnight. Tell me everything. Name, age, description, dorm, last known whereabouts, major, etcetera. Anything you think is relevant, I want to hear it."

Teagan took a breath and pulled one of Harley's fliers from her bag, setting it on the coffee table between them.

For twenty minutes Teagan talked uninterrupted. Nate had asked nothing, simply typed and nodded along. Now he posed a question. "You mentioned earlier she was rushing a sorority. Which one?"

"Rho Upsilon Nu."

"Hmm... RUN. Interesting."

"Run?"

"Yeah, R-U-N. Rho Upsilon Nu."

Teagan frowned.

"It's not the first trouble at Rho Upsilon Nu. I can tell you that much."

"Something else happened with that sorority?"

"Have you heard of Jessica Meyers?"

Teagan shook her head.

"She was an out-of-state student two years ago. It was rush week and she vanished, never been found."

"What? Are you serious?"

"Yeah, truly. Look her up."

"She was rushing Rho Upsilon Nu?"

"Yeah. She left her job at the Husher Student Store to walk back to her dorm and just disappeared."

"And to this day she hasn't been found?"

"Nope."

"I can't believe I've never heard of her."

Nate shrugged. "No one has. She was from Oregon and had a weird family situation. Mom was dead, dad was flakey. The university suppressed the story. It's not exactly good for admissions to have that kind of history in the mainstream. I remember when it happened, but I was a freshman and so green. I kind of believed what everyone believed—that she took off.

"But this summer I saw an editorial written by her cousin printed in the *Husher News* demanding to know what was being done in her case. That's when it struck me. This girl is still missing. She never went home. If she'd run away, she'd have turned up in Oregon by now, called someone, used a social media account, something. She was eighteen. She didn't have the resources to disappear.

"That's the job of investigative journalists, I think. To take a hard look at the facts and then apply some common sense. No one did that with Jessica. They did the 'she was stressed by school and left' line. Which might hold water for a couple of weeks, but then she should have turned up. Especially as an eighteen-year-old girl who didn't have a history of running away."

Teagan leaned forward, pulse quickening. "That's what's

happening with Harley. The cop at the campus police basically said as much."

"An unfortunately common occurrence at universities. To put it simply, it's bad for business, and from what you told me about Harley, Dad is in prison, Mom is... what? Chronically unemployed?"

"I said she's had jobs on and off, not chronically unemployed," Teagan said, annoyed.

"Hey, no judgment. I'm simply trying to point out the myriad justifications the university will have for not launching a full-scale investigation on day one. It's not only universities. Law enforcement is biased. Give them a girl who's gone missing with parents who donated a hundred thousand to the school last year and that girl's name will be on everyone's lips within an hour. Offer up a new student from a troubled family and you might see some traction in a week, two weeks, but that's only if someone is pushing for answers. In Meyers' case, that wasn't the situation. The only person who put any effort into pushing for an investigation was Meyers' cousin, who isn't much older than Meyers herself."

"Have you talked to the police about Jessica's case?"

"Yeah, and I got the feeling the detective also suspects something fishy, but he gave me the usual 'can't comment on an ongoing case' B.S. Still, I'm well within my rights to tell the story and that's what I intend to do."

"You're going to write about Jessica Meyers?"

"Yep. I interviewed her cousin last week. The story isn't ready, but honestly, your friend going missing might be what the Meyers case needs."

"How so?"

"One girl vanishing from a campus is an anomaly, easily written off as a coincidence, but two? People will perk up over that, especially parents. Something's not right at Husher."

20

Blair stepped through the front door of Rho Upsilon Nu with several other PNMs she'd encountered during the walk from campus. They all wore formal dresses. Blair's was a sequined gown her mother had had specially made in the sorority's colors of pink and gold.

"That dress is amazing!" another PNM murmured as they stepped into the house.

Blair smiled at her, but before she could speak, a group of Rho Upsilon Nu sisters traipsed into the front hallway. They all wore gold dresses and each held a bouquet of pink flowers.

"This is it, ladies! Preference round," Sloan announced. "And by virtue of standing here before us, you're an elite group of women. Rho Upsilon Nu is top-tier. Fifty girls started this process with you, fifty girls who wanted to be members of Rho Upsilon Nu, and now there are ten. Eighty percent have been deemed unfit to be part of our sisterhood. You're the final ten and tomorrow some of you will join us.

"Each of us has a bouquet of pink roses for one of you. Should you receive a bid tomorrow, whoever bestows you with our signature flower will be your big sister. She'll be your confidante here in the house, your guide, your mentor."

The Rho sisters moved toward the PNMs, each offering a girl of bouquet of pink roses before leading them into a room.

Only Blair and Sloan remained. Sloan's mouth spread into a wide smile. "You know what that means," Sloan said. "It's me and you, Blair."

She handed Blair the roses. The scent of the flowers was strong, the blooms heavy and ripe.

Sloan led her into a sitting room, dimly lit by lamps draped with pink shawls. A small table had been set in the room, one chair on each side, a single candle in the center.

Blair sat across from Sloan, who leaned forward and lit the candle with a match.

"'Bound by sisterhood, sealed by secrets: forever united, forever true,'" Sloan said, eyes boring into Blair's. "That's our motto. That's what you're committing to. You understand that, don't you, Blair?"

Blair nodded. "I do."

"And in Rho Upsilon Nu, we take our secrets to the grave. If a sister confides in you, you will never share that secret. Not with any other sister and especially not with anyone outside these walls."

Blair nodded again. Her dress was too hot, itchy against the skin on her chest and back. She wanted to scratch, to tear the dress off and take a cold shower. Instead, she continued nodding, her mouth curved into a forced smile.

The candlelight in Sloan's eyes flickered. The room was all shadows and too much warmth, and when Blair shifted in her chair, her thighs stuck together. Her mother's voice whispered in her ear: *Thighs should never touch.* She'd go to the gym that night and again in the morning. Two-a-days would shave off those extra couple of pounds.

"I came to Rho as a legacy like you," Sloan said. "And in this sisterhood, I found my home, my community, my purpose. When I leave here, I'll take the skills I've learned, the leadership experience, but most of all I'll take the sisterhood."

Sloan droned on and Blair tried to listen, tried to focus on her words, her face, but she'd begun to feel removed, her body in the chair, but her mind drifting toward the flickering flame. A daze settled over her like a gauzy sheet, casting the world in a mesmerizing orange glow.

The flame of the candle suddenly streaked up and lit the tips of Sloan's long hair on fire. She screamed and Blair fell back, tipping her chair over and smacking the floor. Pink roses scattered across the hardwood. Sloan slapped at her hair, shrieking. The door burst open and Heather and Ginger flew into the room.

"Oh, my God, what just happened?" Heather demanded, looking to Sloan, whose hands were still crushing her singed hair as Blair struggled to roll off the chair and stand up.

"My hair lit on fire. Oh, my gosh. That did not just happen," Sloan blustered.

"I told you you've been using too much hair product," Heather said.

Sloan glared at her, still patting her hair. "Look at my dress. It's all black by the collar. This will never come out."

Blair stood and rubbed her knee, which she'd struck on the edge of the table.

"We're not re-lighting this," Sloan snapped, picking the candle up between two fingers, though the flame had extinguished.

The room stank of burnt hair. After the girls left, Sloan and Blair returned to their chairs, though Sloan had clearly lost her enthusiasm for the ritual.

∾

THAT NIGHT, Blair woke, bladder full, and stood, fumbled through her dorm room to the door.

Groggy, not wanting to allow sleep to ebb away during her night trip to pee, Blair kept her eyes half-lidded as she padded down the hallway and stepped into the girls' bathroom. The lights, which operated on a motion sensor, flicked on, the fluorescent brightness washing away the dark. Blair slitted her eyes further, tucked her chin to her chest, and hurried to one of the stalls. She shivered at the cool of the tile floor beneath her bare feet.

She closed and locked the stall and released a little gasp at the icy toilet seat. The rush of her pee filled the silence and she stared down at the tiles, the bits of dirt and hair clogging the grooves.

Something moved in the bathroom, a shuffling sound, as if someone were sliding their feet along the floor rather than walking. Had there been a girl in another stall? Blair stared at the gap beneath the bathroom door, goosebumps rising along her arms.

Someone stepped into view, as if they stood directly in front of Blair's bathroom stall. White tennis shoes appeared tattered, the toes scuffed. A mossy green grew over the top and snaked up the legs that Blair realized were putrid, the pale flesh wrinkled. Skin hung from the bare legs in peels. A fleshy glob dropped off and landed on the tile with a barely perceptible thud. Knees appeared. The person, the thing was kneeling, bending down.

Allowing her shorts and underwear to slip off her feet, Blair pulled her knees up to her chest, stared in horror, lips raked back from her teeth, eyes bulging as the legs bent and two hands, fingernails broken, braced against the floor. The face of the girl appeared next, cocked at a weird angle, lips bruised and chapped-looking. Bits of bone protruded from the side of her mushy-looking face.

Blair's mouth fell open. A scream tried to emerge but caught somewhere deep in her ribs, as if it were a balloon that had snagged and deflated.

The girl's opaque eyes locked on Blair and, scrambling on hands and knees, she pushed beneath the stall.

The lights in the bathroom went dark.

Blair screamed and plunged off the toilet, climbed, putting one foot on the toilet seat and then reaching blindly for the top of the stall door. Her screams grew louder, hysterical.

She found the hard edge and pulled herself up just as something cold and slippery took hold of her ankle. Blair shrieked and kicked it away, scrambled over the top of the stall, straddling the hard partition, which dug painfully between her ribs and into her pelvis. Struggling for breath, she hoisted her leg over and dropped into the next stall.

The lights flickered on, washed away the black.

"Hello?" A girl's voice, timid, spoke into the bathroom.

A second followed, louder, more gruff. "Who's in here? What's going on?"

Legs wobbling, naked from the waist down, Blair shot from the stall into the bathroom. The R.A. and another girl from her floor stood in the doorway, sleepy-eyed. The R.A. had a look of annoyance. The other girl clung to the R.A.'s arm.

At the sight of Blair, a flash of apprehension crossed the R.A.'s face. Her gaze darted to the locked stall door.

"Is there someone in there?" she demanded.

"I..." Blair too turned to look at the stall and then at the floor.

A part of her wanted to see a trail of blood and dirt, remnants of the girl, but the tile was bare. There were no dirty handprints, no streak of grime that surely, had the girl been real, would remain on the floor.

It's happening again.

Blair's mind reeled. She was fully awake now and already

minutes ahead to the potential outcomes of this moment. If she admitted what she'd seen, someone would call her mother. They'd say, 'Blair's buckling under the pressure, it happens to a lot of freshmen, the overwhelm. It might be best if she comes home.'

"The lights went out," Blair blurted. "And I thought I heard something outside the stall. It was so dark and I freaked and just"—she gestured at the stall she'd walked through—"climbed over the top."

The R.A. appeared skeptical. The other girl looked relieved.

After a moment, they helped Blair fish her underwear and shorts from beneath the locked stall, and then the R.A. crawled under and unlocked it.

As Blair returned to her room, she glanced back at the two girls, sure she'd see them watching her, their eyes full of suspicion, but they'd walked the other way.

BLAIR DIDN'T SLEEP that night. Though fatigue dragged her down, turned her eyelids heavy, she forced them to stay open. She feared the vulnerability of sleep.

21

After another long night, Teagan forced herself out of bed. She laced up her shoes, took a long swig from her water bottle and left the dorm. She'd never been a fitness runner.

She ran to burn off the rage, the anger that sometimes took up residence in her body like a stream of lava flowing beneath her skin. When that anger started simmering, running or punching a bag were two of the only things that helped. Her punching bag sat abandoned in the basement of her grandmother's house, which left running as her sole means of releasing some of the energy, which had contributed to yet another night of restless sleep.

By the time Teagan reached the sidewalk, morning fog obscured the dorm and blanketed the campus. Cool and white and surreal, it scattered as she jogged along the road edge.

Outside the dorm, two girls from her hall waved and called hello. Teagan threw them a nod and turned the opposite direction and picked up her pace. Her shoes slapped the concrete and filled her ears. She hadn't brought headphones, rarely did, but especially not now with Harley missing. She needed thinking time and music obliterated her thoughts.

As she ran, the hundreds of scenarios she'd considered in the previous days marched in formation across her brain. Nothing, save one, resonated. Harley had been taken. She'd been abducted and either been murdered or was, at that very moment, being held against her will. Another option did not, could not, exist.

Teagan ran to the route Harley would have taken that night from Curly's, and as Teagan turned onto the tree-lined path, she slowed. Up ahead, largely obscured by fog, she spotted the shape of a girl with long blonde hair. Teagan blinked and then picked up her pace, running harder, but as she grew closer to the girl, the shape that had moments before seemed solid dissipated.

There was no girl. No one at all on the path.

At the Den, Teagan turned and jogged off campus toward Greek Row.

All the poles Teagan and her grandma had peppered the day before with posters of Harley were now covered over by hot pink fliers which read *'Toga Party! Hosted by Rho Upsilon Nu and the Alpha Lambda Fraternity.'*

Teagan stared at the graphic of a man and woman wearing togas, leaf crowns on their heads, gyrating to soundless music. Her chest constricted, and she snatched the flier from the pole and ripped it to shreds. She ran to the next and the next, tearing each flier down, scattering bits of pink paper along the sidewalk, so furious she gave not a thought to the trouble she'd get in if she were caught.

As she ripped another free her finger snagged on a splinter. She swore and jerked her hand away, watching the spot of blood that formed at the wound. Hand shaking, she pressed it against her gray t-shirt. The rage in her chest shifted into a sob that lodged into her throat. She gritted her teeth and stared at the ground, wishing she could break something, stomp the sidewalk until cracks formed in its surface.

"Teagan?" A man's voice spoke behind her, but she remained perfectly still, willing the sob to slip back down and stay buried behind her ribs.

After several more seconds of silence, when Teagan felt confident the emotion had passed, she straightened.

Lex watched her, worry creasing his forehead. "Are you okay?" he asked.

She gave him a curt nod. "I'm fine. Just"—she gestured at the poles—"putting up fliers." An obvious lie.

"And taking some down too, I see."

"Fuck their toga party," she spat.

He frowned and nodded. "Pretty inconsiderate for them to hang those fliers up with everything that's going on."

"Yeah, well, I don't think compassion makes the list for qualities in a good sorority sister. The only real requirement is razor-sharp nails so you can stab your sister in the back when she's not looking."

Lex peered at her nails. "Based on those stubby things you call fingernails, I suspect you're safe from being recruited."

She glared at him, but he only continued smiling at her.

"Care to join me for a cup of coffee? I'm walking over to the Java Jon's."

"Clearly coffee is what I need," she muttered, gesturing at the fragments of paper strewn across the lawn.

He chuckled. "We'll see if they have any tranquilizers on the menu."

Teagan fell into step beside him.

"Any news at all on your friend?" he asked.

"No."

"No leads through the Facebook page?"

"Nothing."

"There will be. You just need the right person to see the page or Nate's article. It'll happen."

Teagan said nothing. She'd felt so hopeful after the meeting with Nate the night before, but the instant she'd returned to her dorm room, empty of Harley, the disturbing alternate reality she now lived in had taken hold.

"What is all this?" Teagan murmured as they walked toward a section of street where the sidewalks were crowded with guys.

"It's bid day, aka the running of the bulls," Lex told her. "Today the PNMs receive their bids and find out which sorority chose them."

The doors on a tall, mostly glass, building opened and girls swarmed out and down the steps. Many laughed and cheered. In the throng, Teagan caught sight of girls not celebrating, but crying, red-faced, filled with despair.

"Those ones didn't get into the houses they wanted," Lex explained.

All the girls wore white t-shirts and jean shorts or pants. Frat guys who crowded the sidewalks clapped and hooted. Some of them held water guns and squirted the fleeing girls.

"Harley should be here," Teagan murmured. "Harley should be in that group and she's not."

To Teagan the mass of girls was the last place she'd have wanted to be, but she'd wanted it for Harley, for her friend, and Harley wasn't there and each big event that Harley missed pushed Teagan closer to some dark, irreversible truth.

22

Blair moved down the street, stumbling, hazy, swept along by the current of girls. A boy on her right, Ken or Kent, grinned at her before taking aim at her chest and blasting her with a stream of cool water. She gasped and stared down at her white shirt, at the dark shadow moving across it, and for an instant the stain was scarlet, oozing and hot.

Blair tripped, got tangled in the feet of the girl beside her, and they both tumbled to the sidewalk. The other girl yelped in pain, eyes welling up as she clutched her ankle.

"I'm sorry," Blair murmured, climbing to her feet while the girls around them parted and streamed by, a school of sharks swarming to the kill site.

Blair offered her hand and the girl took it, frowning. She limped away from Blair without a word.

As the Rho Upsilon Nu house came into view, Blair froze. A long dark red mark ran the length of the sidewalk, up the cement steps to the front door. Blood. A trail, as if a body had been dragged into the house. Around her girls jostled and cried out and laughed. They bumped against her, but she couldn't move. No one noticed it, no one screamed in horror.

The door swung open revealing the dark cavity within the sorority house. There was someone in there... something.

Suddenly arms wrapped around her from behind and the sound trapped in her chest broke out. Blair screamed and pushed away, realized it was her mother who'd embraced her, who now had an expression of embarrassment bordering on anger.

"What's wrong with you?" Blair's mother hissed.

"Margo!" another Rho Upsilon Nu mother yelled across the lawn, and Margo plastered on an enormous smile.

Blair's mother jumped up and down and grabbed Blair in a rib-crushing hug, the tightest hug her mother had ever given her, and for those seconds, her face buried in her mother's hair, sweet with the smell of her orange-scented shampoo, Blair thought she might be okay. But then her mother's arms fell away and she turned and embraced the mother of another girl, a sorority sister from her own time at Rho Upsilon Nu, and Blair stood alone surrounded by her new sisters.

The blood trail was gone. It had never been there, not for anyone except Blair, who nodded and smiled as each member of Rho Upsilon Nu took hold of her and hugged her.

When it was over and they'd been ushered into the house and handed a plethora of Rho Upsilon Nu monogrammed gifts, Blair walked with her mother outside.

"I cannot believe that is what you chose to wear for bid day. Those jeans are old," her mother said, fingernails digging into her arm as she marched Blair toward her car. "I told you what to wear. And your hair! Did you curl it at all? My God, it's so stringy and limp. Ugh."

Blair climbed into the passenger seat and shoved her hands between her knees. Her eyes drifted back to the house. She remembered those streaks of dark red and shuddered.

"What's wrong with you? Aren't you even happy? You're basically in. You're a Rho now. You should be jumping for joy."

Blair's lower lip quivered. She bit it between her teeth. "I think... umm..."

"Don't say 'umm,'" her mother snapped.

"I might need to talk to Dr. Maynard."

Her mother slammed on the brake and Blair, who'd forgotten to buckle her seatbelt, hurtled forward and nearly hit her head on the dashboard.

Her mother put up a hand to silence her before Blair could speak again. She rolled her window down as Sloan's mother, Paige, appeared, her red lips stretched wide. "Where are you girls going? We're having brunch!"

"Just a quick run to Blair's dorm to get a different pair of jeans. We'll be back in a blink."

"Okay, you hurry. We've got mimosas and a Bloody Mary bar all set up on the back lawn."

Paige held up a tall glass filled with red liquid. Beads of perspiration rolled down the glass and the ice cubes clanked as she wiggled it from side to side.

Blair's stomach twisted and she forced her eyes away. It was only tomato juice, a Bloody Mary, but a dense coppery odor filled her nostrils and for an instant she imagined all the sorority mothers and daughters slurping glasses of blood, red dribbling over their painted lips and spilling down their white t-shirts.

"Save one for me," Blair's mother called, shifting into drive and pulling down the street. The skin near her temple pulsed and her lips were thinned to a line. She said nothing until she parked in front of Willow Hall.

"Why do you want an appointment with Dr. Maynard?" she demanded.

"I've been seeing—" Blair started.

"Never mind. Don't tell me. I don't want to hear about your

fantasies. Jesus, Blair. Are you intent on ruining everything? Is that it?"

"Mom, I'm not trying to ruin anything. Maybe if I talk to him—"

"I'll talk to him and ask him to write you a script. You can pick it up at the campus pharmacy."

"But I'd like to talk to him and—"

Before Blair could finish, her mother climbed from the SUV and stalked up the steps toward the dorm. Blair followed her.

At the corkboard in the front hall, Blair's mother glared at the missing picture of Harley Rand. "Ridiculous. Those disgusting things are posted everywhere."

"She's missing. Her friend is worried about her."

"If she were so worried about her friend," Margo seethed, "I'd imagine she'd be creating allies, not enemies here on campus. Not to mention Paige said the girl's mother is trailer trash, so..." Margo gave Blair a significant look but said nothing more.

"So...?" Blair replied.

"So, it's not any surprise she took off. According to Sloan the girl was desperate to get into a sorority and things were not looking good for her. Probably figured 'what's the point?' and bailed. It runs in her family, for God's sake."

23

Teagan sat across from Lex in the coffee shop. She'd ordered something called Tranquil Sunset, an herbal tea that tasted mostly of peppermint. Lex had opted for a large black coffee, requesting a separate glass of ice, which he spooned into the steaming liquid.

"Why didn't you just order an iced coffee?" Teagan asked.

"Because then it's cold. I prefer lukewarm."

"Sounds gross."

"To each their own." He bent over and pulled something from his bag, laid it on the table between them. "Have you seen this?"

Teagan leaned forward and spun that day's copy of the *Husher Student Newspaper* toward her. Harley's story fell just above the fold on the front page.

Husher University Freshman Missing Since Wednesday

Harley Rand, 18, of Baldwin, Michigan, has not been seen or heard from since leaving her job at Curly's Sandwich Shop in the Den, Wednesday night at nine p.m. She is a freshman living in Willow Hall on the northeast side of campus. Harley was also partic-

ipating in rush week and had attended several activities on Greek Row.

According to Harley's best friend and roommate, fellow freshman Teagan Kelso, her absence is highly unusual, and Teagan is concerned foul play may be involved in Harley's disappearance. A request for information from the campus police went unanswered.

Just two years ago, Jessica Meyers vanished during rush week after attending an evening recruitment event at the sorority Rho Upsilon Nu. (Jessica's story continues on page 4.)

If you have any information about the disappearance of Harley Rand, please contact Husher Campus Police. Harley's friend has set up a Facebook page, 'Find Harley Rand,' with more information, including a map of the path Harley would likely have walked after work the night she vanished as well as more photos of Harley.

"This is good." Teagan studied the picture she'd given Nate. It was different than the one on Harley's missing poster. Teagan's grandma had taken it on their move-in day at Husher. Harley stood next to the Husher University sign, smiling, hopeful.

Teagan turned to page four, where another face peered out: Jessica Meyers'.

"Did you know about this girl?" Teagan asked, pointing at Jessica's photo.

"Yeah. I was a sophomore. It was a big deal for a few weeks and then faded, like everything does, I guess."

"How can someone vanish and after a few weeks everyone stops looking?"

Lex took a drink of his coffee, added another ice cube and swirled it with his spoon. "It's the nature of human beings, especially the nature of teenagers and young adults. We're a self-absorbed bunch, wouldn't you say? I think she was an out-of-state girl."

"You never wondered what happened to her?"

"I did at the time, sure. Everyone did, but when nothing

much showed up in the news, I sort of figured she went back home, resurfaced or whatever. Until I read this article, I honestly didn't even realize she was still missing."

"That is so screwed up," Teagan muttered. "What kind of school lets something like that happen? What kind of police? Isn't there someone who holds them accountable for stuff like that?"

"Hypothetically, sure. But everyone is fallible. People slip through the cracks."

Teagan pushed her fingers into the hollows of her eyes. The tea, rather than calming her, was setting her on edge. She wanted to fling it across the room, hear the satisfying crack as the cup shattered against the wall.

"What time do you have class?" Lex asked.

Teagan looked up from the paper. "Who cares?"

He leaned back and folded his arms across his chest. "I suspect future medical schools won't look favorably on a candidate who flunked their first semester in college."

"What does any of that matter right now? Harley is missing. She is missing! She might be hurt or..." Teagan stood, hit the table with her hip and sent a splash of tea across the surface.

"Okay." Lex held up his hands. "Just sit down for a minute. Hear me out."

But Teagan couldn't sit down. She couldn't have idle chitchat in a cafe as they hurtled toward another night without Harley.

"I have to go." She turned and strode from the coffee shop, pushed the door so hard it smacked the wall outside.

She ran down the street, sprinting until a stitch worked its way into her side. She slowed and massaged the taut muscle, wishing the blood pumping in her ears could drown out her thoughts of Harley.

∽

TEAGAN RETURNED to her dorm and sat at her desk, opened her laptop and searched for everything she could find about Jessica Meyers.

The articles were minimal. The latest had been the editorial Nate mentioned from the *Husher News*. In it, Jessica's cousin, Erica Griggs, outlined the last day Jessica was seen alive.

Where is Jessica?

This morning two years ago Jessica, my cousin who was more like a sister to me, hugged me goodbye at the airport in Oregon and promised to make her famous chocolate pecan pie when she visited over Thanksgiving. It was the last time I ever saw her.

Her first days at Husher University were lovely. She called me and described the lingering warmth of summer, the campus apple trees heavy with fruit, the classes and the Greek parties and the new friends. She was bubbling over with excitement and I could not have been happier for her.

The last morning I spoke with her was a Thursday, and I will admit she sounded a little less enthused. Maybe the late-night sorority recruitment activities combined with classes had caught up with her. The truth is, I may never know what was bringing her down that morning two years ago.

What I know from witness accounts is that Jessica skipped her nine a.m. math class, but attended her noon English and a two p.m. sociology classes. She attended a rush interview at Rho Upsilon Nu on Greek Row and then worked her shift at the Husher Student Store. She left on foot for her dorm at ten p.m. She has never been seen again.

I live over two thousand miles away. When Jessica disappeared, I was studying for my PhD. I knew within two days of Jessica's disappearance that something was wrong, but the students at Husher University were not informed she'd gone missing for nearly two weeks despite my constant calls.

One month after she vanished, her case was transferred to the Husher Police Department, where it remains. My calls go unre-

turned. When I beg for details, I am stonewalled. My next plan of action is to hire a private investigator. I have saved almost enough money to do so. Is that really my only hope?

Do you have a child, sister, or cousin at Husher? How do you feel about the possibility that they might walk out of their dorm one night and disappear forever?

Teagan finished reading the editorial, disturbed by the similarities between Jessica's disappearance and Harley's. Teagan continued reading everything she could find on Jessica Meyers.

She searched for her name in the Husher University Student Forum. The forum was a nightmare to sift through. Half the time Teagan typed in keywords, unrelated topics popped up. When she searched 'Jessica Meyers,' every post or comment that mentioned anyone named Jessica populated, and Teagan had to painstakingly click and read each to identify its relevancy.

Finally, after a half hour of reading random student gripes, she found a post left nearly a year before that mentioned Jessica Meyers.

Insomniac989: *I have a story to share about that girl who disappeared last year, Jessica Meyers. I never told anyone initially and really regret that now and I'm thinking about going to the police, but not sure if they'll believe me.*

Let me preface this by saying I was walking home from Tamarack Hall and a couple of my friends and I had just gotten pretty high. I was walking back across campus. It was about eleven o'clock and, being stoned, I was just really enjoying the feel of the breeze and the leaves rustling in the trees. You know, all that little stuff you hardly notice when you're not high.

Anyway, I sort of wandered into the woods because I wanted to touch the trees. I know what you're thinking, but as I mentioned, I was stoned. I was standing there marveling at how ridged the bark felt on this oak tree when another girl came down the sidewalk I just vacated. It was Jessica Meyers. I'm like 98% sure because after she disappeared I immediately recognized her picture from that night because she had the long curly reddish hair and, remember, I was as high as a hot air balloon, so I was picking up on all kinds of weird little details. I remember thinking her hair was the color of a fox tail and even had the insane idea of going to ask her if I could pet it, which, for the record, I didn't do because she probably would have freaked out.

I heard the sound of footsteps in the woods on the other side of the sidewalk and so I was watching trying to see who was there and I totally caught a glimpse of what is to this day the scariest shit I have ever seen in my life! It was a person wearing a black robe and a weird-looking mask, like a scarecrow made from that itchy burlap stuff.

This person in the mask was legit stalking Jessica Meyers, keeping pace with her from the woods. I should have followed and tried to see what was up, but the paranoia got hold of me then and I could not will my legs to move. I watched them until they disappeared and she had totally started to walk faster and like a minute later I heard her scream and then nothing.

I know this story sounds made up, but I swear it's not. So, what do you think I should do?

Beneath the anonymous poster, more than a dozen comments had been added. Several called out the poster for lying, trying to seek attention. Several others said they should go to the police ASAP.

FluffyBuns333 posted: *I heard Jessica Meyers was dating a drug dealer and ran off with him.*

Poster Doggo11 replied: *No way! Jessica lived two dorm rooms down from me in Pine Hall. She did not have a boyfriend, though she liked some guy from the Alpha Lambda frat.*

Teagan's eyes lingered on the words 'Alpha Lambda frat.'

Teagan considered the story and whether it could possibly be true. The poster admitted they'd been high, which put the entire scenario into question. Maybe it had simply been a person walking in the woods and the poster had mistaken their regular face for a costume.

Teagan had only smoked pot twice in her life and neither time had she enjoyed it. She'd felt too far away, like her body was firmly planted on earth, but her brain had been set free, connected to some invisible wire and allowed to float up into the sky. Both times she'd been with Harley, who had described a similar discomfort with the experience.

Teagan jotted down a note about the sighting and closed her laptop.

24

Blair stood with the six other girls who'd been invited to pledge Rho Upsilon Nu. None of them spoke, all sensing the tension in the air, the beginning of something important.

Night had fallen and most of the lights, save a few lamps, had been extinguished in the big brick house. A sound emerged from upstairs, and Blair looked up to see her sorority sisters in groups of two walking slowly down the high staircase. They wore long maroon robes, hoods covering their hair. Each held a red candle before her. They stepped into the foyer, and though her face was largely hidden, Blair recognized Sloan's voice when she spoke.

"It's time. Come." Sloan turned and Blair and the other pledges, all wearing white dresses, trailed behind her. The rows of sisters on the stairs parted and Sloan walked between them, the pledges following. Her hands shook and she clutched the skirt of her dress.

They ascended the first flight of stairs and then a second, more narrow set. At the top of the second flight, Sloan held up a hand for the pledges to stop. From behind them, other sorority sisters slipped red silk blindfolds over their eyes. A bit of Blair's hair got caught as the girl tied her blindfold and she winced. The fabric pressed against her eyes, blotted out the shadowy landing. A door creaked open and she was gently pushed forward.

Through a tiny gap at the bottom of her blindfold, Blair saw the feet of the other girls in the room. If she tilted her head up slightly, she could see the hems of the pledges' white dresses and the sisters' maroon robes, long and brushing the wood floor.

Candlelight flickered. Blair's head seemed to float above her body. She wanted to reach to a wall or chair and steady herself but there was nothing to grab hold of. She wobbled and planted her feet wider, trying to ground herself. She imagined her mother doing this same thing decades before, standing in this room, blindfolded. Had she been as terrified as Blair felt now?

The robed figures began to chant. "Sisters by choice, secrets forever, our bond stronger than blood. Sisters by choice, secrets forever, our bond stronger than blood..."

The room felt stifling. Blair swallowed, thirsty. Her mouth had gone dry. Black spots popped and exploded behind her eyes. She struggled to concentrate on the words, slowly trudged forward, bare feet sliding along the scarred wooden floor. She saw globs of dried candle wax on the wood, red, some of it gooey, fresh, and for a moment it wasn't wax. It was blood—splotches of blood all over the floor, and Blair was slipping in it.

She gasped and her head shot up and she ran forward, hands outstretched in search of the door. She ran into the back of another girl, who grunted as Blair tried to maintain her balance, but she'd lost it, was falling back. She hit the floor hard, her head smacking the wood.

Someone ripped the blindfold from Blair's face. Sloan

towered over her, features ghoulish in the candlelight. "Get up," she hissed.

The other girls in the room were eerily still, as if somehow they'd turned off their fight-or-flight response. None of them reacted to Blair's outburst.

Blair gulped breath and winced as Sloan dragged her to her feet and jerked her into the hall.

"What are you doing?" Sloan demanded.

"The blood... I..." Blair gestured at the room.

"What blood?" Sloan scanned Blair.

Blair didn't repeat her words. There'd been no blood.

It's happening again.

"Nothing. I'm sorry. I got hot and dizzy and panicked."

Sloan glared at her for another moment. "You're a pledge. You're not in yet, so I suggest nothing like that ever happens again."

"It won't. I swear."

Sloan yanked Blair's blindfold back over her face, twisted the knob on the door and shoved her into the room.

Sloan started the chant a second time, repeating the oath, and then the Rho Upsilon Nu sisters joined and finally the pledges. "Sisters by choice, secrets forever, our bond stronger than blood."

Blair mumbled the words, the oath, ten times, twenty. She wasn't sure how many times in all, but then the blindfold was loosened and pulled away. Each of the pledges were handed a lit candle. They were arranged in a circle, the pledges on the inside, the Rho Upsilon Nu sisters surrounding them.

"Sisters by choice, secrets forever, our bond stronger than blood. Sisters by choice, secrets forever, our bond stronger than blood. Sisters by choice, secrets forever, our bond stronger than blood."

Their words became a stream, unending, unbroken. Blair could no longer decipher her voice among the rest. Sweat dripped into her eyes, but she didn't dare lift a hand to brush it away. Wax from the candle slid hot over her fingers, soft, mushy, and when she glanced down, the candle was flesh, skin sinking in, blood pouring out. She shut her eyes, sucked in a breath, felt someone pressing close behind her. She'd stopped chanting. She searched for the thread of words, found it and started again.

"These candles," Sloan said, ending the chant, "represent our spirits. On this night the individual becomes one. One sisterhood, one purpose. Each of you will walk to the cauldron, tilt your candle sideways and allow the wax to drip until the flame goes out. The candle of every Rho who has ever been rests in this vessel." She walked across the room where an enormous black iron pot sat on a heavy wood table.

"Come," she said. "Join us."

One by one, the pledges moved to the cauldron. Blair's fingers burned as she turned her candle and the wax poured hot over her skin and into the basin, the bottom thick with red wax.

And then it was over and the girls flooded into the cool air of the hall and rushed down the stairs. They laughed and hugged.

Blair forced smiles at her sisters, but her legs were shaky as she descended to the first floor, where the girls discarded their candles on a table and tossed their robes over a chair.

"It's toga party time at Alpha Lambda," Sloan announced. "Togas on this rack here." She gestured at a rolling wardrobe hung with white togas someone had put in the room while they'd been upstairs. "Let's celebrate!"

25

Wearing their togas, the Rho Upsilon Nu girls walked together, many hand in hand, down the block toward the Alpha Lambda frat house.

As Blair stepped through the front door, a wash of emotion coursed through her. Her brother had lived in this house. She drifted toward a wall of pictures, imagined his face would be captured there in a former class, but Sloan grabbed her hand and yanked her away.

"The party's out back," Sloan said, sounding annoyed.

Blair followed the girls through the house and out to the backyard.

White twinkle lights entwined with garlands had been strung from the trees. The Alpha Lambda guys cheered as they arrived. The guys wore white sarongs and held red solo cups. Music blasted from two enormous speakers and numerous drinking games from flip cup to cornhole were already underway.

As Blair neared the pool, she realized a girl floated face down in the calm surface. Golden hair fanned out from her head. The water around the body had turned pink, but close to the girl's head, crimson rivulets snaked away from her hair.

Blair screamed and jumped into the pool, swam towards the girl. "Help! Help me. Someone call 911," Blair shrieked, flailing through the water, her sarong wet and heavy, pulling her down.

She reached the girl and flipped her over. The bloated dead face of Harley Rand gazed back at her. Her eyes were bulging white orbs, her lips two purplish pouches protruding from her mottled skin.

Blair opened her mouth to scream again, but another sound broke through her thoughts—laughter. She looked up, shocked, to see dozens of students staring down at her, laughing, pointing. Sloan looked furious, her lips curled back from her teeth.

Struck dumb, Blair could do nothing, but shift her horrified gaze to her peers, to their faces twisted in cruel laughter.

What was wrong with them?

But as she had the thought, the texture of the body beneath her hands registered. Not the slimy spongy flesh she'd originally felt. It was hard and... plastic.

Blair stared down at the body, a shiny pink, not the color of skin at all. Smooth and slippery and filled with air. The face of the blow-up doll stared at Blair with its huge painted blue eyes and mouth open in a wide O.

The swim across the pool was endless, and when Blair dragged herself up the steps, dripping, the Alpha Lambda guys clapped and made catcalls. Some of her Rho sisters laughed, others looked unsure whether it had been a joke.

Blair forced a smile and did a curtsy, hoping, praying, they'd believe it had all been a prank. More laughter and clapping.

"Brilliant," a guy told her. He was tall and tan and chiseled, his hair wavy and dark. "I'm Corbin." He offered his hand and she shook it, dripping water onto him.

"Blair," she said, trying to still her quaking voice.

"Come with me. I'll get you a towel."

Blair followed him into the house. He ducked into the bathroom and emerged a moment later with a large white towel. She pushed her face into the soft fabric and tried not to cry.

"Any chance you brought a change of clothes for that little stunt?" he asked.

She shook her head. "No."

"I've got something in my room. Hold on." He disappeared for several minutes and when he returned, some of Blair's nerves had settled. He handed her an Alpha Lambda t-shirt and pair of gray sweatpants with a drawstring. "You won't be winning any fashion contests, but it's dry."

"Thanks," she told him, slipping into the bathroom and locking the door.

She looked at her reflection in the mirror, her blonde hair wet and stringy, the skin beneath her eyes dark with her running makeup. If her mother saw her, she'd throw a blanket over her head and drag her from the party in humiliation.

After Blair had made herself mildly presentable, she returned to the hall where Corbin waited.

"I think you need a drink. Yeah?"

Blair nodded. "Yeah. Thanks."

26

It was nearly ten p.m. when Teagan decided to crash the Alpha Lambda-Rho Upsilon Nu toga party.

She didn't have a toga, but opened the closet hoping Harley had an extra set of sheets somewhere in her stuff. The mere sight of Harley's dresses and skirts arranged on hangers made Teagan want to scream, rip the pain out and stomp on it until it died.

Never in her life had she felt the amount of despair that now lived in her body, as familiar as the beat of her own pulse. It sat in the corner behind her ribs, sharpening its little claws, reaching out now and then to prick her in the heart.

Teagan sat on her chair and clutched her knees and rocked back and forth until the screams and the tears trying to break free receded into the depths. Teagan didn't open the closet again. She pulled jeans and t-shirt from her dresser, put on a bit of mascara and left.

The night was warm and fragrant and loud. Students swarmed the houses along Greek Row. Tiki torches lined the sidewalks. The party had started hours before and Teagan assumed non-Greeks had been welcomed in by now. When she arrived at the Alpha Lambda house it was packed with people. They filled the front lawn, dancing, kissing, and drinking.

Teagan moved slowly through the crowd. When she twisted the knob on the front door of the house, part of her thought she'd find it locked, shut out by these people who wanted nothing to do with her and her missing friend, but it opened easily. Like the front lawn, the interior of the house was crowded. Rap music blared from the living room where more students danced and yelled. The furniture lay buried beneath bodies—everyone held cups of beer.

She paused next to a group of sorority girls with shirts that displayed Greek letters in glittery silver. "Hey," she said, hoping the girls were intoxicated enough to not immediately get suspicious at her question. "Did any of you know Jessica Meyers? I think she rushed a couple years ago."

Two of the girls shook their heads. The third bobbed slowly up and down, eyes widening. "I rushed that year too. I think she moved back to like... some other state."

"She disappeared from Husher and no one ever found her," Teagan said.

"No way," one of the other girls gasped.

"Yeah." Teagan continued focusing on the girl who'd known Jessica Meyers. "Did you know her pretty well?"

The girl caught the eye of a shirtless Alpha Lambda, who'd started to beckon her over. She moved toward him, but Teagan caught the hem of her shirt. The girl twisted and scowled at Teagan's hand.

"Sorry," Teagan said, "but really quick. Did you know her well, know if she had a boyfriend or—"

"Lauren Jacobs," the girl said.

"That was her boyfriend?" Teagan asked.

The girl rolled her eyes, seemingly annoyed that Teagan was preventing her from rushing into the arms of the glistening Alpha Lambda who'd started to bong a beer. "It was like her best friend or whatever. They never left each other's side during rush week and Lauren got into Rho Upsilon Nu. I'm sure they regretted that choice. They totally passed over me and like ten other girls to take Lauren, who then got kicked out last year."

"She got kicked out of the sorority? Why?"

"For hiding puke in her closet."

Teagan screwed up her eyes. "That's a joke?"

"No. It's true. It got out because an Alpha Lambda guy went in there with her to hook up and saw containers of puke stashed in her closet. Disgusting."

The girl didn't wait for Teagan to ask more. She hurried over to the guy, who picked her up and whirled her in a circle, her head swinging dangerously close to the wall.

Teagan took out her cell phone and put the name 'Lauren Jacobs' in her notes app.

For a half hour, she walked through the crowd, ears perked for Harley's name, Jessica's name, or the word 'missing.' Someone knew something. Teagan had seen many of the girls from Rho Upsilon Nu at the party, many still wearing togas, others in swimsuits and skimpy dresses.

The music was so loud Teagan's eyes began to pulse with the beat and a headache took root in the center of her brain. The fervor with which she'd entered the party had begun to fade and a hopelessness crept behind her.

"Shots! Come on, you shitfaces. It's time for shots!" A freckled guy, wearing a toga that had mostly come undone, wiggled through the crowd carrying a tray of little plastic cups. He stopped in front of Teagan.

"Whoa, Nellie! Hold up." He neighed like a horse as he brought the tray in front of Teagan's nose. "You need two of these. Tequila. It'll loosen you right up."

"I'm good. Thanks."

The guy neighed again, pawed the floor with one bare foot.

"Don't make me turn into a bucking bronco, girl. Take two so I can move on."

Teagan snatched two little cups from the tray. "There. Happy?" she demanded.

He grinned. "Happy as a horse in pig shit. Or wait... is it happy as a hog in horse shit? Who cares. Shots!"

He moved along. The pungent smell of the tequila pricked sharp in Teagan's nose. She stared at the two little cups. She'd never been a drinker. Both she and Harley had been too up close and personal with alcohol dependence, and though they'd each had an occasional drink at parties in high school, they'd agreed it didn't taste great and hardly seemed worth the effort of trying to obtain it.

Still, as she stared at the honey-colored liquid, some piece of her wanted the lie it sold. *Takes the edge off, relaxes you, makes the hard stuff less hard.* She knew all the reasons people drank, had heard them first hand as her grandmother, an AA sponsor, talked her latest member away from a bottle or a bar.

Her grandma herself had chosen alcohol as her escape of choice after Teagan's mother's death more than a decade before, and those had been some rough years. But not all bad. Teagan had fond memories of her inebriated grandma putting up the Christmas tree in April or letting Teagan walk to the corner store to buy candy for dinner.

"Fuck it," she muttered, and took both shots. The tequila sent a fireball into her stomach and she gasped and steadied her hand on the counter.

She'd come to the party as a spy, seeking any shred of evidence about what had happened to Harley, but like so many of her searches, this too seemed futile. She was chasing ghosts, shadows, perhaps nothing at all. The tequila could dull the sharp edges a bit and she desperately needed a reprieve from herself.

What if Harley did leave? Run away to start a new life?

The thought wriggled its way into her consciousness. It was something people did. Teagan's dad had done it—left before she'd even been born. And even though every cell of Teagan's body resisted the idea that Harley had up and left, some tiny piece of her wanted to believe it because though it would hurt, the terrible rejection and abandonment, it wouldn't hurt as bad as the alternative—never seeing Harley again, knowing she was gone forever.

Teagan eyed the keg, the tequila already fuzzing her better sense. She grabbed a plastic cup and shoved it beneath the spout, watched the beer and foam rise. She took a long drink and another, then put the cup beneath a second time.

"Oh, damn," a guy said, nodding his approval at Teagan. "Get after it, girl."

Teagan stared at him, vaguely remembered him from the night she'd visited the frat party with Harley. Branden or Brady. It didn't matter. He leered at her, his white sheet turned toga revealing his muscled chest.

"Want a tour of the upstairs?" he asked, grinning. "Let me get you a refill first."

Teagan started to shake her head no, then nodded instead and handed him her cup. She had a looseness to her, a calmness, but she wasn't wasted. This was a guy who could give her information, who was so distracted by delusions of his own greatness, he'd never recognize she was manipulating him.

She followed him to the second floor, caught sight of his name on the door; Brody. He pushed the door open and stepped inside. The room was surprisingly tasteful for a frat boy. Diplomas and awards hung in glass frames on his walls. His desk was neatly stacked with text books, his bed made, his dirty clothes hidden perhaps in a closet hamper.

Teagan took a drink of her beer and walked the perimeter of his room, feigning interest in his many accolades.

"Do you remember me?" she asked.

Brody tilted his head and smiled. "Oh, I'd remember you, baby. I can tell you that much."

"How about my friend, Harley? Do you remember her? We met you here at a party during welcome week."

He grinned. "Oh, yeah? You've got a friend, huh? Go get her. Let's have some fun."

Teagan, in her usual state of mind, would have been enraged at his comment, but now ignored it. "Friend of yours?" She picked up a bobblehead statue, the only quirky thing in the guy's oddly perfect room. It was a three-headed dog, tongues lolling from the side of its' mouths.

"Cerberus," he said. "The hounds of Hell. I call him Fido. He's our Alpha Lambda mascot."

Teagan finished her beer as she walked, scanning the floor, the shelves. Nothing that pointed to Harley having been there.

"So anyway," Teagan murmured, a little unsteady on her feet, "about my friend Harley..."

Her vision blurred, steadied, then blurred again. The beer and tequila fizzed in her belly. She burped and didn't bother covering her mouth or saying excuse me.

Brody patted the bed. "Here, sit down. You can lie down if you need to. You look a little pale."

Teagan brushed a hand across her forehead, touched a lock of hair, sweaty against her clammy forehead. Her skin felt hot beneath her fingers. Something was wrong. The knowledge jolted her. Teagan needed to get out of there and now, but something was wrong with her legs. They were stiff, heavy. Her stomach cramped and she doubled over, grimaced.

"I'm gonna be sick," she slurred.

Brody made a face and hurried to his door, pulled it open.

Teagan lurched out and down the stairs.

27

B lair recognized the dark-haired girl who'd been searching for Harley Rand and posting fliers over the previous days.

"Teagan..." Blair whispered as the girl plunged from the steps, her legs nearly buckling as she landed hard in the front hallway at Alpha Lambda.

Blair shot forward and caught her, pulling her upright and snaking an arm around her back.

"Huh?" Teagan's head lolled forward and then she craned sideways, blinking at Blair.

"Teagan, are you okay?"

"Hmmm..." She shook her head slowly. "Gonna be sick," she muttered.

"Okay. Come on. This way." Blair steered Teagan, who tripped over her own feet, toward the front door. They'd barely made it down the steps before Teagan turned and vomited into the grass. Two guys who'd climbed into a tree and were shaking acorns onto people's heads made gagging sounds as Teagan threw up.

When the puking had stopped, Blair helped Teagan to her

feet. Teagan leaned heavily on Blair as they walked back to the dorm. She wasn't dead weight, but close, her feet dragging, her arm so heavy on Blair's shoulder, Blair gritted her teeth against the ache.

When they reached Willow Hall, Blair took them through the back door using her key card so they could bypass the woman in the front foyer. The steps were the hardest of all. Twice Teagan doubled over, spit dribbling from her lips, and Blair feared she'd vomit in the hall. She didn't.

"What room are you in?" Blair asked as she pushed open the door to the second floor.

"Room? Umm…. 217."

She fished Teagan's keys from the pocket of her jeans and opened the dorm room, helped her inside and then frowned at the loft bed. She'd never be able to get her up there.

"Here. Just lie on a bean bag," Blair said, easing her down onto one of the large bean bags beneath the loft.

Teagan collapsed and curled into a ball, buried her face into the black fabric and closed her eyes. "So dizzy," she murmured.

"Yeah, hold on. Let me get you some water. Don't sleep yet." Blair opened the mini fridge and took out a bottle of water, unscrewing the cap and holding it to Teagan's lips. "Take a drink. As much as you can."

Teagan drank, though more water ended up on her shirt than in her mouth. She slumped back into the beanbag, eyes closed.

Blair stood and eyed the door for a moment, before returning her gaze to Teagan, who was very drunk. She didn't want to leave her, so instead flopped down on the opposite beanbag and closed her eyes.

～

"HI. GOOD MORNING."

Teagan blinked at the girl who sat on Harley's bean bag. She was vaguely familiar. As Teagan sat up, a fire poker stabbed into the center of her brain. "Oh, fuck," she muttered, laying her head back and putting a hand to her temple. "Ugh."

"Headache?" the girl asked.

"Mmm... hmmm."

"Here." The girl uncurled Teagan's fingers and put two little pills in her palm.

Teagan opened her eyes and gazed at the pills. "What are these?"

"Ibuprofen. And here's some water." She handed Teagan a bottle of water.

Painfully, Teagan sat up, shoved the pills in her mouth and took a drink. Her stomach churned. "I don't even remember what happened last night. I followed that guy Brody upstairs and then"—she waved her hand—"nothing."

"I don't know what happened up there, but you came down at the Alpha Lambda house and threw up outside. I walked you back here, figured I'd stay just in case you got sick in the night."

"Thanks," Teagan mumbled. "That guy, Brody, he must have given me something. No way was I just drunk."

"I don't really know him," the girl admitted. "But you were pretty out of it. Still no word on your friend?"

Teagan closed her eyes. "No."

"I'm really sorry."

Teagan nodded, but that sent a jolt of pain ripping through her head. "What was your name? I forgot it."

"Blair. Blair Davenport."

"Teagan Kelso," Teagan said.

"I remember," Blair told her. "I have to head back to my room and change and then go to class, but I'd be happy to stop by after and check on you."

"You don't need to do that. I'll be fine."

"Are you sure?"

"Yeah."

Teagan listened as Blair stood, crossed the room and left. She too needed to get up, check her messages, call her grandma. She needed food and coffee and a shower, but the pounding in her head and rolling in her stomach rendered all those options impossible. She closed her eyes and struggled back into sleep.

IT WAS noon when Teagan finally dragged herself off the beanbag and down to the community bathroom. She showered and put on clean sweatpants and a t-shirt. When she returned to her room, she checked her phone and realized she had four missed calls from her grandma. She called her back, but got her grandma's voicemail, which meant she was likely with a patient. Teagan sent her a quick text.

Teagan: *Sorry I missed your calls. Slept late.*

Her grandma responded: *At doctor appointment with Sally Bloom. Made some calls yesterday and found a TV station willing to do a press conference with us at Husher today at four.*

Teagan: *A press conference? Awesome. That just made my whole day.*

Grandma: *Fingers crossed. Lisa and Buzz are coming too. I'll call you in a couple hours.*

Teagan turned on her laptop. She opened the student directory and searched for the name of the student the girl at the party had mentioned the night before: Lauren Jacobs, supposedly the best friend of Jessica Meyers. There was only one Lauren Jacobs listed, a junior. Teagan sent her an email asking if they could talk.

She then navigated to the 'Find Harley Rand' Facebook page. She posted an update: *Press conference at Husher University about Harley's disappearance today at four. More details to come soon. Please spread the word.*

A little red eight hovered above the inbox, which meant she'd received eight private messages. Before she could open them, someone knocked on her dorm door.

28

Teagan found Blair standing in the hallway, two paper cups in her hands. "Coffee?" Blair asked.

"Oh, uh, sure. Yeah."

"I'm not interrupting, am I? I didn't have your number or I would have texted first."

"No. You're good. Come in. Thanks for the coffee. I can use it, that's for sure."

"Cream or no cream?"

"No cream," Teagan said.

Blair handed her one of the cups and followed her into the room. Teagan returned to her computer chair, but fought the urge to open the messages. "Thanks for last night. I'm not sure where I would have ended up if you hadn't helped me," Teagan said.

"Oh, sure, yeah, no big deal. I mean, I live here in Willow Hall too, so it wasn't like a big inconvenience."

"Still, I appreciate it. I never do that, get drunk. I can't imagine what kind of an ass I made of myself."

"Not any worse than I did," Blair murmured.

"Oh, yeah? Well, whatever you did, at least you remember it."

Blair picked at the lid on her coffee cup. "That's not always a good thing."

"True enough. Still, I don't know what I was thinking getting wasted in some random frat house."

"Probably about your friend," Blair said. "I'm really sorry you're going through all that. It must be scary."

"It is, and infuriating. If I didn't think the university would slap me with a huge fine, I'd have punched about ten holes in the wall by now."

"Has there been any news at all?"

"Maybe. I was actually just checking the page I set up and I have messages. I don't know if there's any tips, but do you mind if I look?"

"No, gosh. Not at all. Go ahead."

Teagan opened each message, her disappointment growing. Five of the messages were from high school friends, shocked to hear about Harley and asking what happened. Three were from Husher students who'd met Harley in class and hoped she was found safe.

Teagan sighed and turned back to Blair, who sat perched on the edge of Harley's desk chair.

"Nothing?"

"No. Lots of thoughts and prayers," Teagan muttered.

"At least you're getting the word out," Blair said.

"I guess. You were at Rho Upsilon Nu the other day when we were hanging fliers. Were you rushing that sorority?"

Blair's cheeks turned pink. "Yeah. I'm a pledge now."

"What does that mean exactly?"

"It means they invited me to join as a pledge, which is sort of like a probationary period where I'm pretty sure they get away with torturing us for the next four weeks. If we survive it, we're officially sisters."

"Torturing you? Sounds miserable."

"It is," Blair murmured. "But... who knows. Maybe it will all be worth it."

"Why do I get the sense you don't actually want to be in a sorority?" Teagan asked.

Blair tugged on her long blonde hair swept over one shoulder. She glanced down at it and grimaced. "My hair is actually much darker than this," she said. "My mom has appointments set up for me every three weeks to get the roots done."

Teagan frowned. "Why?"

"Because sororities prefer blondes, and so do fraternities. They won't admit that, of course, but there was a big anonymous survey in the Greek community a while back and across the board, all the Greeks wanted blonde girls."

"Who cares what your hair color is? That's mental."

"Hair, nails, outfits, the works. My mom was a Rho and it was the highlight of her life. If I hadn't rushed, she would have totally flipped out," Blair said.

"I can't even comprehend that. I would have told her to stick it where the sun doesn't shine."

Blair giggled. "What about you? No helicopter mom guilting you into rushing?"

Teagan snorted. "No. No mom at all. She died of cancer when I was six. My dad split before I even vacated the womb. My grandma raised me."

"Oh..." Blair's mouth turned down. "I'm sorry."

Teagan shrugged. "It's fine. My grandma's great. If my mom had lived, she wouldn't have been pushing me to join a sorority though. She never went to college. She bagged groceries for a living, not exactly the kind of stock those Greek girls are looking for."

Blair smiled. "But your best friend was rushing? How did you feel about that?"

"The truth? I hated the idea of Harley joining a sorority,

getting emotionally kicked in the teeth by a bunch of girls who'd never slept on sheets with a thread count of less than fifteen hundred, girls who'd do their best to strip away her identity and turn her into another Barbie. No offense," she added.

"All that being said, Harley is my best friend in the world, and that word doesn't even come close to explaining what she means to me. What she wants matters to me, and she's wanted this her whole life. Was it scary watching her go for it?" Teagan nodded. "Terrifying. I was afraid I'd lose her, that she'd begin to slip away, but fear is a liar. Nothing slips away. We let it go. I wasn't going to let her go, not ever, not even if she became the president of one of those damn sororities." Teagan frowned, the truth dawning on her. "But I did let her go. I let her go and now she's gone."

"No..." Blair shook her head. "You're searching. You're doing more than... most people would. I don't think I've ever had a friend like that."

"Harley and I have been close since we were young. We had a sort of shared orphan experience."

"Orphan? Are Harley's parents dead?"

"No. Harley's dad's in prison. Her mom is... inconsistent. I mean, we all are, right? But Lisa, that's Harley's mom, was a drug addict and alcoholic for a long time. She's clean now, but Harley was always the adult in their relationship. People say that kids of addicts either become addicts themselves or they become over-achievers, perfectionists. Harley's the latter. That's why she wants to be in a sorority. She's borderline obsessed with Ruth Bader Ginsburg."

"The judge?"

"Yep."

"Is Harley planning on studying law?"

Teagan smiled. "You'd think so, right? But no. She wants to be a teacher, which is another sorority link for her, I guess. She had a really amazing teacher in elementary school who helped her and her mom with all these social programs to get food and help with bills. That teacher had also been in a sorority and talked about it like this dream experience. So, Harley was hooked on the idea from a pretty young age."

"Sounds like my mom. Was Rho Upsilon Nu her first choice?"

"Yeah."

"How come?"

"Beats me. All of a sudden, this summer she homed in on them. I'm sure she did loads of research. That's Harley's personality. Nothing is ever half-assed."

"And do you have a major?" Blair asked.

"Pre-med."

"Wow, really? You want to be a doctor?"

"Yep. Oncology."

"That's cancer stuff?"

Teagan nodded. "Yeah. My mom died of breast cancer and I still remember her doctor. We send each other letters a couple times a year. How about you?"

Blair sighed and picked at her fingernail. A flake of pink polish came off and she blanched. "Oh, no," she murmured. "I'll have to fix this."

Teagan leaned over to her desk and plucked a pink marker from her drawer. "Here. Color it in. Good as new."

Blair smiled and colored the light spot. It was clearly mismatched, but from afar no one would notice. "I'm majoring in business. That's what my mom wanted, so..."

"What do *you* want?"

"Well... if I could pick anything, I'd choose art history or something that could prepare me to do an MFA."

"What's an MFA?"

"A masters in fine arts. Basically, an art degree."

"You like to, what? Paint, draw? That kind of thing?"

"I like to sculpt things with clay. That's my favorite, but I enjoy drawing too."

"Sculpting. That's really cool. My art abilities end at stick figures."

Blair's phone pinged and she looked at it and sighed. "That's my alarm. I have to be to Rho Upsilon Nu in a half hour for pledge stuff. I better get going."

Teagan stood and walked her to the door. "Hey, Blair," she said before the girl started away.

"Yeah?"

"Could you do me a favor and ask around about Harley at the sorority? Just see if anyone saw her the day she went missing?"

Blair looked concerned at the prospect, but after a moment she nodded. "Sure."

"Thanks. And there's a press conference at four in front of the Den if you want to come by."

"I'll try to be there," Blair said.

29

"To the attic, pledges," Ginger said when Blair and the other pledges arrived at the Rho Upsilon Nu house.

Sloan and three other sisters waited for them when they stepped through the door into the attic room. "Take off your clothes," Sloan said.

Blair frowned at her, unsure if she'd misheard. She glanced at the faces of her fellow pledges, saw similar expressions of misgiving.

"What are you, deaf?" Sloan shouted. "I said take off your clothes!"

"All of them?" a tall slender girl named Amy asked.

"Everything except bra and underwear," Sloan said.

Uneasily, the girls stripped. Blair resisted, but then caught the scathing look on Sloan's face and with shaky hands pulled her shirt over her head. She unbuttoned and unzipped her shorts and let them fall to the floor, stepped out and slid them aside.

All the pledges stood naked save bras and underwear. Blair tried not to look at them. She focused on the floor, on the grooves between the wood planks. Bits of red wax remained from their ritual the night before.

A pungent chemical aroma filled the air and she looked up. The Rho sisters held markers in their hands, caps removed, and they descended on the pledges, drawing on their skin. Sonya, a shorter girl with wide hips, stood beside Blair, eyes welling with tears. Two sisters drew big circles on her hips, her thighs. They marked X's across the spray of freckles on her chest.

Sloan poked Blair's stomach. "No muscle," she muttered, scribbling x's across her skin. She drew an x around a birthmark on her lower back and then added more circles to her upper arms—flabby, according to Sloan.

The faces of her fellow pledges were pale, some streaked in tears and mascara. Blair's own face felt like stone. She could move her mouth, blink her eyes, but that was all. She stared straight ahead as Sloan's marker swiped hot across her skin.

The scent of the markers was heady, chemical.

The opposite wall grew fuzzy, indistinct and there in the whorls and grooves a shape emerged.

It was a girl-a girl with black empty eyes and a stitched mouth.

Blair gaped at the girl, rocked unsteady on her feet, felt her mouth go dry.

They stared at each other-Blair and this shadow girl trapped in the wall. This girl who wanted something from Blair-something she couldn't say because she'd been silenced forever.

A whimper slipped between Blair's lips and when a hand clamped on her elbow, she jumped and cried out.

"Jesus, Blair. Relax," Heather said. "You can get dressed now."

Blair realized all the pledges had put their clothes back on, were filtering into the hall behind the Rho sisters.

Trembling, Blair grabbed her shirt and pulled it over head. She slipped on her shorts and followed Heather into the hall.

"There's my little sister," Sloan said pulling Blair into a hug. When she withdrew her smile vanished. "Hey, what's wrong?"

Blair said nothing, but her eyes darted to the room they'd all just stood in, many of the girls crying as their Rho Upsilon Nu sisters pointed out their imperfections and trouble areas.

"That?" Sloan said, shaking her head. "Don't get hung up on that. We've all been through it. It makes us stronger, and you know what?" Sloan looped her arm through Blair's and guided her toward the stairs. "Most of us go through our whole lives without any true friend who will say 'hey, you've gained a few pounds,' or 'that haircut makes your forehead look huge.' We need that, all of us. We need some real brutal honesty, and that's just a little activity to show you that in this house we tell it like it is."

Blair allowed Sloan to guide her down the stairs and into the kitchen, where a spread of food had been laid out. Blair eyed the options warily. Huge blueberry muffins and chocolate croissants, donuts and trays of cookies.

"Help yourself, pledges. This was brought in for you."

Blair took nothing. She filled a glass of lemon water and sipped it, only half listening as Sloan laid out the pledge events in the days ahead. She tried to concentrate, but her mind drifted to the shape of the girl in the attic room.

As Blair hurried away from the house, her textbooks fell out and hit the sidewalk. She'd forgotten to zip her backpack up after putting her pledge calendar inside. She turned and bent over, gathering the books.

"What the heck is that?" A man's voice rose behind her and Blair straightened up and turned to see Corbin frowning at her.

"What?" she asked.

He marched over and lifted up her shirt. She took a step back and swatted at his hand.

He held his palms up. "I'm sorry. That was out of line. I saw the"—he gestured at her waist—"marker spots and realized the girls must have done their humiliating ritual of telling you about all your flaws That's not a flaw, by the way."

Blair frowned, put a hand on her lower back, pressing her fingers over the little eye-shaped birth mark. "It's fine. This is part of the process, right? Getting broken down so they can build us up again."

"Yeah, it is, but it still sucks."

Blair leaned back down and swiped her book from the grass. "I have to get going. I have class in twenty minutes."

"I'll walk you," he said.

"Aren't you going in?" Blair gestured at the Rho house. Someone watched from a downstairs window, and though Blair couldn't see them well, she suspected it was Sloan.

"Nope."

Blair cast a final self-conscious glance at the house, then started away. Corbin fell into step beside her.

"You're dating Sloan, aren't you?"

"Sometimes," he admitted.

"Is that how she'd describe it?"

"Probably. She went on a date with Brody the other night. Neither of us feels the need to own each other."

"Oh. Okay."

"Does that bother you?"

Blair shook her head. Blair had only had one boyfriend in her life and ultimately her mother had scared him away. "So why did you join Alpha Lambda?"

He tilted his head, thoughtful. "For the brotherhood, the camaraderie. My uncle was a Lambda down in Florida. He loved it. I've actually met a lot of his frat brothers because he brings them up to family Christmas. He went into business with one, married the sister of another. He and like twenty of his frat brothers take a big trip together every year. It's been a family for him and I wanted that too."

"Because your actual family isn't great?"

He shook his head. "No, they are. I mean, they're not perfect, but they're good. My parents are divorced, both remarried. I have one biological brother and then a half-sister on my mom's side and a half-brother on my dad's side. We all get along pretty well, but the frat just represented a different kind of family, a chosen family, you know?"

Blair nodded, but in truth she didn't know. The last family she'd have chosen were her sisters at Rho Upsilon Nu.

"How about you?" he asked. "You look the part of a Rho, but I get the sense you're not as into it as some of the other girls."

Blair sighed, adjusted the straps on her backpack. "I'm not sure I fit in."

"Would you have preferred a different sorority?"

Blair shook her head, almost said she would have preferred no sorority, but then remembered she was confiding secrets to the sometimes-boyfriend of Sloan, a girl he'd likely tell everything she said. "No. I'm happy with the sorority. It's just a lot to adjust to."

"True enough. It's been three years since I pledged. I've forgotten how demanding it was, but it really will make you closer with the girls. So..." He raised an eyebrow. "I wanted to ask you about the party last night, the pool thing."

Warmth flooded Blair's face and she allowed a sheet of blonde hair to fall from behind her ear to hide her embarrassment.

"Were you really joking about the girl in the pool? There was something in your face. You looked truly terrified for a minute."

"It was a long day yesterday and I'd had a couple drinks

and... yeah. I thought it was real. I wish I'd been joking." She shrugged.

"Don't sweat it. When I was pledging, we had to strip off everything but our underwear and run the length of the sorority houses with all the girls outside throwing water balloons at us. My problem? I'd gone commando that day, which meant I had to run buck naked down this whole street." He laughed. "So, if any of your new sorority sisters are talking about my junk, it's not because I get around. They've seen every bit of me of there is to see."

Blair laughed and glanced at Corbin, who didn't look at all embarrassed as he recalled the story.

"That's what makes the Greek experience unique. You're called to do things you'd never do in ordinary life and you do it together and you're stronger for it."

30

Teagan dressed in black shorts and a short-sleeved red flannel with a white t-shirt beneath. She pulled her dark hair into a ponytail.

Her hangover had largely subsided, but remnants of the previous night's activities made her stomach feel mushy as she gathered fliers and left the dorm. Her grandma was meeting her at the Den, where the press conference was scheduled to be held on the lawn outside at four.

The street in the front of the Den was surprisingly crowded as Teagan turned the corner. People stood in groups around the lawn and others loitered on the steps that led up to the student building.

Someone had erected a small podium with a microphone on it. Three separate news vans were parked on the street. Teagan spotted Nate from the *Husher Student Newspaper* standing near the sidewalk talking to Lex.

As she got closer, her grandma appeared from a crowd of people. Teagan hurried toward her. "There's a lot more people than I expected," Teagan said.

"Me too. I made some calls this morning as well. Do you

remember Polly from AA? Her husband was an editor for a Cadillac newspaper for years. I'd totally forgotten. He reached out to a few friends and helped spread the word. Finally we might get some traction here."

"Yeah, I hope so."

Teagan's grandma hugged her, patting her back for a long moment. "How were classes this morning? Have you been making sure to eat?"

Teagan pulled away and shook her head. "I haven't been to classes. I can't with all this happening."

"TT." Her grandma took her hand and squeezed, looked like she might say something more, but then the sound of a motorcycle split the air and they both watched as Buzz, Lisa riding behind him, pulled to the curb.

Teagan lifted her hand to wave, then froze as Lisa plummeted off the motorcycle and landed hard on one knee. She stood, brushed Buzz angrily away, and wove through the crowd toward Teagan. She was inebriated, barely able to walk a straight line. Her shoulders bumped against several other people, her head drooped forward and her legs wobbled with every step.

"I'll go," Teagan's grandmother said, hurrying toward the woman.

Before Teagan's grandma could intercept Lisa, Lisa turned and lunged toward a girl in the throng of people. Teagan gasped as the girl jumped back. It was Blair and she was wearing one of the signature pink and gold Rho Upsilon Nu t-shirts.

"You know!" Lisa shrieked. "Your sorority knows what happened to my daughter. You know!"

Teagan's grandma took hold of Lisa, who collapsed in tears, leaning against her, weeping so loudly people turned to stare. Buzz didn't approach the women, but hovered near his bike, red-faced and glassy-eyed. He too appeared drunk.

Blair, her face pale, backed away and disappeared into the crowd.

Teagan's hands felt sweaty and her stomach roiled. The nightmares, the not sleeping, now combined with a hangover had taken a toll. Her brain was thick, foggy and the most prevalent emotion coursing through her was anger. Anger at Lisa for getting drunk and showing up at Harley's press conference barely able to walk. Anger at herself for not having more compassion for her best friend's mother. Anger most of all at whoever had taken Harley, stolen her, likely killed her.

The message she was about to say would not be a tear-filled plea to bring Harley home alive. She no longer believed such a thing was possible.

Hands balled into a fist, she funneled her rage and marched onto the platform.

"This is my friend!" she half yelled into the mic, holding high a missing poster of Harley. "Harley Marie Rand. She's five feet six inches tall, slender, with green eyes and dark blonde hair. She was last seen here"—Teagan pointed at the Den behind her—"on Wednesday after her shift at nine p.m. She worked her shift at Curly's and likely took that path." Teagan pointed toward the sidewalk that wound its way toward Willow Hall.

"The last known person to see her was the guy she worked with at Curly's—Paul. No one has come forward saying they saw her after that time. She does not own a car. I've checked the buses that came through campus that night. None of the drivers remember her. She was rushing several sororities with hopes of getting into Rho Upsilon Nu. She might have been near that sorority the night she went missing, though the sorority sisters claim they didn't see her."

A reporter standing in front of a Husher news camera shouted a question. "Where are her parents?"

Teagan's gaze darted to Lisa, who her grandmother had

settled on a bench and now held a bottle of water to her lips. "Her mother is devastated and very emotional right now, so I am speaking on her behalf."

"Did she have any reason to run away?" another reporter called.

"No!" Teagan said more loudly than was necessary. "She absolutely did not run away, and anyone saying otherwise is spreading lies."

"How do you know?" the first reporter asked.

"Because I know my friend. Harley was so excited for this school year and she had absolutely no reason to leave, and if she had left, she would have been in contact with me or her mother or another of our friends."

"Is it true her father is incarcerated? We received a tip that her father is in prison?"

Lisa released a fresh wail of despair at the comment.

31

Teagan stared at the reporter, who seemed to be referring to a clipboard of notes. Fury ripped through her, but she bit it back. "Yes. And he's been there since Harley was a baby. She doesn't know him and his choices have no bearing on what's happening with Harley right now."

Teagan's grandmother suddenly appeared beside the little stage. "May I?" Connie asked, stepping up next to Teagan.

Teagan nodded, outrage muddling her ability to speak.

"Hi, everyone. I'm Connie Kelso," Teagan's grandmother said. "I've had the good fortune of being very close with Harley as she grew up, thanks to her and Teagan's friendship. I can assure you she is not the type of girl to run away, and if our assurances of her character are not enough for you, consider this. In high school Harley was a 4.0 student who had nearly perfect attendance. Such good attendance she received an award at graduation. She has now missed nearly a week of classes.

"Harley loves children and animals. She stands up for what she believes in, is a loving and loyal friend." Her grandmother squeezed Teagan's hand and Teagan, fighting emotion, looked to the sky in an attempt to shove the tears down. "She has never, not once, not even for an afternoon, been unaccounted for by the people who love her.

"Please use your common sense. This is an eighteen-year-old girl, a girl like many of you standing here. What would you want the community to do if this happened to you or one of your friends? To your daughter? To your sister? What we need now are people searching, asking questions and calling in tips. Teagan has set up a Facebook page, 'Find Harley Rand.' There are details of Harley's last known whereabouts, the route she would have walked, and more photos.

"Talk to your friends, find out if anyone saw anything. No tip is too small, no rumor should be disregarded. We"— Connie wrapped an arm around Teagan and pulled her close —"cannot do this alone. We are begging for help in finding this lovely young woman we miss and are terribly worried about."

"Why isn't there a police presence here?" a reporter asked.

Teagan, fuming, leaned toward the mic, but her grand-mother beat her to it.

"Teagan has filed a missing person's report and we trust they have opened an investigation. I can't say why they're not here today, as we did contact them and let them know we'd be holding this press conference; however, my sincere hope is they aren't here because they're out there looking for our Harley. Please do whatever you can to assist the police, and if you'd prefer to call tips in to them or have questions for them, their number is on the fliers and the Facebook page."

Several people in the crowd turned and scanned, as if surprised the police had not attended.

As Teagan and her grandmother stepped off the little podium, people crowded around them. Some asked questions, others spoke words of encouragement. Teagan's grandma continued answering questions and Teagan walked to the edge of the lawn. Her head ached and she suddenly couldn't stand the cacophony of voices.

She glanced up to see Nate and Lex approaching her. "People are listening," Nate said. "That's good."

"Who's that reporter?" Teagan demanded, pointing at the man who'd mentioned receiving a tip about Harley's dad.

"I don't know," Nate admitted. "But I think I saw him by the Around Town Van over there. They put out the *Free Weekly* on all the happenings in Husher. I'm surprised they'd be here."

"Well, he was an asshole," Teagan grumbled.

Nate chuckled. "I'm going to head back to the newsroom and get some of the video from today's press conference posted on our Facebook page. The gears are turning. Keep your head up."

He walked away, leaving Teagan standing beside Lex, whose gaze paused on Lisa. Harley's mom had stretched across the park bench, feet dangling off one end, a balled-up sweatshirt beneath her head.

"Is that Harley's mom?" he asked.

Teagan stared at her, unable to hide the disgust on her face. "Yeah. She's been clean for two years and now this. I'm so pissed at her. Why can't she hold it together for one fucking day? Why can't she show up here and tell these people that Harley matters, that her life matters?"

"You did that and your grandma did and, honestly, people will relate to her mom falling apart. Who wouldn't want to do that if their kid disappeared?"

Teagan eyed Lisa for another moment, doubtful anyone would relate to her in her current state. "Maybe." Teagan blew out a breath.

The crowd began to disperse, students back across campus, others to their cars.

"Now what?" Teagan asked. "For five minutes this felt like a big deal and now everyone is leaving."

Teagan's grandma walked over, her expression drawn. "I brought the van and I'm going to take Lisa with me, see if I can't help her get back on track. Are you okay here, TT? You could come with us."

Teagan imagined the hours ahead at her grandma's house as she attempted to detox Lisa. Grief, guilt, a torrent of emotion that Teagan didn't want to witness and frankly had no patience for. Her daughter was the victim, but Lisa had once again chosen soothing herself instead of helping her only child. "No. I can't. I'd say things to Lisa I can't take back. Better if I'm not around her."

Her grandma drew her in for a hug and rubbed her back. "I understand. But remember not all of us have the strength of the lion. Some of us are kittens, no matter how old we get." She kissed Teagan on the temple.

Teagan, remembering Lex still stood beside her, gestured at him. "This is Lex, Grandma. Grandma, Lex."

"Hi," he said. "Nice to meet you."

"Call me Connie," she told him. "Or Grandma. You keep an eye on my little TT. Even if she tells you not to."

"I'll do my best," he said.

Teagan watched her grandma return to Lisa, help her to her feet and start for the van. When she scanned the crowd for Buzz, she didn't find him or his motorcycle.

"Your grandma seems nice."

"She's great. Thanks again for coming." Teagan started away, but Lex caught up to her.

"Where are you headed now? Can I help with anything?"

Teagan shook her head. "No, I'm good. I want to be alone."

TEAGAN SPOTTED Blair walking toward Willow Hall. "Blair, hey, wait up."

Blair stopped and turned. Her face looked blotchy as if she'd been crying. She swiped beneath her eyes and smiled.

"I'm really sorry about that," Teagan told her. "That was Harley's mom and she's clearly fallen off the wagon."

"No, it's okay. You don't need to apologize."

"I know, but still. That wasn't fair to you."

Blair tucked her hair behind her ears. "I was a little startled."

"She singled you out because of your shirt."

Blair looked down. "She thinks Rho Upsilon Nu is somehow involved?"

"She brought some nutter psychic to campus the other day. You probably saw us. The psychic, Ramona, sort of fixated on the sorority house." Teagan didn't mention that she'd focused specifically on Blair.

"A psychic? Really?"

"Yeah. Lisa..." Teagan sighed. "She buys into all kinds of weird shit. It doesn't matter. Again, I'm just... sorry."

Blair waved toward an open window. Teagan followed her gaze to where a girl in a baseball cap waved back.

"Whose room is that?" Teagan asked, gooseflesh creeping up her spine. It was the same room the psychic had pointed to when she'd visited the campus.

32

"I t's my room," Blair said. "That's my roommate Colette. I need to run up and drop off my books. Do you want to walk with me?"

"Sure," Teagan murmured, casting a final glance at the window.

They met Blair's roommate in the hall outside their room.

"I'm off to math lab," she told Blair. "Not to be confused with meth lab, which would probably be more fun."

Blair laughed and gestured at Teagan. "This is Teagan. She lives on the second floor."

"Hi, Teagan. See you guys later."

Teagan followed Blair into her dorm room. It was a mirror image of hers and Harley's, though Blair and Colette hadn't lofted their beds.

"So, not giving any credence to the psychic whatsoever," Teagan said, "have you heard anything around Rho Upsilon Nu about Harley? Have they talked about her at all?"

"Not really, no." Blair unloaded her books and set them on her desk.

"I mean, even that seems weird to me. Doesn't it?" Teagan

asked. "A girl who was rushing their sorority has disappeared and they don't even talk about it?"

"Well..." Blair fidgeted, zipping and unzipping her backpack before finally hanging it from a post on her bed. "They always have a zillion sorority things going on. There's not a lot of time for deep discussions. You know?"

"I guess," Teagan muttered. She sat on the bed and flopped back onto Blair's pillow. Something hard and poked between her sharp shoulder blades. She sat up, pulled back the covers to reveal a tarnished silver box.

"What is this?" Teagan asked.

Blair's face flushed.

Teagan took her hands from the box. "I won't look."

Blair bit her lip and shook her head. "No, it's okay. You can open it."

Teagan lifted the lid. "Tarot cards, feathers, bones." She sifted through the stuff, raising an eyebrow. "What is this your secret goth stash?"

Blair smiled, but her eyes looked sad. "Kind of. I've always loved this stuff, just felt really drawn to it, you know? Hopefully that doesn't weird you out. I know you don't believe in all that."

Teagan took out the tarot cards and studied the picture of the Hanged Man on the front. "Because of what I said about the psychic? I just didn't believe in her, well... okay, maybe I lean toward the skeptical side of things, but this stuff is cool. Harley and I had our tarot cards read a couple times. I can't say there were any groundbreaking revelations, but it was fun. I'm curious why this stuff is tucked under your pillow though? Is your roommate anti-New Agey stuff?"

Blair sat in her desk chair. "Not my roommate, no. My mom. If she knew I had those, she'd get very upset. The first time I ever showed any kind of interest in"—she did air quotes—"'weird things,' my mom totally went berserk. I'd bought a

Magic 8 Ball, for God's sake. Those are like the tamest version of fortune telling that exists."

"What'd she do?"

"Ran it over it with my dad's Escalade."

"No way. Seriously?"

"Swear on my life. Even my dad thought she was being nuts. And then I had to clean it up, which was a nightmare because they're full of blue ink and it spewed all over the driveway."

"That's a pretty bizarre reaction. Why do you think?"

"She grew up in a pretty religious family. I think her parents were very anti-anything unconventional."

"Well, jeez. I'm sorry I was being such a hater about the psychic earlier."

Blair picked up the box and carried it to her desk. "Don't be. I'm skeptical too. I just kind of... enjoy quirky things."

"So, you have to keep all this stuff secret from your mom. You have to dye your hair and paint your nails and pretend to be someone you're not. Why don't you say screw it? You're in college now. You're out from under your mom's control."

Blair stared at her, eyes wide. "The moment I did that she'd stop paying for my school. She'd stop paying for everything. She'd make sure I had to move back home."

Teagan shook her head. "My grandma's not paying for my school. Are you kidding me? On a home healthcare salary? I have loans and grants and I'm doing work study."

"Except that funding is based on our parents' finances. My parents have money. The university will not be giving me any grants."

Teagan nodded. "Yeah, that might be an issue. You need to talk to someone who could help with that."

"Maybe," Blair murmured, though Teagan felt the resistance in her new friend.

A little ting came from Blair's laptop and she peered at the screen, her face paling.

"What?" Teagan asked.

"It's another email from the dean. A second student was reported missing today. Cassie Ward hasn't been seen since yesterday evening."

Teagan grabbed her cellphone from her pocket and opened her email. Cassie, also a freshman, had last been seen at her dorm just after eight p.m.

"She was rushing," Blair said, frowning.

"You're kidding me. Was she rushing Rho Upsilon Nu?"

"She didn't get invited back after the first round, or she didn't choose Rho. I'm not sure. I only saw her there during the open house round at Rho, but I know she was still involved because I passed her going into a sorority house on philanthropy day too."

Teagan's mind reeled. "I have to go."

"Where?" Blair asked.

"I don't know. I need to walk and think."

"Do you want me to join you?"

Teagan shook her head. "No. Thanks. I'll talk to you later."

33

Teagan returned to her room and checked her email again, rereading the message from the dean about Cassie Ward. The details were as scant as those offered in Harley's case.

On Facebook, Teagan found a profile for Cassie. She had shoulder-length red-blonde hair and big brown eyes. Her 'about' info listed a hometown of Grand Rapids, but she hadn't posted anything new on her profile in over a year, so Teagan found few details there. On another social media site, she discovered Cassie was a more regular user, posting photos and short video clips of her outfits for rush week and images of her gathered with other rushes, none of whom Teagan recognized from Rho Upsilon Nu.

On Harley's missing page, someone had posted a comment about Cassie. Melanie Jones had asked: *Are these missing girls connected?*

Nothing new had come into the page in terms of tips and after an hour of·scouring the internet for any details regarding Cassie, Teagan gave up and left the dorm.

Night had fallen and a light drizzle had sent most of the

students at Husher University into the buildings. Teagan passed no one as she returned once again to the path that led from the Den to Willow Hall. It looked different at night, largely dark, as the streetlamps lay too far apart to offer much light. Everything was made fuzzier by the rain. The world felt sodden and sad.

She stared at everything, the dark shape of the trees on one side of the path, the black empty road on the other.

A car passed her and slowed.

Teagan froze and stared at it, brake lights illuminating the puddles of water as it pulled to the curb and stopped. The driver was waiting for her to walk up, pass within mere feet of the car, close enough for someone to reach out and grab her.

Had that happened to Harley? Had she been walking this path when that car pulled to the curb? Had the person offered her a ride and she'd climbed in?

No. Never. Harley would never have jumped into the passenger seat of a car with a person she didn't know. But what if they had a gun and forced her? Or maybe they'd lured her to the car by asking for directions, then dragged her inside?

Teagan's instincts told her to turn and run the other direction, cut through the path that led back into campus. Instead, she took a step forward and another. She drew close enough to the car to read the license plate number and commit it to memory.

Now was the time to flee. She had enough to give Officer Key a plate number, a way to track down the owner of the car, but she couldn't force herself to turn away. If this was the person who'd abducted Harley, she wanted to get close enough to see their face.

As she came abreast of the car, the passenger window rolled down and a familiar voice called out. "Hey, need a ride? It's about to pour." Lex sat behind the wheel.

Above the trees a bolt of lightning lit the sky in a purplish streak. Thunder followed seconds later.

Teagan nodded and walked to the passenger door, climbed in. The leather seats were warm. The car smelled of the coconut breeze air freshener hanging from the rearview mirror.

"Do this often?" Teagan asked as Lex shifted into drive and pulled forward.

"What?" He glanced at her sidelong.

"Pick up random girls at night?"

"I'd hardly call you a random girl, and no, I don't make it a habit, but considering you were seconds away from a storm that might have washed you into the sewers, I figured I'd be a good Samaritan. Headed to the Den?"

Teagan nodded and studied the dashboard of his car, then the floor well beneath her sneakers. It wasn't that she suspected Lex of picking up Harley. But for those moments as she approached the car, she almost felt as if she'd stepped into Harley's skin that night, was seeing and feeling what she experienced, and Teagan wanted to hold onto the sensation a bit longer.

Had Harley sat and studied the inside of the man's car, noticed the smells? Had she picked up on something in his voice? Some threat?

Teagan blinked through the windshield at the sparkling pools of water in the road. The rain, formerly a patter, picked up and drummed loud against the roof of the car.

Lex turned his windshield wipers to full speed. He slowed at the stop sign at the end of the street and flicked on his right blinker. The road would take them into campus. Another right and they'd be headed toward her dorm.

"Turn left," Teagan said.

"Huh?" He stared at her. "Why?"

"Just do it." She didn't say more, didn't want to explain and risk breaking the trance, the tendril of insight into that night.

Was that what this was? Or her own imagination leading her on some fictional quest, a trail produced out of desperation to know the truth?

Lex flipped the left blinker on and turned. The road led them away from campus. Towering oak trees banked the sidewalk. Behind them stood houses, but soon the houses grew further apart and then gave way to isolated fields and forests.

Teagan stared hard through the window at a world blurred by rain. Was Harley out there? Had something terrible happened and she'd been killed and carried into those woods? Dumped or, worse, buried? What if they never found her? What if Teagan had to live the rest of her life without knowing?

"Care to tell me where we're going?" Lex asked.

Teagan said nothing. In her mind she waited for a voice, a sign, something to guide her to her friend, but no divine clue arose. Nothing but her own relentless thoughts.

Teagan collapsed back against the seat, the tension, the hope draining out of her. "I don't know," she finally answered. "I thought maybe if we drove this way, I'd get some... sense of where Harley might have gone if she'd gotten into a car that night."

Lex nodded, glanced her way. "This road is pretty rural from here until a little town called Manton, which is also pretty rural."

"She could be anywhere," Teagan murmured.

"Yeah," Lex sighed. "But if it helps to ride, I'm happy to drive you."

"Okay." She turned her head and watched the bleary trees rushing by. "Did you hear there's another girl missing?"

"I saw the email, yes."

"And?"

"And it's concerning."

Teagan leaned her head back and gripped the seat. "I'm so angry."

"At who?"

"At everyone, everything. The campus police for starters. What if they'd sent the email the first day I reported Harley missing? And really put some effort into making it clear that something bad might have happened to her? What if they'd done their fucking jobs and looked for her? I just don't get it. How many girls have to disappear?"

Teagan rubbed her eyes. Heat poured from the vents and she yawned, covering her mouth. She hadn't slept well since Harley vanished. Every night had been a turmoil of thoughts and nightmares and startling awake at every sound hoping it was Harley, but it never was.

"Hey."

Teagan heard Lex's voice, felt something warm on her arm. She opened her eyes to see his hand resting there, his eyes watching her.

"Where are we?" She blinked and rubbed her face. She'd fallen asleep.

"Willow Hall. I pulled up about twenty minutes ago, but figured you needed to sleep."

"How long have I been out?" She leaned down and collected her backpack from the floor.

"Almost an hour. I drove to Manton, circled through town, came back and drove around Husher for a bit. Now here we are."

"Thanks." She pushed open her car door.

"Not a problem."

She offered a half smile, still groggy from her nap. The rain had stopped, but a misty dampness clung to the air. "See ya later," she told him.

He stepped from the car, walked to where she stood. "It's okay to ask for help, you know."

"I have asked for help," Teagan snapped, instantly defensive. "The police, the press conference, the Facebook page. I'm practically begging for help."

Lex stared at her. "No, you're not. You're storming around like an angry bull that's been released into the streets of Madrid. You're constantly seeing red and I suspect you're making more enemies than friends."

"I'm not here to make friends."

Lex sighed and looked up at the sky as if she were missing the point. "Actually, you kind of are, Teagan. This is your freshman year at college. Whatever the outcome with Harley, this is the beginning of your journey too."

Teagan glared at him, his words sharp and hot in her overwrought brain. "Do you think I care?" she demanded. "Without Harley none of this matters." She caught on her words, the despair delivering a sudden jolt of grief up her throat and through her lips. She shoved her fist into her mouth, bit her knuckles hard enough to break the skin. Tears poured over her cheeks.

Lex stepped closer, hesitated, and then grabbed her hard and pulled her against him.

She shoved her face into her hands, shuddering with sobs as he awkwardly held her. Teagan did not fold into him, soften. She was stiff, solid. She broke away and ran up the wide steps to Willow Hall.

34

The day had been busy for Blair. After a morning workout and back-to-back classes, she'd just sat down for a quick lunch when a text came in from Sloan.

Sloan: *Pledges to Rho Upsilon Nu STAT!*

Blair threw her food away and ran up the stairs of Willow Hall two at a time, wanting to change before walking to the sorority house. She found her dorm room slightly ajar and, when she pushed inside, Colette was dragging her green tote toward the door.

"Oh, hey, Blair." She smiled, face flushing. "I've actually been moved to another room. I was going to leave you a note."

Blair scanned the space, saw Colette's pictures, computer and books were gone. Her twin bed had been stripped of its boho-style bedding.

"Okay, yeah. That's fine." Blair thought of her mother the very first day demanding Blair have a different roommate. Apparently, her request had been granted. "Are you still in Willow Hall?"

Colette nodded. "First floor, so definitely stop by. Okay?"

"Yeah. I will. Thanks, Colette."

After Colette left, Blair stood in the little room. Her sketchpad, which had been tucked between two books on her bookshelf, now sat on her desk. She eyed the book and wondered if Colette had paged through it. Probably not. More than likely it had fallen out when she was getting her own books from the shelf.

WHEN BLAIR ARRIVED at the sorority house, the other pledges were already there. They stood in the hall, passing curious glances to one another.

"All right, girls," Sloan announced, sweeping into the hall with a broom in hand. "Your big sisters are off for a much-needed spa day. While we go out, you'll be cleaning this place from top to bottom."

Winona, another pledge, put up a shaky hand.

"What?" Sloan asked, clearly irritated.

"I have an English paper due tomorrow. I'm not even halfway done and—"

Sloan glared at her. "Then you better get started cleaning now. And FYI, girls, this isn't a suggestion. This is a probationary period for all of you and whether you become a Rho Upsilon Nu is going to depend on what happens over the next few weeks."

The sisters, dressed in matching pink sweat suits, left the house and trailed down the sidewalk laughing.

"THIS IS DISGUSTING," Paula said, wiping a glob of toothpaste from the sink.

"Yeah," Blair murmured. "Does it make you... like, regret rushing?"

Paula shook her head. "No way. Rho Upsilon Nu is the best sorority at Husher. I'll wipe the girls' asses if that's what it takes to live here."

Blair laughed. "God, I hope that's not on the schedule for tomorrow night."

"Nah. They balance out the shitshow with a party. This weekend we'll get to party with the Alpha Lambdas. Can't complain about that."

"They seem like pretty cool guys," Blair said, though her thoughts wandered to Teagan staggering off the porch steps and her later admission that she suspected Brody had drugged her.

"Pretty hot guys. Have you met Dane? Or Corbin? I wouldn't mind gettin' a piece of either of those two."

"Yeah. I've talked to Corbin a bit. He's really nice, but... I sort of think he and Sloan are a thing."

"Yeah, maybe. That's the rumor, though I never see them making out or anything. How boring. That being said, I'd never in a million years go after Corbin if it meant inviting the wrath of Sloan. She's hardcore."

"Yeah. She's... intense."

They cleaned together in silence for several minutes, and Blair thought about Harley Rand. "What do you think about the girl who disappeared?"

"Cassie?"

"Well, her too, but I actually meant the first girl, Harley. She was rushing Rho."

"Oh, yeah, I know. I saw her. She was super pretty and seemed cool. I talked to her a few times, but... I don't know. She acted a little skittish. I think Sloan's right and she just got overwhelmed and took off."

"But don't you think her family and friends would have heard from her by now?"

Paula shrugged. "Not if she didn't want them to. Maybe she had a secret boyfriend or something."

"Yeah. So, you haven't heard any of the girls talking about her? Sloan or anyone?"

Paula glanced at Blair, puzzled. "No. I mean, other than complaining about all the fliers her friend keeps putting up and how it's totally dampening the vibe around school."

Blair bent over to spray behind the toilet, but only a spritz of air came out. "It's empty," she said, shaking the bottle.

"Sloan said there's more bleach in the basement."

"I'll grab some," Blair told her, relieved for a few moments away from the cramped bathroom, nauseatingly pungent with the smell of disinfectant.

Blair opened the basement door, flipped on the light, and followed the narrow wood steps down. Though large, the space was cluttered. Plastic shelves lined the walls, filled with cardboard boxes. One side of the basement consisted entirely of bicycles and sports gear—skiing equipment, tennis rackets, a box of volleyballs.

Blair maneuvered through the stuff to a shelf filled with bottles of cleaners. The bottom shelf held four half gallons of bleach.

The lights flickered and Blair grabbed a bottle of bleach and stood, hurried back toward the stairs. They flickered again and went out. She froze, bleach clutched in her hand. The room grew cold, and she wanted to book it for the stairs, but in the total darkness, she was afraid she'd trip or run into something.

Her skin prickled, and she heard a sound—a scraping along the cement floor.

The lights flickered back on. Several feet away, a girl dragged herself toward Blair. She used only her arms; the rest of her body, shriveled, bloody, stretched behind her. The girl had blonde hair darkened with blood, her face drooped, her lips peeled back from her teeth.

"Peggy," she croaked.

The lights blinked out again. Blair clutched the bleach and listened to the sound and wanted to scream as it got closer and then she felt the hands of the girl, sharp nails digging into her bare legs as the thing clawed her way up Blair's body.

Blair dropped the bleach, shoved the dead thing away and ran. She rushed full speed into a heavy object that stopped just above her knees. Blair launched over the top of whatever had tripped her, sprawled forward, and landed hard, palms first on the floor. Fear sweat poured into her eyes as she pushed onto hands and knees and crawled forward, terrified that the dead girl would soon overtake her.

The lights blinked and came back on. Blair froze, inches from smacking head first into a concrete wall. Shaking, crying, she twisted around, searched for the dead girl, but she wasn't there.

It's happening again.

And it was, and Blair could not stop it, could not make it go away. She turned over and pushed her back against the icy wall, pulled her knees to her chest.

"Blair?" Paula called from upstairs. "Did you find the bleach?"

Blair swallowed, swiped her hands beneath her eyes, and gathered her voice. "Yep. Got it. I'll be right up."

As she stood, she saw what she'd run into—an enormous black steamer chest. Something shiny poked from beneath it. Blair knelt and wriggled it free. She stared at the cracked face of a Minnie Mouse watch.

∾

WHEN THE SISTERS RETURNED, they weren't alone. The Alpha Lambda fraternity guys flooded into the house behind them. Blair swiped self-consciously at her hair. There was no mirror nearby, but she knew she looked rough, sweaty and dirty, more like she'd been hit by a truck than cleaned a bathroom.

"Okay, pledges, get up, come on. Up, up, up!" Heather yelled, walking down the hall. "Shirts off, up against the wall."

Blair looked at Paula, who climbed hesitantly to her feet, looking to the other pledges, who all appeared equally confused.

"Your superior told you shirts off!" Sloan screamed, her voice slightly slurred.

Paula went first, yanking her t-shirt over her head and dropping it on the ground. She wore a black lacy bra and her chest glowed with a sheen of perspiration.

The frat guys watched her and clapped. One of them whistled.

"Definitely a C, maybe a D," Brody said.

Blair caught sight of Corbin near the back of the group. He offered her an apologetic smile.

Sloan moved to stand directly in front of Blair, glared at her. "Get your shirt off now or you're out, Davenport."

Blair blinked at her, wanted to refuse, to run from the house, but every other pledge had stripped out of their shirt. One of them was braless, but seemed unfazed by the hoots of the guys. Blair took off her shirt, held it balled at her stomach, her whole body trembling.

"Ooh, the baby of the group," a guy near her leered. "As flat-chested as a boy."

"Not another anorexic in this house. Sloan, we told you we like curvy girls, not beanpoles."

"Eat a penis, Kurt," Sloan snapped.

"Sure, whip it out," he told her.

Sloan flipped him off. "Go ahead, boys. Put 'em in order."

For five minutes, the fraternity haggled over which girl had the best boobs, or tits as they called them. The braless girl, Jocelyn, ultimately came in first. Blair, unsurprisingly, was last.

When it was over, Jocelyn announced that her prize should be to kiss whichever boy she liked. She selected Corbin and pulled him against her, mashing her face against his.

The rest of the Alpha Lambda guys cheered them on, but Blair put her t-shirt on and slipped out the door.

A heavy cloud cover darkened the evening sky, and as Blair walked back to her dorm, she jumped at every sound. The girl from the basement hovered in her mind's eye, a grisly, terrible image that wouldn't leave her.

It had happened before, the visions, but never as intensely as they were coming now.

Footsteps suddenly registered behind her-heavy, fast. She glanced back as a figure, hood covering their head, gained on her. She froze, eyes wide, as the man brushed past her, not even glancing in her direction.

For several moments, Blair remained still, her heart hammering, watching the figure turn onto a side street and disappear from view.

35

After another sleepless night, Teagan walked downstairs to the cafeteria and forced down a plate of scrambled eggs. On her way back to her room, she spotted a copy of that day's student newspaper in the community room.

Three girls gone in two years. What's going on at Husher University?

Teagan snatched the newspaper from the rack and read the article published that day by Nate Dryden.

It started on a warm September evening in 2015. Jessica Meyers, a freshman at Husher University, studying here from out of state, left her job at the Husher Student Store to return to her dorm. She never arrived. It would be two days before her roommate reported her missing to campus police, two weeks before campus police notified students and staff that a freshman had disappeared. It's now been two years and no sign of Jessica Meyers has been found. The Husher police say the investigation is ongoing. Jessica's cousin in Oregon says 'what investigation?'

Why is Jessica's case especially concerning right now? Because in the last seven days, two more Husher University coeds have vanished from campus. Like Jessica Meyers, both girls were rushing sororities, both were freshman and both were last seen on campus after dark.

Harley Rand is an eighteen-year-old from Baldwin living in Willow Hall. Last Wednesday, she worked her shift at Curly's Sandwich Shop and she has not been seen or heard from since.

Disturbingly, a campus-wide email went out yesterday about a second missing girl, Cassie Ward, also eighteen, from Muskegon, Michigan.

Teagan's cell phone rang. Her grandma.

"Hi, Gran," she said, tucking the paper under one arm and taking the stairs back to her room.

"Hey, TT. I'm just checking in. How are you holding up?"

"Another girl disappeared."

"What?"

"Yeah, it's true. Also a freshman, also rushing a sorority. It's so crazy and yet everyone is walking around like nothing has changed."

Her grandma was silent for several moments. "Maybe you should come home."

"Come home? And do what? Harley went missing from school. I can't come home."

"Honey, I know how desperate you are to find her, but you're eighteen. You don't even have a vehicle there. I'm worried about you."

"Don't worry. Okay? I'm fine. I have to stay here."

Her grandma sighed. "All right. You've never been one to back down. I don't see why I thought you would now."

"I won't. Not until I find her."

"That could take a long time, honey."

Teagan ignored the comment. "How's Lisa?" she asked.

"Not well. I've been trying to coax her back into AA, but she refuses. She's ignoring my calls. No matter how many times I learn that you can't force a person to change, the lesson never seems to stick."

"I can't believe she'd do this to Harley. When we find Harley, she is going to be heartbroken. Lisa is being so selfish."

Teagan's grandma said nothing and Teagan gripped the phone tighter, understood her grandma's silence, the fear that Harley would not be coming back.

"We'll cross that bridge when we come to it," her grandma said finally.

"Yeah." Teagan's call waiting beeped. The caller I.D. displayed 'Husher University.' "I have another call coming in, Gran. I'll call you back later."

"Bye, TT. Be safe."

Teagan ended the call with her grandma and clicked over. "Hello?"

"Teagan, it's Officer Key. I need you to come to campus police."

"Why? Did you get a tip? Do you know where Harley is?"

"Someone brought in a backpack. We need confirmation that it's Harley's. We've been unable to reach her mother."

"You found her backpack..." It wasn't a question. The teal flowery backpack rose in Teagan's mind, made the thump of her heart a thunder in her ears.

"We suspect it's hers, yes."

"Who found it? Where did they find it?"

"We can cover those details when you come into the office."

"Was her cell phone inside?"

"We can discuss that when you come in."

"Fine. I'm coming right now. I'll be there in ten minutes." Teagan stood and ran from the dorm.

36

Teagan didn't stop running until she'd pounded up the steps to the building that housed the campus police and stood panting in front of the door. She caught her breath, then pushed into the air-conditioned office.

The boy who'd been there the first day when Teagan reported Harley missing again sat behind the desk. He smiled, but the expression fell away when he remembered her. He pushed back in his chair as if she might start yelling at him.

"Is Officer Key in there?" Teagan asked, bypassing the front desk and heading straight for Key's office.

The front desk guy didn't say a word, just watched as she walked to the office door, turned the knob and pushed inside.

Key stood at his desk, cell phone pressed to his ear.

"Mm... hmmm. Yes. I understand. I'll send someone over this afternoon." He ended the call and set his cell phone on his desk. Purplish shadows hovered beneath his eyes. His skin looked sallower than when Teagan had previously seen him. He put a hand over his mouth and muffled a cough, waving her in.

Teagan's eyes shifted from the phone to the item sitting next to it, which had been shoved into a large, sheer plastic bag. She wanted to reach for it, but her body no longer listened to her mind's commands as she stared until her eyes burned at the too-familiar backpack.

"Is it Harley Rand's?"

Teagan blinked, opened her mouth, wished she could unsee it. The bits of mud clinging to the teal fabric. The little cow keychain dangling from the zipper.

"Yes," she breathed.

"We found identification inside, but I wanted to ensure the bag was a match."

Teagan's eyes slipped up to Key's. "Identification? Her wallet?"

"Yes. Her wallet, which included her student I.D., her driver's license and a few other cards."

"Her punch card for Sweet Scoop."

Officer Key frowned, then nodded slowly. "Yes, I believe I did see a card like that in there."

Harley chose a different flavor every time. Green tea, bubble gum, watermelon sorbet. Teagan stuck to her tried-and-true favorite, mint chocolate chip. She never veered. When Harley challenged her to try other flavors, she refused. 'I like what I like,' Teagan would say. There were probably eight punches on the card. Two more and Harley would have had a free cone.

"Now she never will," Teagan said.

Key studied her. "What was that?"

Teagan shook her head and stepped back from the table. She no longer wanted to look at the bag, didn't want to notice the discolorations—just dirt, she told herself. "Where was her bag?"

"I can't disclose specifics, but a student found it discarded on the side of a county road near a cornfield."

"Not on campus?"

"No. About six miles away."

"But a student found it?"

"Yes. He's a commuter to school here. His parents own the farm where the bag was found. It looked as if it had been thrown from a car window, but obviously that's speculation. He looked inside, saw Harley's I.D. and immediately brought the backpack in."

"Was there anything else inside? Her phone?"

"No cell phone."

"Well, did you search the cornfield and the house that kid lives in?"

"A ground search of the cornfield is underway. There won't be a search of the farm house because we'd need a warrant for that and there's no probable cause."

"No probable cause? Her stuff was on their property!"

"Currently we have no reason to suspect they have knowledge of Harley's whereabouts. If new evidence comes to light an investigation will be conducted."

"Okay, and in the meantime, they can do whatever they want? Hide or destroy evidence, strengthen their alibis?"

Key shot an exasperated look at the ceiling. "Harley's bag was discarded on the side of the road. Any person who drove down County Road 41 might have tossed it out. Harley herself might have—"

"No!" Teagan shouted before he could finish. "No. Harley herself did not throw her backpack, which she saved for weeks to buy, working two jobs last summer, out a goddamn window. Forget it."

Teagan turned and stormed from the office. The rage, the adrenaline, had dissipated within a block. Her body grew heavy, her brain a fog of images. Harley's beloved backpack lying in the mud, rain pelting the fabric, washing away any evidence her abductor might have left behind.

Zombie-like, Teagan walked back to her dorm. She pushed open the door to her room, unchanged from when she'd left it less than an hour before and yet...

She stepped into the room and sniffed the air. A whisper of a scent lingered in the space—Harley's scent, the grapefruit cotton candy body spray. It hadn't been touched since Harley disappeared, but Teagan smelled it now, smelled it as if sometime in the previous hours someone had depressed the nozzle and sent a mist of the overly sweet scent into the air.

Harley's bean bag chair sat in the corner beneath her loft bed. A slight depression marred the purple fabric. Teagan studied it, felt sure it hadn't been there before. Whenever Harley sat on the bag, she puffed it out again after standing.

Teagan sagged against the wall. Was her mind conjuring all this? A desperate delusion to convince herself Harley was not gone forever? In the back of her thoughts, a black hole beckoned. She could sink to the floor, curl into a ball and scream. She could scream until someone came and took her away and pumped her full of some narcotic that would numb it all, make it all disappear.

But even as the thought flitted through her mind, she killed it. No one was looking for Harley. Not really. No one except Teagan. And if there was even a sliver of hope that Harley was still alive somewhere, captive perhaps, Teagan would be the one to save her.

Teagan took a breath, balled her fists, and marched to her laptop. She maneuvered to the 'Find Harley Rand' Facebook page and rapid-fire posted an update.

Today I was called to the Husher campus police office with news that Harley's backpack had been located six miles away from campus, on County Road 41 near a cornfield, likely thrown by a person in a passing car. I don't have a specific location, but if you're the person who turned in this bag, I want to talk to you ASAP!

Teagan posted her phone number and email beneath the update and then she left, needed to get away from her and Harley's room. She walked to the third floor.

Teagan started to knock on Blair's door, but realized the door was slightly ajar. "Blair?" she called through the opening.

No one responded, but Teagan stuck her head inside.

Blair stood perfectly still, staring at a wall, hands in fists at her stomach.

"Blair?" Teagan stepped toward her, saw that Blair's eyes had rolled up into her head. Her lips were parted, moving but making no sound. When she released a breath, it puffed out pale and shimmery, like fog rolling between her pink lips.

Teagan reached to touch Blair's arm. Her skin was ice cold and clammy. "Blair," she said, louder, grabbing hold of both Blair's arms and squeezing. "Hey!" She pushed close to Blair's face, shouted in her ear. "Blair!"

Teagan pressed her fingers against Blair's neck, found her pulse. It was rapid, too fast.

"Okay, I'm calling 911." She started away, then turned back. If Blair's condition worsened, she might fall. She was in range of the dresser and the bed. She could hit her head, get hurt or worse.

Teagan grabbed her, tried to ease her down, but it was as if all Blair's muscles were taut, rigid. She couldn't get her to bend her knees, fold at the waist. She was wooden.

The cold seeped off of Blair's icy skin. The entire room had gone cold. Teagan's breath crystalized in front of her. The window held a sheen of frost.

"What is happening? What in the fuck is happening?" she said, her own pulse quickening.

Teagan took out her phone, started punching the emergency numbers, when Blair suddenly gasped. Her eyes popped wide and her hand opened. Something fell from her fist and landed on the carpet. In an instant, her body changed, soft-ened, shoulders hunching forward. She took a step back, eyes locking on Teagan.

"It's happening again," Blair whispered.

37

Blair sank onto the edge of her bed, lifting a hand to her temple, frowning. Her head pulsed and her mouth was dry.

Teagan stood across the room, staring at her as if she'd sprouted horns from her forehead. "What's happening again?" Teagan asked.

"I'm not sure... umm... when did you come in?"

"When did I come in?" Teagan demanded. "Like two minutes ago, and you were... I don't know. What was that? Some kind of seizure? Do you get seizures?"

Blair stood and moved shakily to her desk, where she picked up her water bottle and took a long drink. Her notebook was still open to her sketch of the dead girl at Rho Upsilon Nu. She quickly closed the cover.

"No. It wasn't a seizure." Blair didn't look at Teagan, didn't want to explain what had just occurred. The vision of the overgrown field, the running, a horrified scream piercing the quiet night followed her still.

Teagan stood, watching, waiting for an explanation.

"Sometimes... umm... I have these..." Blair touched her

throat. The flesh felt tender and she had the distinct sensation that someone had just ripped a necklace from around her neck. "Sort of like out-of-body experiences. I don't know how else to describe it."

Teagan watched her uneasily. "I don't understand."

"It's a long story," Blair murmured. A long, strange story that was so unbelievable she'd never told it to anyone.

Teagan crossed her legs, rested her hands on her knees. "I have time."

Blair took another sip of water, wondered if she was about to alienate the only friend she'd made at Husher University.

"When I was seven," Blair said, "my parents took me to this big fall festival party put on by the private school they were trying to get me into. There was a huge bonfire, a hayride, apple picking, the whole deal. Somehow, I got separated from my mom and dad. This middle-aged guy took my hand and asked me if I was lost. He seemed so normal and nice. I told him I couldn't find my parents, and he said he'd just seen them and they asked him to take me to the next place—another orchard up the road. It didn't even cross my mind to question him. He was an adult and acted like he knew my parents, so I went with him. He led me away across the grass, away from the property to the roadside where this old dark-colored car sat. I knew it was old because it was big and boxy, like a boat on wheels, you know?"

Teagan nodded.

"Anyway, he let go of my hand and got out his keys to unlock the car. All of a sudden, I wasn't behind the car anymore. I was in the backseat looking out through the back window."

"He kidnapped you?"

Blair blinked, looked at Teagan. She'd begun to drift, had almost forgotten another person sat in the room with her. "I was in the car looking out through this grimy back window, a scream bubbling in my chest, but it wasn't me. I was still outside the car staring at that back window. It was like I'd"— Blair held up her fingers as if reaching to touch someone—"I'd stepped into that other little girl's body and she'd once been real and she'd been trapped in that backseat, watching her house fade from view and knowing in her guts that she'd made a terrible mistake getting into that man's car.

"All these thoughts and feelings happened in like half a second. I was in her, the memory of her, or the ghost of her, and then I was back in my body knowing she was dead and this man had killed her and he was bad, very bad, and suddenly he had the back door open and he was stepping toward me and I ran. I bolted for the black woods, which before that moment had been the most terrifying thing I might ever have done because I was afraid of the dark and especially the woods at night, but I didn't even care."

"Did he follow you?"

Blair nodded, squeezed her upper arms so tight it hurt, but also lightened the sensation of that horrible memory, of crouching in those dark woods and hearing his heavy feet on twigs and leaves, feeling the cool October wind in the branches, watching the far-off flames of the bonfire and fearing she'd never hear her mother's voice again.

"Yes, for what seemed like an eternity, but then I heard voices calling and they got closer and they were yelling for me. And that guy still didn't give up right away. He'd been swearing under his breath and breathing heavy. He sounded like an animal.

"When the voices started, he got really still. He thought I'd run out and go toward the voices, but something in me knew to stay put, to not move a muscle. I waited so long I peed my pants, but once the people searching got into the woods, he finally took off. I heard his car start and drive away, and only when I heard my dad's voice did I come out.

"I was crying and blubbering and wet with pee and my dad scooped me up and just"—Blair blew out a breath—"hugged me so tight. It's weird, but that's one of my favorite memories of him, just holding me and carrying me back to my mom, who was wild with fear. They took me to the hospital, which obviously was unnecessary, but my mom was always a little over the top."

"Did you tell them what happened?"

Blair frowned, remembered the fear in her mother's eyes that night, and shook her head. "No. I wish I had now. You know, because... for all I know, he went out that night and stole some other little girl. I didn't want to tell because I thought my mom would get mad at me for being so stupid and following a stranger." Blair tucked a strand of hair behind her ear. "I've really regretted that."

Teagan sat on the bed. "I don't quite understand how that relates to what just happened to you."

Blair sighed. "Ever since that night I have... my mom calls them episodes. I'll see things, feel things, and once in a while I sort of... umm... like step into another... person."

"Step into another person?"

Blair released an uncomfortable laugh. "Ready to run screaming from my room yet?"

Teagan raised an eyebrow. "I'm too curious to leave now."

"It's like being inside that little girl in the back of that guy's car. Sometimes I feel like I'm in someone else's memory."

"Just now that was happening? You were in someone else's memory?"

Blair frowned. "I was... uh... running through a field at night, weirdly enough."

"That's it?"

"It was dark and I was afraid, and then... suddenly you were here and I was back in my room."

"That's really strange," Teagan said. "I'm not saying you're strange, but that experience? I don't know how to process that. Are you sure it's not your imagination? Maybe narcolepsy? You're falling asleep and slipping into a nightmare."

"I was tested for narcolepsy, did two separate sleep studies, but it wasn't that. And anyway, that little girl in the back of that man's car... she wasn't a dream. She was real. I know it. I used to see a doctor, and I was on medicine, but it made me really... not here, you know? I always felt as if I'd just woken up from a really long nap and I couldn't seem to shake the brain fog."

"How often does it happen?"

"Not often."

"What do your parents think?"

"I'm sure you can imagine my mother is not thrilled about it. I'd call her primary reaction denial. She won't even talk about it. If I bring it up, she wants me medicated. And until lately it hadn't happened in a couple years and now all of sudden it's back."

"And you think it's what then? Like you're actually some-how... what?"

Blair's cheeks colored, and she didn't meet Teagan's eyes. "I sort of think... that it's... spirits. I'm glimpsing what people who died felt before they died."

Teagan stared at her, mouth agape. "Spirits. Ghosts?"

Blair nodded.

"This conversation is getting weirder by the second."

"We don't have to talk about it. I know it doesn't make sense."

"But it's real. Something was happening to you. I saw it. I just wonder... could there be some medical explanation for it?"

"I wish there was. When I first went to the doctor, they ran a bunch of tests, did an MRI, sleep studies, the works. They decided it was mental, and I needed a psychiatrist, who put me on the meds and so I took those for a while, but like I said, the meds made me not feel like myself so I stopped taking them."

"Does something trigger it? Did anything happen today that might have caused it?"

Blair stood and walked across the room, bent to pick up the item that had slipped out of her hand. She handed it to Teagan, who studied the watch.

"Whose is it?"

"I don't know. I was in the basement at Rho yesterday getting cleaner and found it wedged beneath the corner of a trunk. I stuck it in my pocket. I meant to give it to the house mother and forgot. I found it today, took it out and..." Blair shook her head. "That's the last thing I did before I opened my eyes and you were standing there."

Teagan handed the watch back. "Do you think it belonged to someone who died?"

Blair bit her lip, thought of the dead girl dragging herself across the basement of the sorority house-a girl she'd first had visions of in high school nearly two years before. Medication had made her go away, but now she was back. "I don't know." She slipped it back into her pocket.

"I don't think it'd be a terrible idea to see a doctor again," Teagan murmured.

Blair sighed, unsurprised by Teagan's response, but disappointed nevertheless.

Teagan, perhaps sensing her disappointment, changed the subject. "They found Harley's backpack today."

"They did?"

Teagan nodded.

"But not Harley?"

"No. It looked like someone had tossed the bag through a car window out in some rural stretch of nowhere."

"Oh, no." Blair sagged onto her bed. "I'm sorry. Do the police have any idea who might have done that?"

"No. Nothing. I got pissed at the cop and stormed out. I

probably should have stayed and listened to him, but he made some comment about how Harley might have done it herself."

"What a jerk."

"Exactly."

A text beeped on Teagan's phone. She read it and then started typing.

"Is it news about Harley?" Blair asked.

Teagan looked up, clearly distracted. "I don't know. It's this guy Lex. His friend works for the student newspaper and they want me to meet them at the newspaper. I should go." Teagan paused in the doorway. "You can come if you want."

Blair smiled and shook her head, her thoughts sticky, a headache oozing behind her eyes. "I think I'll lie down for a bit."

38

I t was nearly seven o'clock and the student newsroom was quiet. The dim lights reflected the office in the large glass windows as Nate led Teagan to Lex, already seated on a couch.

"Have you ever heard of the Husher Harvester?" Lex asked.

Teagan's heart did a little jump at the name. "No. What is it?"

"Not what, who," Nate said. "The Husher Harvester was a serial killer who killed girls here at Husher in the late 90s. They caught him in '99 and sent him to prison."

"Husher had a serial killer?"

Lex nodded. "I remember my parents talking about him forever ago when I was a little kid. I'm guessing it was around the time the trial was happening."

"Why the name Husher Harvester?"

"He dumped his victims' bodies in cornfields."

Teagan frowned, thought again of Harley's bag. "Harley's backpack was found near a cornfield, not in one."

"The Harvester's victims' stuff was found in ditches along the road next to cornfields," Lex said.

"How do you know all this?"

"As soon as we saw your post, I went into the newspaper archive and started searching," Nate explained. "It was the cornfield thing that got us thinking about him. That was his M.O., but stranger still, the victims' bodies weren't found in the same cornfield where he'd tossed their stuff. At the time, people speculated he was a farmer, but he wasn't. He'd been a student at Husher when the killings started and they continued for about three years after he graduated."

"He was a student?"

"Yep." Nate turned his laptop to face Teagan and Lex.

"Robert Thomas, a 1996 graduate with a major in finance, member of Alpha Lambda fraternity, and a real estate agent in Husher," Lex read.

Teagan leaned closer to the article, eyes widening. There was something oddly familiar in his face, but she couldn't place him. "He was in Alpha Lambda?"

"Yep. And not just in Alpha Lambda. When he graduated, he was the president."

"And he was murdering girls on campus."

"Five total. Three from Husher, two non-university girls who worked in town."

"That's sick," Teagan murmured, "but it happened almost twenty years ago and you said yourself the guy went to prison. I mean, surely, they didn't let a serial killer out."

"No, he's in for life," Lex said, "but we were mulling it over after dinner and thought, what if he had an accomplice?"

"An accomplice? Who's just now killing people a decade-plus later?" The conversation bothered her. It was one thing to discuss Harley as a missing person. It was another thing to link her to a serial killer, to talk about her as if she were the victim of a murderer. "Was anyone else ever implicated when this Robert guy got caught?"

"I don't know," Nate admitted. "The truth is, I've never dug into this case at all. Weirdly, no one ever talks about it. There are no anniversary articles, but Husher is like that. True to their name, they like to keep things hush-hush, especially any news that reflects poorly on the university. Husher is the number one employer in town. Local politicians insist Husher is the reason property values have increased. It's the town's golden goose, so to speak."

"I grew up not far from here," Lex said. "As a kid the Husher Harvester was like an urban legend. I knew he'd been real, but he took on that sort of 'man with the hook' quality. We'd do these games in the cornfield at night and one person was the Harvester, kind of like hide-and-seek tag. Frankly, it scared the hell out of me."

"A game inspired by a serial killer. Sounds fun," Teagan quipped.

"No, it makes sense," Nate added. "I grew up near Detroit and there'd been a string of kid killings in the late 70s. The Babysitter Killer, they called him. He was never caught and me and my friends did the same thing. When we'd walk to the corner store or to the park, we'd pretend every car was the guy and we'd run and jump in dumpsters or scoot under parked cars. My dad used to say it's how kids process the boogeyman."

"It feels like a stretch trying to connect this guy to Harley and Cassie," Teagan said, staring again at the picture of Robert Thomas.

"Maybe not though," Nate said. "I found an article that speculated Thomas had an accomplice-that he couldn't possibly have done all the killings alone because he had at least one alibi placing him somewhere else during an abduction."

"He had an alibi and was still convicted?" Teagan asked.

"They only tried him for three of the murders," Nate explained. "The police cases for the first two murders, committed while he was a Husher Student, were weaker. They had less evidence and more time had passed. It's pretty typical with serial murderers. Take Ted Bundy for instance. Police believe he murdered more then thirty women, but he was only convicted of killing three."

"I'm afraid if you write about this Thomas guy, the whole case will get derailed," Teagan said. "Everyone will be too busy rehashing details about an old serial killer to focus on what's actually happening."

"I disagree," Lex said. "What better way to put some fire under the ass of the police than to bring up Husher's darkest history and remind people of what's at stake? If this is a serial killer, there will be more victims. Every day that Harley and Cassie aren't found is a day closer to a potential next victim."

Teagan crossed her arms over her chest. She didn't want this to be Harley's story, didn't want her name remotely connected to a serial killer called the Husher Harvester, and yet Lex was right. The university and the police had continued to keep mostly quiet about the fact that two freshmen had vanished from Husher.

Her cellphone rang, and she saw a number she didn't recognize. "Hello?"

"Hi, is this Teagan?"

"Yeah."

"My name is Adam Gallagher. I found your friend's backpack."

ADAM GALLAGHER AGREED to meet Teagan, Lex and Nate in the student newspaper office.

When he arrived, Teagan studied him, searched for any evidence of guilt in his face. There was none. He looked young, freckled with ruddy skin and curly brown hair.

"Hey, I'm Adam," he said.

"I'm Nate."

Lex bent forward and extended his hand. "Lex."

They shook hands and Adam turned to Teagan, who did not offer her hand. She was suspicious of this guy, even if he looked like a Boy Scout. He'd found Harley's bag. For all she knew, he was the one who'd tossed it on the roadside.

"I'm Teagan," she said. "Where exactly did you find Harley's backpack?"

Nate and Lex exchanged a look, but Teagan ignored them, focusing on Adam.

"Uh... County Road 41, about a mile west of the Pine Trail intersection."

"I have no idea where that is. Here, show me on a map." She opened her phone.

"Have a seat, Adam," Lex told him.

"Let me open a larger map on my laptop," Nate said. "Then we can all look."

Teagan set her phone down. Adam perched on the edge of a chair and maneuvered around the map. He pointed to a dark line. "This is County Road 41. This first big stretch is the old Doxon farm, mostly gone back to nature. My family's farm runs along this whole section here. This is all cornfields. If we open the street view, you can see."

Nate clicked an icon, and the screen filled with a camera image of the road edge—towering stalks of corn in the background, waist-high grass separating the field from the road.

"How did you even see her bag? The grass is really tall."

"It was tall when this photo was taken, but it's not right now. My dad mowed it at the end of summer."

"That's weird," Lex murmured when they'd navigated back to the map and looked at the route from Husher University to the farm.

"What?" Teagan asked.

"The other night when we took that drive in the rain, we went right by this place."

"And you saw nothing on the side of the road?" Teagan narrowed her eyes at Adam, who shifted uncomfortably.

"It was dark and raining," Lex said. "I didn't see much of anything. It's just strange, we drove right by there."

"How did *you* see the bag?" Teagan demanded of Adam.

"I was walking our dog. Normally, I don't because he runs free on the property. We have a hundred acres, but my dad likes us to walk the perimeter of the fields now and then, so I took Dundee—that's our Saint Bernard—out for a walk. He dragged me into the ditch and there it was."

"How did it look?" Nate asked. "Dirty? Were the straps broken? Anything you noticed?"

Adam shook his head. "Not really. It looked pretty good, especially considering it had been out in the elements. Muddy on the bottom, but nothing was broken. I carried it back to the house and left it sitting on the porch for half the day, kind of forgot about it. Then around dinner, my mom asked whose it was, so I unzipped it and found that girl's wallet with her I.D. and stuff. Harley."

"Did you recognize her name?" Nate asked.

"Yeah, because I'd seen the fliers and the email from the dean. I don't know her," he added quickly. "But I recognized the name and my parents said I better run it into the campus police right away, so I did."

"And you never met Harley?" Teagan demanded.

"Never, no. I live off campus and just come in for classes. I'm not around much."

"And the police told me they're searching the cornfield. Is that true?" Teagan asked.

Adam nodded slowly. "Yeah, and we've been helping. It's easy to get lost in there, so we set up the search rows. They brought dogs and everything. They haven't found anything. I don't think she's out there."

Teagan frowned.

"Did you guys see anything suspicious around the time she went missing?" Nate asked. "Unfamiliar cars? That kind of thing?"

"No. Our house is quite a way back from the road and there are a lot of trees in the yard. Even if we'd been looking, we likely wouldn't have seen anything, especially since it probably happened at night."

"How long has your family lived there?" Lex asked.

"In our house? Oh, jeez, ummm... since my dad was a kid. He grew up there and bought the farm from my grandparents. Me and my brother grew up there too."

"So, you've heard of the Husher Harvester?" Lex continued.

Adam's eyes widened, but then he looked perplexed. "Oh, yeah, I've heard all about him. But he's in prison. There's no way it's him."

"But it could be an accomplice," Nate added.

Adam tilted his head sideways, but his expression looked doubtful. "No bodies have been found."

Teagan glared at him and he, seeing her stare, quickly looked away.

"It just seems like a leap is all," he mumbled. "Though my dad always said this place," Adam pointed at a spot on the map, "The Doxon farm was a murder site. Apparently, the Husher Harvester killed one of his victims in the farmhouse. It was already abandoned by then, but after the bodies were found, police did a pretty massive search and they found blood and clothing belonging to one of the girls in that house."

"And Harley's backpack was less than a half mile from that property," Lex murmured, shooting Teagan a grim look.

39

B lair tried to focus on the professor's voice as she spoke about sculpture as a way to tap into the creative unconscious.

Eyes gritty, a headache still percolating, Blair sank her hands into the clay. It was cool and slippery and instantly soothing. She drifted into a lull, her hands moving and molding, fingers pinching.

"Whoa! What is that?"

The voice broke Blair from her reverie. She looked up to see another girl from her class, Monique, standing and staring at her sculpture.

Blair turned to look at it and recoiled. She'd molded a tall cornstalk, the leaves dropping away from the ear of corn and in the center of the stalk a human face, a girl's face, the mouth twisted in a scream of terror, eyes melting into her cheeks. "I... umm..."

"This is intriguing," the professor said, pausing behind Blair and nodding her approval. "It's abstract and, frankly, a little chilling. Well done, Blair."

It was dark as Blair walked home from class. Wind rushed

through the trees and caused Blair's hair to fly around her face. She tucked it behind her ears, bowed her head, and hurried onward.

As she walked, she heard footsteps behind her, but when she glanced back, the sidewalk stood empty. Still, she picked up her pace, and when she turned onto the isolated sidewalk bordered by woods that took her back to Willow Hall, she slowed and considered a different route. No one occupied the sidewalk as far as she could see.

Pulling her backpack tighter, she started down the path, half jogging, which was nearly impossible in her heeled boots. Wind rushed up her skirt, and she swatted at it, trying to keep it down. In the woods to her left, something moved. She turned, not slowing her pace, and studied the dark forest.

For an instant she saw a face there, a scarecrow face, and then it was only the arrangement of leaves and branches and nothing more.

Blair... It was a whisper, warm against her ear. Blair spun, but no one stood behind her. The wind whipped harder.

Blair... Blair... Blair... The wind called out to her in a hundred voices, girls' voices, pleading voices, and now there was more movement in the trees, the constant appearance and vanishing of the scarecrow face keeping pace with her as she fled down the sidewalk.

When she finally moved out of the dark path into the halo of a streetlamp, the wind had dulled, perhaps blocked by the high dorm buildings.

A group of girls from Willow Hall approached. "Hi, Blair," one of them called.

Blair lifted a hand. It trembled so badly, she glued it to her side and hurried up the steps to her dorm.

～

An hour later, a knock sounded on the door to Blair's room. She stood and opened it. Teagan stood outside, and Blair struggled to focus on her face.

"Hey, is everything okay?" Teagan asked. "I tried calling you, but got your voicemail."

Blair nodded. "Sure, yeah. Just studying."

"Can I come in?"

"Mmm-hmmm."

Teagan walked into the room, staring intently at Blair. "Why are your eyes glassy?"

Blair blinked, rubbed her face. "Are they?"

"What is that?" Teagan asked.

A silty white powder coated the lap desk on Blair's bed. Blair swiped the powder away and shook her head. "Nothing... I don't know... umm, powdered sugar. I ate a donut earlier."

"Bullshit. Did you eat it through your nose?"

Blair brushed a hand under her nose, felt nothing, but looked at her fingertips anyway.

"What are you on?" Teagan demanded.

Blair struggled to bring Teagan into focus. "What are you talking about?"

"I'm talking about what you're high on. I know what it looks like. Just tell me."

"Look, it's not a big deal. I get scattered, find it hard to focus. It's the only way I can get my homework done. Why do you care anyway?" Blair's face had grown hot. Shame made her want to tell Teagan to get out, leave her alone.

"I care because you're my friend and I don't want you to fry your brains on drugs."

"I'm not going to fry my brain. It's Adderall, not meth."

"Why in the hell are you putting it up your nose?"

Blair thought of the one guy she'd dated in high school—Josh. He'd been the Adderall user, snorted it so he could stay up all night sketching horror scenes and writing black poetry.

When her mother discovered Blair was dating him, she'd called his parents and threatened to turn him in for using drugs if he went anywhere near Blair again.

"It hits different," Blair murmured, quoting her former boyfriend.

"Jesus!" Teagan pushed her hands through her hair. "Not only are you risking the cartilage in your nose, if anyone caught you, you could get expelled."

"Look, you just don't get it, Teagan."

"I don't get it? My mom fucking died. My grandma was an alcoholic who struggled to put food on the table. My best friend in the world has vanished from the face of the earth. You think I don't get why someone would want to numb out?"

"It's not because my life is so hard," Blair said, eyes flooding with tears. "It's because of... the... the thing that happens, seeing things and sometimes losing touch with my body. This" —Blair gestured at the residue—"makes it happen less."

Teagan sat in Blair's computer chair. "Did it happen again?"

Blair shook her head, but the sculpture from class hung in the back corner of her mind. The mouth opened and the voices of the wind in the trees—"Blair..."—rippled through her mind. She shook her head, banished it. "No, but... it will. It'll happen again."

"Okay, fine, but... you still shouldn't do it. There has to be another way that doesn't involve snorting things up your nose."

"You can't exactly search this problem on WebMD. 'Home remedies to stop seeing dead people.'"

Teagan shuddered and Blair wished she'd used different words, but different words wouldn't soften the truth.

"Someone can help you with this, Blair," Teagan said.

Blair looked away. "I don't know, Teagan. Can we just not talk about it right now?"

"Okay," Teagan agreed, though Blair suspected she wouldn't actually drop it. "Where are you from, Blair?"

Blair frowned, unsure where the question was coming from. "Grand Rapids. Why?"

"Have you ever heard of the Husher Harvester?"

Blair shook her head.

"He was a serial killer here in Husher in the late 90s. He targeted girls that went to school here."

"A serial killer?" Blair breathed.

"Yeah. And he used to throw their stuff out the window next to cornfields."

"Was Harley's stuff found next to a cornfield?"

"Yes."

Blair swallowed, seeing the vision again of her sculpture, the hideous cornstalk with a girl's face trapped between the leaves. "Do you think it's the same guy, then? The serial killer?"

"No. He's in prison, but Lex and Nate think he might have had an accomplice."

"An accomplice?"

"Yes." Teagan stared at her and then looked away. Blair sensed she wanted to say something more.

"What is it?" Blair asked. "Did they find something else?"

"No, but yesterday when you had that experience, when you'd gone all cold, you said you were in a field."

Blair bit her lip, nodded.

"Do you think you might have... somehow been experiencing what Harley went through?"

Blair dropped her eyes to the floor, felt that cold finger of dread trace down her spine. For an instant, the image of Harley's battered face floated dreamlike behind her eyes. "I don't know, Teagan. The truth is I don't understand it any more than you do."

40

Blair opened her door the following morning to Teagan, who stood holding two cups of coffee. "Get dressed. My grandma is picking us up."

Blair blinked at her, took the coffee and moved aside as she pushed into the room. "She's picking us up? Why? Where are we going?"

"The woman who came to campus the other day, the psychic. She might be able to help you."

"Help me with what?" Blair sipped her coffee and winced when it scalded her top lip.

"With the"—Teagan twirled her finger near her head—"visions and stuff."

Blair frowned. "I don't know, Teagan. I don't like to tell people, because if my mom found out—"

"She won't. My grandma was an alcoholic. She's a sponsor now. Ramona was in the program. That's how she met Lisa. These people know how to keep a secret."

~

TEAGAN'S GRANDMA parked outside A&W and led Blair and Teagan inside. She walked up to the counter and returned a moment later.

"Here you go, girls. This will make you feel better." Teagan's grandmother slid chilled glasses in front of the girls. On top of each sat a glob of vanilla ice cream.

"It's a root beer float," Teagan explained. "The root beer remedy."

"Cures all your woes," her grandma agreed, then placed a third in front of her own seat. She reached for Teagan's hand and squeezed. "Or at least a bit of salve on the wound."

"Thank you, Mrs. Kelso," Blair said.

"Connie, please."

"I've never had a root beer float," Blair admitted. "My mom is a sugar nazi." It seemed odd to be drinking a root beer float at ten in the morning, but she smiled when she took a drink. "It's really good," Blair murmured, enjoying the fizzy burst followed by the smooth cool ice cream.

"Thank you for helping Teagan through this. It's been a rough couple of weeks and I know you've been a true friend to her."

Warmth climbed into Blair's cheeks and she glanced at Teagan, who seemed only half there, her gaze fixed on the plate-glass window, the cars zooming by in the street.

"I like your bracelet," Blair told Teagan's grandmother.

Connie held her wrist up so the little silver feather charms caught the sun. "One feather for every year sober," she explained.

"Oh..." Blair closed her mouth, unsure how to respond.

"Don't feel embarrassed," Connie told her. "I'm proud of my sobriety. It's one of the hardest things I've ever done, giving up alcohol. Teagan's mother, Robin, died twelve years ago, and I'd been a drinker before that, casual, social, that kind of thing, but losing my only daughter just... broke me. I lost control, and I almost lost Teagan. As if she hadn't been through enough." Connie sighed.

"They say you can't learn from other people's mistakes, but I'm living proof that you can. A friend of mine from the bar got into an accident one night. I'd been up there too, drinking. I used to take Teagan with me and she'd just wander among the tables and the regulars. She was a bar baby, thanks to my addiction.

"My friend Theo left. We'd shared about five pitchers of beer. He had no business driving, and neither did I, especially with Teagan, but I ended up doing it not ten minutes after he'd left. She and I made it home safe, but the next day I got a call from Theo's sister. He'd swerved across the center line and hit a family head-on. Theo lived, but the other family—a mom, dad and two little girls—all died. Theo never walked again, and two years after the accident, he took his own life."

Blair stared at Connie, searched for an appropriate response, found none. Teagan sighed and leaned her head on her grandma's shoulder. Connie patted the side of her head.

Connie smiled. "You're probably wondering why I'd tell you such a terrible story, why I'd share details about the kind of person I've been. I do it as a reminder to myself and to anyone who might need to hear it. I was on the same trajectory as Theo and that night it could as easily have been me, but I was spared. Whether by luck or the grace of God, I might never know.

"But the moment I hung up the phone with Theo's sister, I packed Teagan in her car seat and drove to the Methodist church. I hadn't been to church in twenty years. I cried through the whole thing, me and Teagan both. Pretty disruptive for the service, but at the end, the pastor took me aside and he helped me get set up with the local AA chapter and a sponsor. Now I'm a sponsor. I get to pay it forward."

For a moment, Blair slipped into her own memories. Two paramedics walking through the front door of her family's big, immaculate brick house. A stretcher between them. A white sheet with an impossibly still shape beneath. Blair remembered falling... falling.

"We can learn from each other's mistakes," Connie went on. "I'm living proof."

"Did you ever miss it? The alcohol?" Blair thought of her little bottle of Adderall, how the pills seemed to push the shadows away, edge them back, make room for light.

"Oh, I missed it. I had more than a few close calls. There's a reason recovered addicts call it 'practicing sobriety.' Most of us will open the door to see that demon lurking outside every day. Except instead of a demon, he looks like Prince Charming, arriving to carry you away from all your problems. It's only when you slam the door in his face and then peek at him through the window that you see him for what he really is, a devil in disguise, a monster who wants nothing less than your life in exchange for that little reprieve from this all-too-sharp reality.

"When he appears, you have to hold fast to your angels." Connie pulled Teagan close, kissed her temple. Then her gaze lifted and she smiled. "There she is." Connie stood and waved as the woman Blair had seen previously at the sorority house walked in. She wore a hot pink off-the-shoulder t-shirt and ripped jeans.

"Ramona," Connie said, giving her a half hug. "Thank you so much for coming."

"Good to see you again," Ramona told Connie. "And you as well, Teagan. I haven't had a coney dog in ages," she said, eyeing the counter.

"This is Blair," Teagan said, grabbing Blair's hand and pulling her to her feet.

"Blair." Ramona leaned close, a little too close, and stared deeply into Blair's eyes. "It's a genuine pleasure."

"Nice to meet you." Blair took a step back, caught Teagan's expression, a mix of exasperation and curiosity.

"I'm going to pop up to the counter and get a root beer and coney dog," Ramona announced. "Anyone want a coney dog?"

"Girls?" Connie asked.

Both Teagan and Blair shook their heads no.

When Ramona returned, Teagan and Connie went to a table on the opposite side of the room. Blair settled on the padded seat across from Ramona.

41

"How are you feeling, Blair?" Ramona asked.

Blair bit her thumbnail and then, imagining her mother's furious gaze, stuffed her hands beneath her thighs. "I'm fine. How are you?"

"Can't complain, though I just came off of an overnight shift at the packaging company I work for and I am starving." She took a massive bite of her coney dog and watched Blair as she chewed. Blair felt a bit like an animal at the zoo.

"You're not psychic for a living then?"

Ramona swallowed, took a drink of root beer and shook her head. "I wish, but it's not exactly an in-demand position."

Blair glanced at Teagan and her grandma—absorbed in their own conversation—then swept her eyes toward the window, anywhere but at Ramona.

"I'm picking up on a male figure," Ramona said. "Let's see, with an N name. Nate or Noah...?"

Blair looked back at Ramona, confused.

"Nolan. Definitely Nolan. Who was Nolan, Blair?"

Blair's breath caught. "My brother," she whispered.

Ramona's face fell. "I see. I'm sorry. He's with us now, and

I'm getting... hmm, well, he's jumbled. I can't quite make out what he wants to say, but I think..." Ramona touched her mouth. "He died of... did he choke or eat something?"

"He overdosed." Blair murmured the words so low Ramona had to lean forward to hear her.

"Yes... okay. I see it now. Pills and maybe some alcohol. Okay. I'm sorry, love. I don't mean to be so blunt. I'm just telling you what's coming. That's all."

"Is he saying anything else?" Blair clutched the table in her hands.

It had been more than a year since Nolan had died, but within weeks of his burial, their mother had taken down his photos, cleared out his room and ceased speaking his name. Some days Blair felt as if he'd never existed at all.

Ramona frowned, squinted. "No. I'm afraid not. He's nearby, but not giving me a message. I think he just wants you to know he's here."

Tears fell over Blair's cheeks. Ramona handed her a wad of napkins. Blair mopped at her face, turning it slightly so Teagan and her grandmother wouldn't see her crying.

"Go on. Cry. It's good for the soul. He's here, even if you can't see him right now. He's never come through for you?"

Blair blinked at the woman, then shook her head. "I tried once a few weeks after he died. I tried to speak to him, but..." Blair shook her head. "Nothing."

"Spirit is weird that way. You know how I think of it? When somebody we love tries to make contact, they're so excited, so full of energy, they can't focus it enough for us to perceive it. They scatter their attention all around us like drops of rain. But if they reach out to someone who they're not emotionally linked to, they can turn the faucet on and hold the energy long enough to get a message across."

"Is there anyone else?" Blair's eyes again darted toward Teagan and her grandma.

Ramona followed her gaze and then shifted back to Blair and closed her eyes. "There is, yes, but they're very unclear. A shadow far in the back, a female, perhaps. She's not coming forward."

Blair let out a little sigh of relief that her dead visitors were not revealing themselves to Ramona.

"Have you always been able to.... see people who have passed?" Blair asked.

"For as long as I can remember. I came from a family who didn't understand, so I spent many, many years numbing myself. Alcohol mostly, but there was some harder stuff, too. Your family isn't comfortable with what you see, right?"

"No. My mom especially."

"It's always the moms," Ramona murmured, shaking her head. "I have a theory about that, you know? Women are the more intuitive gender, closer to the source of all energy, to spirit, because they're the vessels for spirit to come into the physical world and they're often the midwives at the death bed. They're linked to the whole cycle. But some women take that power and fuel it toward denial. They seek eternal youth, deny death as if it were avoidable. They wall themselves away from their essential nature and they hate anything that reminds them we are not immortal, that we are all going to die."

Blair thought of her mother, who'd refused to have a funeral for Nolan. Who'd insisted he be cremated. Instead of welcoming family into their home to grieve, Margo had taken Blair on a girls' trip to a spa in Arizona while Blair's dad stayed behind to dispose of Nolan's ashes.

"I won't lecture you on how to cope with this skill," Ramona went on, "but that's what it is. It's a skill. I've watched people develop it like learning to play a piano. When I was young, I saw it as a disability, an affliction, but when I got older, I found others, got involved in a group. They helped me get clean, and I started to see there's value in this skill, so long as you control it and not the other way around."

Blair thought of the girls, the dead girls who came at night and sometimes during the day. Who took hold of her body, who peered out from her sculptures, who whispered in her ear.

"I can't control it," she murmured.

"It takes practice, and before you can close it off, you have it to open it up. Have you ever heard the saying 'what we resist persists?'"

Blair nodded.

"Spirit is like that. When I was young, I pushed it away, so it pushed back, needled its way in any moment I was distracted. At night was the worst, which led to insomnia, which led to exhaustion, which I handled by drinking more—you know the cycle.

"In group, I learned the practice of visualizing a door. Behind that door is the energy of spirit. In meditation, I would open that door just a crack and, with a tape recorder running, I'd allow the messages to come through me. Then I'd visualize the door closing, and I'd walk to it, turn a key in the lock, and call out, 'I'm busy today, but I can see you on Saturday at noon.'" Ramona laughed. "It sounds absurd, doesn't it? But it started to work. Not always right on time, but in the vicinity. It was less about them showing up than me willingly going in and opening the door, giving them some time, some presence. And then I'd close it again. I've been doing that for over ten years now. It hasn't failed me yet."

Blair's eyes drifted to the large ceramic A&W Bear positioned near the parking lot entrance. She considered Ramona's story. It was so simple. It'd never work for her. The spirits who visited her weren't Nolan, a quiet, distant bit of static. They were vengeful, angry. They were real.

"I wonder if you could tune in to me for a moment and tell me who you see," Ramona urged. "Tell me if anyone comes in."

"Tune in?"

"Yes. I want to close your eyes and visualize the door, but I want you to ask, silently if you prefer, 'Is anyone here for Ramona?' Open yourself to whoever might want to speak to you on my behalf. Ancestors, departed friends."

Blair closed her eyes. She shoved her hands, which had begun to shake, into her lap. Silently, she posed the question: *Is there someone here for Ramona? And no one else, please, no one else...*

For a moment there was nothing, only darkness and her own incessant thoughts about sitting in A&W having such a ridiculous conversation. Her mother would be furious if she knew. The scents of French fries in oil and the sharp little pungent onions from Ramona's coney dog filled her nose. From the kitchen a man shouted, "Dogs are done."

Then something materialized. There at the far end of a long dark hall—a red door. A little crack fractured the darkness, light spilled through the opening and in came a woman. Her hair was long and dark and curly and she held a tiny wriggling white dog in her arms.

"Julia," Blair murmured.

"Very good. What do you see? Tell me every detail."

"Umm... she has..." Blair curled her finger in the air. "Long curly hair, black, and she's holding a little dog." Blair spoke the dog's name at the same moment that Ramona did.

"Pee Wee," they both said.

Blair's eyes opened. Ramona was smiling, studying her.

"That's my mother and our chihuahua, Pee Wee. Is she still there?"

Blair closed her eyes. Darkness again, but then after a second, that crack of light appeared. Blair stared at the door, breath held, and suddenly it hurled open all the way and a flood of something dark and fast poured through.

Blair pressed back against the vinyl seat, felt the cold as the shadow rushed through her and suddenly she was gone, no longer in the booth at A&W.

She pulled open a white door, eyes skimming over the Minnie Mouse watch encircling her wrist as she stepped onto a narrow staircase. A musty smell greeted her as she descended into the basement at Rho Upsilon Nu. Gingerly, she walked down, squinting toward the dark beneath her.

Suddenly from behind, two hands shoved her. Screaming, she flailed, lost her footing, and plunged toward the concrete floor below.

42

Blair shrieked and flung out her arms, eyes popping open. Her hand hit her root beer float and sent it flying. Pop and ice cream splattered Ramona and the glass rolled off the table and shattered on the floor.

Across the room Teagan and her grandma bolted from their booth and hurried over.

"Oh, gosh... I'm so sorry," Blair sputtered. The vision receded, but the sense of falling remained.

Ramona grabbed a napkin and dabbed at her face. She plucked a glob of ice cream from the front of her shirt and plopped it on the table. "It's okay. Don't get upset. Can you tell me what you saw or heard?"

Blair glanced sidelong at Teagan and shook her head. "I don't really know. Shadows."

Ramona tilted her head and nodded. A yawn seized her and she covered her mouth. "Let's do this. I have to get home and get some sleep, but I want you to practice the door visualization. Okay? I'm going to give you my number and you can call me if you want to talk through this some more. Maybe you can even join us for group."

"DID IT HELP?" Teagan asked as they walked to her grandma's van.

Blair stared at her feet. "I don't know. I'll try the things she said."

"And she gave you her number if you need help."

"Yeah. She's part of a group that works with all that stuff. I don't know. I could never tell my mother."

"So don't tell her."

"Yeah." Blair had no intention of telling her, but her mother had a way of finding out things. Even as they climbed into Connie's van, Blair scanned the parking lot for any sign of her mother's black SUV.

TEAGAN'S GRANDMA parked at the curb in front of Willow Hall. Teagan and Blair climbed out.

"Lovely to spend a little time with you today, Blair," Connie said, hugging Blair goodbye.

"You too. And thank you for everything."

"Here." Connie tucked something into her hand.

Blair unfurled her fingers. A silver token sat in her palm, words etched into the surface.

"It's the serenity prayer," Connie said. "It's gotten me through some tough times."

"Thank you."

"TT, call me later?" Connie hugged Teagan, who nodded.

"I will. I promise."

"I wish I could stay longer, but I'm taking care of Edna Fuller for the rest of the day."

"Don't feel bad. I'll call you tonight, or sooner if anything develops."

Teagan's grandma climbed back into her van and both girls waved goodbye.

Blair turned the coin over. The back side read, 'One day at a time.'

"Oh, shit," Teagan muttered.

"Wha—?" Blair didn't have a chance to get the word out. Her mother was suddenly there, hand gripping her upper arm, face a display of rage covered over by the most insincere, disturbing smile Blair had ever seen.

"Who was that? Whose van was that?" she hissed.

"It was... umm..."

"My grandma's van," Teagan said, more loudly than necessary, stepping closer to Blair and her mother, eyes fixed on Margo's fingernails digging into Blair's skin.

She released Blair's arm and took hold of her hand. "Isn't that lovely?" She didn't give Teagan a chance to respond or Blair an opportunity to say goodbye. Margo dragged her daughter toward the entrance to Willow Hall.

"Why aren't your dressed?" she demanded. "The legacy luncheon is in a half hour at Rho Upsilon Nu. All the mothers are going to be there. This is unacceptable. My God, look at your hair and your face. Hurry up, we don't have much time."

In her dorm room, Blair's mother scrubbed her face with disposable cleaning wipes. She yanked a brush through her hair and then grabbed a dress and shoes from Blair's closet.

Blair stood, legs wobbly, head fuzzy, and allowed her mother to jerk off her clothes and force the dress over her head.

"Where were you? What were you doing with *those people*?" She spoke the words those people as if Teagan and her grandma were something she'd found on the bottom of her shoe.

"Teagan's grandma took us to breakfast," Blair lied.

Margo grabbed her chin and pinched it. "Hold still. I need to fix your makeup." Blair's eyes watered as her mother hastily applied mascara, nearly poking her in one eye. "You won't go anywhere with them again. Do you understand?"

Blair, fighting tears, nodded.

THE LONG DINING table had been set at Rho Upsilon Nu. Candles flickered in gold candelabras placed on a silk pink runner. Dishes of salads, bread and sliced turkey lay on large platters.

Everyone talked at once, their voices rising and falling as the mothers shared stories of their own time at Rho Upsilon Nu.

"I have to use the bathroom." Blair excused herself and bypassed the bathroom nearest the dining room, opting for the one at the back of the house. Mostly she needed to breathe, to calm down, to take a couple of pills.

Blair dropped two pills on the vanity top, crushed them beneath the heel of her hand, leaned down and snorted the powder. She stood, leaned close to the mirror and wiped the dusting from beneath her nose.

She thought of the coin Teagan's grandma had given her. It remained in the pocket of the shorts she'd been wearing.

"I can do this," she murmured, staring at her reflection, her perfectly applied makeup, expertly styled hair. It was *her* there in the glass, but she felt as if she looked at a stranger.

Blair slipped from the room and moved down the hall, already feeling the Adderall streaming through her blood, chasing out the fog.

As she passed the sitting room, she heard a sound—a creak.

Blair peered into the empty room. No one sat inside, but the white antique rocking chair, which had apparently been in the house since the very first chapter of Rho Upsilon Nu at Husher, rocked back and forth.

"Hello?" Blair called stepping inside.

The long white curtains rippled as if shifted by a breeze. She crossed the room, pulled back the curtains and peered at the windows—both closed, locks fastened.

A crash resounded behind her. She spun to see the bone china fox, an antique also in the house for decades, had fallen from the mantel and smashed on the floor.

"Oh, God," she murmured hurrying to gather the pieces.

Before she'd made it halfway across the room, the massive framed photo of Margo and her Rho sisters broke free from the wall and shattered on the wood floor. Glass skittered toward her and the image settled face down. A mirror fell and then a candle. Framed pictures, lamps, trophies all tipped and crashed to the ground.

The white curtains billowed and for an instant, tucked into the shroud of sheer fabric, Blair saw the outline of a young woman, the sheet sucked in as if she'd taken a breath and inhaled. Her arms flailed and her body twisted. She was being smothered by the curtain—was fighting for her life. Blair ripped the curtain free. No one stood behind it, but the fabric whooshed up, ensnared Blair, who for a startling moment was not alone inside that white shroud.

The girl's face was half skeletal, mud and peeled skin and white bone, and the other side weirdly perfect with red lipstick and peach eyeshadow. Her body was a similar imbalance, one side skeletal, wasted, the other pristine in a lemon-yellow dress, fingernails bubblegum-pink. The smell then—rotted, foul, dead.

Blair screamed, thrashed out of the curtain, and raced for the door, but it slammed just as she reached for it. She wrenched the knob, but it didn't turn. It wasn't locked, but frozen. She hammered against it and screamed.

43

Teagan strode across campus to Monroe Hall in search of Lauren Jacobs. Lauren—who'd been Jessica Meyers' best friend—had sent her an email agreeing to meet.

"Are you Lauren?" Teagan asked.

The girl sat against an oak tree, a chemistry textbook opened in her lap. Nestled within the larger book, Teagan spotted a paperback.

She looked up. "Teagan?"

"Yeah. Do you mind if I sit?"

Lauren shook her head, dog-eared the page in the paperback and closed the cover. It was a Harlequin romance with a bare-chested man standing at the top of a grand staircase. "Go for it, free country and all."

Teagan dropped into the grass and gestured at the book. "How is it?"

Lauren shrugged. "Better than chemistry."

"I bet. So, you were good friends with Jessica Meyers?"

"Best friends."

"Okay, and you were also a sister in Rho Upsilon Nu?"

Lauren stiffened. "I'm not a member anymore, and I prefer not to talk about them."

"You were, though, right?"

Lauren's eyes narrowed. "Barely. Who told you to talk to me? Was it Sloan? You can tell her I'm sick of the pledges harassing me. I'm not telling Rho's secrets and I don't intend to."

Teagan leaned in. "I'm not part of the sorority. I swear. Are they harassing you?"

Lauren looked beyond Teagan, scanned the quad as if checking to see who watched them. "No, they're fine."

"Please, listen..." Teagan pulled a folded flier from her back pocket and opened it. "This is my best friend who's missing— Harley Rand. She was rushing Rho. I'm worried that whatever happened to her had something to do with them. I know Jessica also went missing during rush week."

Lauren's eyes welled at the mention of Jessica having gone missing.

Teagan leaned closer, sensed she'd struck a chord. "Why did you get kicked out of Rho?"

"Why do you think I got kicked out?"

Teagan remembered the story of plastic containers filled with puke in Lauren's closet. "Someone said it happened because you were bulimic."

Lauren snorted. "Half the girls in there are bulimic. That was just their excuse. I struggled after Jessica disappeared. We rushed together, and we'd become really close. I met her at orientation. We were both in Pine Hall. I'd been planning to rush, and she decided to do it too, so we did. It was such a crazy week. During the day you're dressed all proper doing these grown-up-sounding interviews, then at night you're expected to bong beer and flirt with the frat guys. It did my head in. Jessica was handling it better than me, at least I thought she was, but then..."

"She vanished."

"Yeah."

"Did you notice anything weird at all with her around the time she went missing?"

Lauren pursed her lips. "It's hard because I was in the same boat as her. You know? Those first weeks here at Husher were like treading water while fifty sharks circled beneath us. Only later when I looked back did I notice a few things, but... am I making them up in my search for answers or was something really wrong?"

"Like what?"

"A couple nights before she went missing, she came back to the dorm super late, like four a.m. She was out of it, disheveled. I remember she had her skirt on backwards. When I asked her about it the next day, she didn't really remember what had happened the night before, but she'd been at one of the frats drinking, which was the norm. I would have gone too, but I had some kind of stomach bug. We didn't really talk about it and I never did find out what happened."

"Was she dating anyone? Did she have a boyfriend?"

"No. Well, there was an Alpha Lambda guy, Nolan. I think she liked him, but it was all very new."

"And you got the bid for Rho Upsilon Nu. Were they inviting Jessica too?"

"I think so. Heather told me she would have gotten a bid, but then... then she was gone and if I thought rushing was crazy, pledging was like..." Lauren pushed her books into the grass and pulled her knees into her chest. "It was hell. They tortured us. It was like Stockholm syndrome. One day they were so cruel and pointing out how stupid and fat and ugly we were and the next day they showered us with compliments, brought us gifts, surprised us in class with flowers or coffees. It was bizarre."

"Why did you stay in it?"

Lauren bit the side of her thumb. "I don't even know. I was so out of it. Jessica was gone, and I kept thinking she'd come back. Her cousin called me a lot. Jessica's mom was dead and her dad was kind of absent, so her cousin was the only one who even cared she disappeared. The police thought Jessica had taken off. They didn't believe anything bad had happened. My sorority sisters were my only friends. Except not really. They constantly gossiped about each other, slept with each other's boyfriends. They talked about this unbreakable bond, but it was all bullshit. Outside of Jessica, I hadn't made any friends because I devoted every spare moment to Greek life."

"How long were you in the sorority?"

"I made it about a year and then... they started getting on my case about every little thing."

"Did something cause them to turn on you?"

"Yeah. I organized a candlelight vigil for Jessica on the anniversary of her disappearance. Like an idiot, I assumed they'd be excited, proud of me. Just the opposite. They were pissed, said I was bringing down the morale of the whole sorority—the whole campus."

"They didn't want you to hold a vigil?"

"Nope."

"Did they ever talk about Jessica? Drop any hints about what they thought happened to her?"

Lauren shook her head. "They wouldn't talk about her. It was like her name was sacrilegious. I brought her up a few times, and they'd get quiet and then hurry and change the subject."

"Do you think they knew what happened to her?"

Lauren sighed and leaned her head back, staring up into the branches of the tree for several moments. When she returned her gaze to Teagan's it was troubled. "I don't know. Logical me says 'no way'—they're just a bunch of college girls who don't want the vibe killed by talking about one of their own going missing—but then I have a gut feeling, this sense that maybe they do know. Maybe they've known right from the beginning and that's why I got the bid."

"Why would that be?"

"Keep your friends close and your enemies closer."

44

People pounded on the door—Blair's sorority sisters and their mothers.

Blair didn't know when she'd pulled the lipstick from the pocket of her dress, but when the door burst open, she gripped the little tube of Maybelline Red Liberation in her hand. She'd scribbled a word furiously on the white walls: *Peggy, Peggy, Peggy, Peggy.* She'd scrawled the name on the white and pink couches, the floor, the shards of broken mirror.

Sloan rushed in, followed by Blair's mother and the other Rho sisters and their moms. Their faces were white with shock, anger, fear.

For an instant, Blair's mother looked terrified of her daughter, and Blair realized she held a piece of the broken mirror in one hand. It had cut into her palm and blood dripped from her fist.

Margo's fear gave way to fury and then humiliation.

"Peggy!" Blair screamed. She didn't know why. It was the only word she could form. Not help, not 'it wasn't me,' nothing emerged. "Peggy, Peggy!" she shrieked, and she tried to sprint from the room. She needed to tell Teagan, had to tell her, could think of nothing but passing on that message.

Her mother caught her by the hair, yanked her back and grabbed hold of her arms, shook the piece of glass free. It dropped to the wood floor.

"Someone call an ambulance," Margo shouted. "She has a condition." Her mother stared hard into her eyes, dared her to defy her, to move against her.

For a moment, Blair resisted. She had to tell Teagan, but then the adrenaline drained out and she allowed her mother to force her to the floor.

THE PREVIOUS HALF hour had been a blur. The paramedics had arrived at the sorority house and Blair was no longer the hysterical one. It was her mother now, crying, wringing her hands, telling the other Rho sisters and mothers that Blair had a condition, episodes, had always had them, thought they'd been better.

Other students from the surrounding fraternities and sororities had come out. They huddled on their front lawns and watched the commotion.

The paramedic insisted to Margo they had to go as she continued to rattle off excuses to the women at Rho Upsilon Nu. "It's not her fault. She has an illness," Margo sobbed.

Blair seized her moment as she sat alone in the ambulance. She pulled out her cell phone and typed a message to Teagan.

Her mother and the paramedic climbed into the back of the ambulance and Blair didn't have time to hide her phone. Her mother's eyes narrowed on the device still clutched in Blair's bloody hands. She reached forward and snatched it away, stared at the screen, reading Blair's message. She glared at her daughter, but she didn't demand to know what it meant. The paramedic watched Margo, urged her to take a seat.

"You need to sedate her, give her something," Margo told him. "She'll attack you, claw your eyes out. You saw what she did to that room."

The paramedic, a middle-aged man who looked tired beyond his years, eyed Blair, but his concern seemed more for her mother, as if Margo was the one to be wary of.

45

Teagan walked back to Willow Hall, chewing her lip and thinking about Lauren's admissions. The girls of Rho Upsilon Nu were secretive about Jessica Meyers. Why? Why, unless they had something to do with her disappearance?

She took out her cell phone and saw a missed text from Blair. She clicked it open.

Blair: *peggypeggypeggypeggypeggypeggypeggypeggypeggy*

Teagan texted back.

Teagan: *Huh?*

Nothing came back. After several more minutes, Teagan called Blair's number, but it went straight to voicemail. Back at Willow Hall, she walked to Blair's dorm room and knocked on her door. No answer.

She texted her again.

Teagan: *Hey, where are you?*

~

THROUGH A HALL WINDOW, Teagan spotted Blair's roommate walking away from the dorm. She ran downstairs and pushed through the double doors, nearly colliding with several other girls carrying plastic grocery bags.

"Hey!" Teagan called. Blair's roommate, perhaps not having heard her, continued walking. "Hey, you... umm..." Teagan searched for the name of Blair's roommate. Finally, it surfaced. "Colette!"

The girl stopped and turned, stared at Teagan and then walked slowly toward her. "Yeah?" Colette asked.

"I was just upstairs looking for Blair. Do you know where she's at?"

"I don't live with Blair anymore. My mom had me transferred to another room."

"Really, why?"

Colette looked away, stared off in the direction she'd been walking. When she turned back to Teagan, her eyes appeared troubled. "I'd rather not get into it. I have class, so I need to get going."

"I'll walk with you," Teagan said. "I'd really appreciate if you'd tell me."

"Honestly, I don't think it's my place. Blair's really nice."

"Please. We're friends and she sent me a weird message and I'm just trying to find her."

Colette fiddled with the zipper on her sweatshirt, staring at the cracked sidewalk as she walked. "All right, but I'd prefer if you didn't mention to her what I tell you."

"I won't. I swear."

"Okay." Colette sighed. "My mom works for emergency dispatch in Mackinaw City. Her boyfriend is a police detective. Sometimes she can be a little overprotective. She looked into Blair's history. Mostly I think she was worried about her having like a pervy dad or older brother. Like I said, she's a little over-

protective. Anyway, umm... she found out Blair had had some
issues and was institutionalized for a little while."

"Institutionalized?"

"It was a mental health thing when she was in high school. I
really don't want it to get around. She's in that sorority and I
can only imagine how those girls would react to that news."

"Yeah. Sure. Did your mom find out why?"

"Not really. Some kind of an outburst at school. But it's no
big deal. Apparently, Blair's mom put in a transfer request as
well, so... I guess that's that."

"Huh. Okay."

Colette had a look like she might say something, but had
thought better of it.

"Is there something else? I know Blair's struggling. I'm
trying to help her."

"This is such an invasion of privacy," Colette murmured,
"but when I was moving out of our room, her notebook fell off
her bookshelf. It opened I saw some of her drawings and"—
Colette rubbed her arms as if she'd just gotten a chill—"she's
been drawing some pretty disturbing stuff."

"What kind of stuff?"

"I feel really weird sharing this. Maybe you should just ask
her."

"Please?"

Colette sighed. "Torture scenes. Girls, like our age, getting
tortured. Girls who looked dead. Girls running through rows of
corn with like"—Colette brushed a hand over her forehead—
"blood running down their faces. Honestly, it scared me. But I
really have to go. Please don't her I told you that stuff."

Teagan watched Colette walk away, disturbed by what she
claimed to have seen in Blair's notebook.

Girls running through rows of corn-the Husher Harvester-
Harley's backpack near a cornfield. It all had to be connected,
and yet Teagan could not imagine how unless Lex and Nate

were right and Robert Thomas had an accomplice that had resumed his killing spree at Husher University.

She tried again to call Blair, and her phone went straight to voicemail. Her skin prickled, and she fought back the tremor of fear, instantly reminded of so many unanswered calls to Harley's phone.

"Teagan?"

She looked up to see Lex walking toward her, a folder clutched in his hands.

"What's going on?" she asked.

"Have you talked to your friend, Blair?"

"No. I've been trying to get a hold of her."

"Apparently, she flipped out at the Rho Upsilon Nu house earlier and trashed one of the rooms. They called an ambulance and everything."

"You're kidding?"

"No. It's true."

"How did you find out?"

"I just stopped in at Alpha Lambda because Corbin borrowed one of my books. Half the students on Greek Row were outside talking about it. The ambulance had just left."

Teagan thought of what Colette had just told her about Blair being hospitalized in high school. "She sent me a weird text earlier."

"What did it say?"

Teagan opened her messages and showed him the text.

Lex frowned. "That is weird. What does it mean? Is it a name? Peggy?"

"Not a clue."

Lex stared at the message for another moment, then handed her phone back. "I feel bad for her. I can't imagine the Rho Upsilon Nu girls allowing her to stay a pledge after this."

"Maybe that's exactly what she wants."

"Do you think so?"

"Yeah, but her mom was a member and is a total psycho. She's the reason Blair rushed. No wonder she's losing her mind."

Teagan thought of finding Blair in her room, immobile and cold to the touch. She'd described it as being taken over by a spirit. Teagan shuddered.

Lex held up the file. "I brought a bunch of stuff on the Harvester. Want to look through it?"

Teagan tried one last time to reach Blair, then shoved her phone in her pocket, nodding. She considered calling hospitals, but if Blair had experienced a mental health issue, they'd likely not be releasing any of her information, especially to a fellow student. "Yeah. Let's see what you've got."

They went into the dorm, and Teagan led Lex to one of the empty study rooms. They sat side by side on the couch and Lex opened the file.

"Before we get into this, there's one more thing," Lex said.

Teagan glanced at him, saw worry etched there.

"What? Spit it out."

"I heard a rumor."

"Okay... about what?"

"Cassie. The other girl who's missing."

Teagan waited.

"A few of the guys at Alpha Lambda were talking when I showed up today. They didn't realize I was there. One of them said the girl who disappeared, as in Cassie, was, umm... touched, possibly videotaped by one of the Alpha Lambda guys."

"What the hell does that mean? Touched and videotaped?"

"It happened at a party the night before she went missing. I didn't get the details because, obviously, I was eavesdropping and couldn't exactly grill them. It sounded to me like she'd passed out somewhere and one of those guys pulled up her skirt and—"

"Those bastards," Teagan snapped, fuming, sick in her stomach. "What else did they say? Did one of them do something to her? Did they kill her?"

Lex held up his hands, palms out, as if the accusation were lobbed at him. "Whoa. Let's not jump to any conclusions."

"Are you joking? Don't jump to conclusions? She got assaulted, maybe raped, and now she's disappeared? Not to mention it's by the same guys who are like this"—she crossed her fingers—"with the Rho Upsilon Nu girls. The sorority Harley was rushing. Two girls vanished and both were connected to those swine at Alpha Lambda and I'm not supposed to get suspicious."

She thought of what Lauren had told her about Jesscia. She'd been into a guy at Alpha Lambda. "Do you know an Alpha Lambda named Nolan?"

Lex frowned, shook his head. "I've never heard of him. Who is he?"

Teagan shook her head. "I don't know. Maybe it doesn't matter." She gestured at the file. "I can't get into this stuff right now. I'm going to the campus police."

She stood and Lex caught her arm. "It's a rumor, Teagan. It might not even be true."

"Yeah, well, rumors start somewhere, don't they?" She didn't wait for him to respond. She hurried from the room and toward the stairs.

TEAGAN PUSHED through the glass doors into the campus police station. A young woman sat at the desk, dark hair pulled into a tight ponytail. She looked up as Teagan walked in, but didn't smile. "How can I help you?"

"I'm looking for Officer Key."

"What's this pertaining to?"

"The missing girls."

"And what's your name?"

"Teagan Kelso."

The girl remained expressionless. She stood and walked to the office Teagan had sat in before. The girl administered one sharp knock and then pushed the door open. "Teagan Kelso is here to see you." The girl gestured at Teagan to go in.

Key sat at his desk. His skin had a grayish color, his eyes red-rimmed. "What can I do for you?" he asked.

"Have you questioned the Alpha Lambda frat guys about Harley and Cassie?"

"I'm not at liberty to disclose specific interview subjects."

"Well, do you want to know what I just heard? The Alpha Lambda frat boys roofied Cassie and sexually assaulted her and videotaped it. Harley was at their frat just days before she went missing. She was rushing the sorority their friends with. And I think I got drugged there, too."

"Do you have proof?"

"Of what?"

"The drugging? The assault?"

"No. I don't have proof. How the hell would I have proof?"

He wiped at his watery eyes and pulled a tissue from a box, blowing his nose. "Without proof—"

"Are you fucking kidding me? Those guys are behind this. They must have done something to Harley too, and when she threatened to tell, they silenced her." Teagan stood, furious, ready to swipe everything from the man's desk onto the floor.

"And," she slapped a hand on Key's desk. "Jesscia Meyers, the girl who disappeared two years ago, was also involved with an Alpha Lambda guy. That's three girls associated with that frat who have vanished off the face of the earth."

He sucked in his cheeks and glared at her. "Cassie has been found."

Teagan screwed up her eyes. "What? What do you mean she's been found?"

"I mean, she was located safely this morning. She's home with her parents, unharmed."

Teagan shook her head. "No. But—how?"

"She went home, that's how. She spent the last several nights at a friend's house. She hasn't disclosed her reason for disappearing, but if there was an assault, I'm sure that information will come to light. Your theory is incorrect, Teagan."

Teagan stared at him, willed her mouth to close. "But... what about Harley?"

"We have transferred Harley's case to the Husher Police Department. They have more resources and are better equipped to deal with it going forward. I can assure you the Husher police are doing everything in their power to find Harley. I'm not aware of the specifics, as the case is no longer with campus police; however—"

Teagan turned and stormed from his office. She slammed the door so hard it rattled in the frame.

The girl at the desk looked at her, unsurprised, and said nothing as Teagan tore from the building.

She called her grandma. "Grandma, can you come get me? I need to come home."

46

They'd spoken little during their drive. Teagan had given her grandma the basics. Cassie had been found, but Harley had not.

Teagan stepped into her childhood home and her body sagged, tension running out through her feet as she crossed the threshold, kicked off her shoes and felt the familiar worn wood beneath her. She trailed her fingers along the plastered walls painted pale yellow in the front hall and gazed at the array of photos that mostly depicted Teagan and her mother, so alike in girlhood that visitors had often mistaken pictures of a young Robin for photos of Teagan.

"Hi, Mom," Teagan murmured before she walked into the living room. She sank onto the long, mustard-colored sectional and leaned her head back against the tired cushion.

Nails clicked across the floor and their pet corgi appeared in the doorway.

"Chowder!" Teagan opened her arms so the portly little dog could run and spring into them.

He nearly didn't make it, his heavy lower half dragging him back, but Teagan wrapped her arms around the dog and pulled him into her lap. He nuzzled his head under her chin, then flopped across her legs as if the exertion had worn him out.

The front door opened and her grandma appeared, a stack of mail in hand.

"We got a new *National Geographic.*" Her grandma held it up. "Want to read it now?"

Teagan shook her head, leaned over and grabbed a blanket from the back of the couch. "I think I'll take a nap. I'm really tired."

Her grandma smiled. "I'm sure that's what Chowder prefers as well."

Chowder had already closed his eyes. Teagan lay down, folding around the warmth of the dog. Her grandma walked over and kissed her forehead. "I could run into Antonio's and get a pizza? Pepperoni and mushrooms?"

"I'm really not hungry," Teagan murmured.

She shut her eyes, tears swimming up. She and Harley had eaten at Antonio's hundreds of times. They'd sat in the little booths and eaten pepperoni and mushroom pizza, drunk soda and talked about school, weekend plans and the future. They'd been at Antonio's three years before when Lisa had last fallen off the wagon and Harley had told Teagan everything, tears running down her cheeks.

Teagan felt her grandmother's soft fingers graze her cheek and then her footsteps receded. She breathed slow and deep, waiting for the bubble of grief to dissolve. She thought she wouldn't sleep, couldn't possibly with thoughts of Harley so close, but after a while she drifted down and away.

TEAGAN WOKE ON THE COUCH, Chowder still nestled against her belly. Her grandma's voice drifted from the kitchen as she talked on the phone.

"I'm so devastated," her grandma said. "Terrified and sick over this for Teagan. She's already been through so much. She can't lose her best friend."

Teagan moved Chowder aside and stood, chest constricted, heart lodged in her throat. She slipped down the hall and into her bedroom.

Perfectly still, her thoughts a jumble of leftover nightmares and too-hard memories, Teagan stared around her room.

The last time she'd been in the room it had been scattered with shopping bags and plastic totes. She and Harley had spent the previous weeks scouring the discount sales for dorm decor. They'd bought rice paper lanterns, wastebaskets decorated in funky flowers and packs of colored pens and notebooks. The remnants of their tornado remained—receipts on the bed, crumpled shopping bags stuffed in the wicker garbage bin by Teagan's old desk.

Collages of her and Harley hung on the walls, photos they'd meticulously cut over the summers, writing little bubble quotes above their heads before pasting them onto the boards beneath the glass. Shot glasses lined a hanging shelf. A stack of magazines they'd flipped through weeks before sat on the floor. When they'd walked from the room, carrying their totes, laughing, excited, the future had appeared golden, limitless. It all had evaporated in a matter of days.

Teagan's rage-fueled energy of the previous days had dissolved. She was a rag doll, lifeless.

Chowder padded into the room and Teagan hefted him on her bed. He flopped on his side, watching her. She crawled in, curled around him and drifted away.

WHEN TEAGAN WOKE the following morning, her grandma had already left. She'd pinned a note to the refrigerator.

Teagan—

I'm at Mrs. Jericho's this morning until eleven. There's bread for toast and orange juice or some of your oatmeal in the cupboard. Call me if you need anything.

Teagan showered, dressed, and left the house. She'd sold her car to help pay for tuition, but Lisa and Harley's house was only two streets over.

The grass on the front lawn of the faded little bungalow was overgrown. Lisa's Harley motorcycle stood parked inside the open garage.

Teagan knocked several times, and when no one answered, she cracked the door and peered into the dimly lit house.

"Lisa?" she called.

After a moment she heard a sound and Lisa shuffled from the living room into the hall. She looked haggard, wore a wrinkled t-shirt and too big sweatpants. For a moment she stared at Teagan as if she didn't recognize her.

"It's me, Teagan," Teagan told her, stepping into the house.

"Come in then," she grumbled, turning and disappearing into the kitchen.

Teagan followed her. The house smelled musty with the faint odor of cat pee. She doubted Lisa had scooped Dumbo's litter in days.

Lisa spooned instant coffee into a mug, added water from the sink, and stirred it. She sat heavily in a chair and took a sip from her mug—the dark liquid, grounds barely dissolved, dribbled down her chin.

Teagan tried not to stare at her, at her sunken bloodshot eyes and her hair snarled and sticking from her head, her t-shirt a mass of stains. But everywhere else she looked in the drab kitchen reminded her of Harley. The Scooby Doo clock they'd found at a thrift store now hung above the refrigerator. It had never worked, but Lisa had loved it. Scooby Doo was her favorite character. She even had his image tattooed on one of her ankles. Harley's awards, notes, and one of her senior pictures hung haphazardly on the surface of the refrigerator, held by a series of cheap magnets.

Harley had been the touchstone in Lisa's life, the only reason she kept it together, but now Harley was gone and, though neither of them said it, they both knew she wasn't likely to be coming back. Too much time had passed.

Sure, there were girls abducted and found alive days, weeks, even years later, but those were the exception. The rule was those girls were abducted and found days, weeks or years later dead and they'd been dead since the beginning, since the night they vanished.

47

"Have the police given you any updates?" Teagan asked.

Lisa snorted, pushed her coffee away. She patted the pockets of her flannel shirt and pulled out a pack of cigarettes. Rather than a cigarette, she withdrew a joint, propped it on her lower lip and lit it with a pink Bic lighter. Lisa took a drag and then stared at the lighter, her eyes welling with tears.

"Harley bought me this. Pink of all colors. She loved pink." Lisa gave Teagan a funny expression. "I'd sometimes look at her, so perfect and put together and smart and beautiful, and think... how could she be mine? Was there some mix-up at the hospital? Had God given her to me to make up for my hard life? Or was she a test, and I failed it?"

"Someone found her backpack," Teagan said.

Lisa blinked at her, struggled to focus. She held the joint out to Teagan, who shook her head. "But no Harley," Lisa finally said.

"No. Her phone wasn't inside. The bag looked like it was tossed from a window next to a cornfield."

Lisa looked up sharply at that, then shifted her gaze back down, stared at the table. She took another long drag, blew out a puff of smoke.

"Where's Buzz?" Teagan asked.

Lisa gazed around as if just noticing he wasn't there. "Gone."

"Gone for good?"

She shrugged, let her eyes drift closed. The pain in her face made Teagan's chest constrict. Teagan had often been frustrated with Lisa over the years, bothered by her inability to be a better mom to Harley, but she'd always understood that Lisa struggled in ways she'd never comprehend. Harley had known that too and always defended her mother who, despite screwing up in every way imaginable, still strove to make a life for her only child.

At their high school graduation, the previous June, Lisa had given Harley an envelope stuffed with one-dollar and five-dollar bills, money she'd saved returning bottles and cans she'd collected for the previous year—money to pay for Harley's sorority dues at college.

"Do you mind if I go up to Harley's room?" Teagan asked.

Lisa closed her eyes, shook her head. "I don't care about anything anymore."

TEAGAN OPENED the door to Harley's room. Silence filled the space. Even Teagan's footfalls were muted by the carpet. The depth of the quiet unnerved her. In former visits, Lisa always had the TV going downstairs. Harley often left her music playing. Now the entire house had been stripped of sound.

A half bath connected to Harley's room. The door was open and the smell of cat pee was overpowering. Teagan went in, squatted by the box and scooped litter into a little waste paper bag, tying off the top. From the doorway, Dumbo meowed.

"There he is," Teagan said.

She picked up the skinny gray cat with his too-big ears and carried him to the bed. Perched on the edge of the bed, Teagan stroked the cat's back and tried not to let Harley's things get the best of her—photographs of her and Harley, Harley's ragged stuffed cow against the pillows, the laundry sack she'd sewn in high school home ec class, the rhinestone barrettes she'd worn to senior prom. Pale yellow curtains glowed in the afternoon sun. Weeks before they'd both sat cross-legged on the floor sifting through socks, pairing them up, tossing the extras into a box for the thrift store. They'd laughed at how many pairs had animal prints. They'd been so blissfully unaware of what lay ahead.

Harley might never set foot in the room again.

The thought made Teagan's mouth go dry, her heart shrivel behind her ribs. Tears kept at bay for days spilled down her cheeks, dripped onto Dumbo's head. The cat purred, oblivious, unaware that his person had vanished from the world.

Teagan wanted to scream, to sob, but she forced her cries to be quiet, as hushed as the house itself, and when they receded, she stood, left Dumbo on the bed and began searching.

She opened the drawers in Harley's desk. Everything was organized, in its right place. Harley wasn't a keeper. She got rid of things. The drawers' contents included a few pencils, mostly empty notebooks, and high school papers with especially good grades. Harley's dresser held clothes neatly folded. Her closet was color-coordinated, dresses separate from sweaters. Three pairs of shoes lined the floor.

Her jewelry box held two pairs of earrings and three rings. Her bookshelf contained her favorite paperbacks, two photo albums and several colored plastic folders, likely leftovers from high school.

Teagan did not know what she searched for, doubted that anything in the room would offer evidence to Harley's whereabouts, but still she plunged ahead.

Beneath Harley's bed sat a plastic tote filled with extra bedding. Teagan's hand brushed the sharp edge of a wooden box. She had to lie on her stomach and wriggle beneath the low frame to reach it. She stood and sat the box, painted in gold flakes, on the mattress.

Teagan and Harley had created the treasure boxes in girlhood. Teagan's mostly held photos of her mother. Rather than paint her box gold like Harley's, Teagan had spray painted hers green.

Inside Harley's box sat a stack of report cards from high school. Teagan's shoulders fell, her disappointment immediate, as if she'd expected to somehow find Harley herself tucked inside.

Teagan lifted the reports cards out and saw more papers, a stack, stapled together. She read the words across the top: *Family Ancestry—Discover Your DNA.*

One page showed colored maps with highlighted areas where Harley's ancestors originated.

Another page stated: *Relative matches—high percentage of shared DNA.*

Names were listed beneath the headline with varying percentages. Harley had circled the name 'Sabrina Thomas' and written a phone number next to it.

Teagan flipped through the pages, not really understanding what they meant.

Harley had never told Teagan she'd taken a DNA test, and she told Teagan everything. Teagan bit her cheek, sifting a second time through the information with little insight into why it mattered.

48

B lair sat in the hospital bed, her gown too thin, the blanket stiff and cold. Everything about the room made her skin crawl—walls so white her eyes ached, the stink of disinfectant. She wanted to cry, but knew the more important thing now was to act as if everything was fine so they'd release her.

A man appeared in the open doorway, clipboard in hand. His bushy hair and eyebrows matched his white coat. "How are you, Blair? I'm Dr. Horton."

"Hi." Blair smoothed the blanket on her lap. "I'm good. Much better."

"That's splendid news. Amazing what a good night's rest can do, eh?" He pulled a chair closer to her bed, sat and crossed his legs, watching her.

"Yeah. I was exhausted."

"I've been there. Freshman year is very demanding."

"It is," she agreed.

"And how is your hand feeling?"

Blair held up her bandaged hand. She'd needed three

stitches for the cuts from the broken mirror. "It's fine. Doesn't hurt at all."

"Very good. Can you tell me what happened yesterday?"

Blair nodded. She'd already rehearsed the story in her head. "Yes, umm... I went to a lunch event at my new sorority with my mom. I'm a pledge now and we just finished rush week and it's been really draining. Rushing on top of new classes and getting used to living in the dorms has been a lot to adjust to. I went down the hall to use the bathroom and heard a sound in one of the rooms. I realize now it was just an open window, but when I walked in the lock must have gotten stuck on the door and I panicked."

"I see." He wrote something on his notepad. "Your mother said you've had episodes before and spent some time in a facility in Grand Rapids?"

"Yes. I saw Dr. Maynard then."

"And do you see a correlation between what happened yesterday and your previous episodes?"

Blair tilted her head. "Maybe. I remember when that happened in high school it was during the SATs. I think stress causes me to..."

"See things? Your mother mentioned your previous episodes included visions or hallucinations?"

"Yes, but I wasn't seeing things yesterday," Blair lied.

"You weren't?"

"No."

"Well, your mother wants you released ASAP. She's concerned about your missing classes so early in the school year. However, our health must always come first. Stress, as I've learned in my profession, is the worst kind of illness because unlike a cold or a flu we don't go to bed when we're afflicted by it. We often keep on doing the very things that are breaking our backs.

"If you believe you'd be better served by a few days here

with us, I'd be happy to insist on that. We can also consider some medications. Your mother told me she already had Dr. Maynard send in a script for an antipsychotic, which you recently started taking?"

"Yes. Umm... I picked it up, but haven't started taking it."

"Okay, then, I suggest you start taking it.".

"I will, and I'd like to get released. I'll take time for rest. I promise."

He smiled, tapped his pen on his clipboard. "Don't promise me, promise yourself. She's the one that matters."

BLAIR SAT in the passenger seat of her mother's car. Margo drove with both hands braced on the wheel with an intensity that made Blair's knees quake.

"Why aren't we going to my dorm?" Blair asked when her mother bypassed the road that led to Willow Hall.

Margo turned onto Greek Row and pulled to a stop in front of Rho Upsilon Nu. "Because you, young lady, are going to march right into Rho Upsilon Nu and apologize profusely and clean that room top to bottom. You've got one chance to not get dropped as a pledge. Come on."

Blair thought she might throw up as she followed her mother up the sidewalk to the front door.

Margo knocked and then twisted the knob and stepped inside. "Hello, girls!" she called. "It's Margo and Blair Davenport."

Blair's sorority sisters crowded into the hallway and, to her surprise, they were all smiles. Several hugged Blair, though she noticed Sloan and Heather hung back, their expressions wary.

"Thank you again, Mrs. Davenport, for the treats last night. What a surprise," Sloan said.

"Don't thank me, Sloan. I was once one of you girls and I

know every now and then you need some champagne, chocolate-covered strawberries, and in-house pedicures. I see all your toes are looking lovely."

Blair glanced down and saw all the girls' toes were freshly polished.

"Is everything ready in the room?" Margo asked.

Sloan's eyes darted to Blair. "It is."

"Lovely. I'll walk Blair down and get out of your hair. Come on, honey."

She offered her hand to Blair, who took it, avoiding the gazes of her sisters as she followed her mother down the hall, gooseflesh rising along her arms as they approached the room. It had been destroyed the day before, would take hours to clean up.

Blair's mother pushed open the door and Blair frowned as she stepped inside. Everything was in order. The photo of her mother above the fireplace was encased in a new silver-edged frame. Other photos, mirrors and lamps had replaced the broken ones. Even new furniture, all white and pink, was arranged in the room. The lipstick and blood were gone from the floor and walls. "I thought—"

"That I'd let my daughter stoop to the level of a maid?" Her mother's words were cutting. She paused to smooth her hair in the mirror. "Hardly. I paid a cleaning service to come in and take care of it this morning, but I needed you to believe you'd be on your knees scrubbing in here."

"It wouldn't be the first time," Blair grumbled.

"Excuse me?" her mother hissed, grabbing hold of the sensitive skin above her elbow.

Blair gritted her teeth against the pain. "Nothing," she whispered.

"I thought so."

Blair's eyes darted to the white curtains, calm, unmoving. She shivered.

Someone knocked on the door, and Margo released her arm. Blair sucked in a shaky breath and fought the desire to rub the sore skin. Margo opened the door to Sloan. "Come in, Sloan."

Sloan entered the room, smiling coldly at Blair. "How are you, Blair?" she asked.

"I'm okay," Blair murmured.

"Speak up," her mother snapped.

"I'm much better," Blair told her.

"That's wonderful. I'm so happy to hear it," Sloan said.

"Do you have something you'd like to say to Sloan?" Margo demanded, her voice and eyes sharp.

"Yes. I'm very sorry. Truly. From the bottom of my heart."

Sloan nodded, holding her waxy smile. "Apology accepted. I just want to make sure you're okay?"

The question was loaded, less about Blair's health than how much of a danger she was to the other sisters in Rho Upsilon Nu. "I am."

It was a lie. She wasn't okay, not remotely, but Sloan was a snake in the grass, dangerous, and she had Margo's ear. One foot out of line and her mother would know about it.

"The doctor was very clear," Margo said. "It was just a perfectly normal stress response. New classes, new dorm, sorority. I remember those days. Goodness me!" She put a hand to her chest as if breathless. "Bittersweet, so much fun, but a world of new obligations and my Blair is a perfectionist. She doesn't do anything halfway. Many of her doctors when she was young told us to expect such reactions from our gifted child. It's the sacrifice, unfortunately. But she's all better now. Aren't you?"

"I am, yes."

Margo turned her attention to Sloan. "Shall we recite the oath?"

Sloan smiled. "Of course."

Sloan took one of Blair's hands, her mother the other, and then they too joined hands and repeated the Rho Upsilon Nu mantra: "'Sisters by choice, secrets forever, our bond stronger than blood.'"

fter Teagan had returned to her grandma's house, she pulled Harley's file with the DNA results from her bag and opened it. Teagan called the phone number listed on Harley's ancestry sheet and waited. It rang twice and a woman answered.

"Hello?"

"Hi, is this Sabrina Thomas?"

"Yes. Who am I speaking with?"

"My name is Teagan Kelso and I think my best friend reached out to you. Maybe you're related to her. Harley Rand?"

The woman said nothing. Teagan waited, watched Chowder carry his ragged squeaky elephant into the room and drop it at Teagan's feet. She nudged the toy away.

"Are you there?" Teagan asked.

"I am, yes. I did speak to Harley over the summer."

"Can I ask why she called you?"

"I'm sure she'd prefer to tell you herself." The woman sounded guarded, almost cool.

"She's missing," Teagan said.

Silence again. And then, "Missing? What does that mean?"

"It means she's disappeared. We're searching for her. The police are involved. I think something bad happened to her."

"Missing," the woman repeated. "Where did she disappear from?"

"Husher University."

The woman released a soft gasp.

"What? Do you know where she's at?" Teagan demanded.

"No. No, of course I don't. I live in New Hampshire. I moved away from that horrid place for a reason and I prefer not to be contacted. I don't want reporters calling me. Do you understand? If you give out my number—"

"Wait. Hold on." Teagan could sense the woman was about to hang up on her. "Who are you? Why did she call you?"

The woman's breath had changed, grew more rapid. Her voice was low when she next spoke. "I'll tell you, but you must swear you won't share my information. You won't give it to the press."

"I won't. I promise." Teagan didn't want to make any such promises. She wanted to rip the lady a new one for being secretive about something that might help her find Harley.

"Harley was, is... my niece. She is my brother's daughter."

"Okay..."

"She took some kind of family DNA test and found out my information."

"But... why did she want to know? I mean, her dad's been in prison her whole life."

"Yes, that's true, but when Harley called me, she didn't know her dad's real name or his crimes. Her mother, Lisa, who I knew as Angie, gave Harley, who I knew as Ella, a false story about a man imprisoned for burglary."

"Wait. Are you saying Lisa and Harley had different names?"

"Yes. When Lisa, aka Angie, was married to my brother, Robert Thomas, her name was Angie and my niece, the child they had together, was named Ella after my and Robert's mother."

"Robert Thomas..." Teagan's blood ran cold. "As in—?"

"Robert is a convicted serial killer serving a life sentence in the penitentiary in Marquette, Michigan."

Teagan sat up straighter. "The Husher Harvester..."

Sabrina sucked in a breath. "Yes. That was an unfortunate moniker. He was a serial murderer. And I told Harley as much when I spoke to her, which I'm sure clarifies why I do not want reporters calling my home. I've been through this once. I moved away to escape it and I don't intend to go through it again. I have nothing more to tell you. I haven't spoken to Robert in years."

"Did you tell Harley anything else?"

"No. I was twenty-four when Robert went to prison. My mother died from heartbreak; my father went AWOL. There was nothing left for me in Michigan but anguish and I have started a new life, though clearly Angie did one better and even changed their names. Apparently, I should have done the same. Goodbye."

She hung up before Teagan could say more. Teagan almost redialed her number, demanded to know word for word what she'd told Harley, but the bomb had already detonated in Teagan's head and she could do little more than breathe.

Harley had found out her dad was a convicted serial killer and she'd never told Teagan. She'd spoken with Sabrina months before. Harley had been keeping the secret the entire summer.

For several minutes, Teagan stared in horror at the floor, seeing not Chowder pacing about, hopeful she'd throw his elephant, but a replay of the previous weeks, shopping for dorm supplies, packing their stuff for college, moving in. There'd been movie nights and long talks about what lay ahead, and a hundred, no, a thousand opportunities for Harley to confide in Teagan what she'd discovered, but she hadn't said a word.

TEAGAN'S GRANDMA arrived home just before lunch. She held a paper sack from Danny's deli.

"I got you a Cobb salad," her grandma said, bustling into the kitchen. "And I bought each of us one of those enormous chocolate chip cookies." She set the bag on the table and leaned over to kiss Teagan on her forehead. "How are you, honey? Did you get some sleep last night?"

"Robert Thomas was Harley's dad."

Her grandma continued unpacking the brown paper bag. She looked up at Teagan, her brow furrowed. "Robert Thomas? I believe Lisa said his name was Mark or Matt or—"

"Mark Smith. That was the name she gave Harley. Mark Smith, who'd gone away for armed robbery. But it wasn't true. His name was Robert Thomas. Robert Thomas, the Husher Harvester."

Her grandma, who'd begun to unwrap the cellophane from her sandwich, paused. She shook her head. "The serial killer? No. That can't be true. No, gosh, no. Of course not. Lisa would have told me—"

"Her real name isn't Lisa. It's Angie. She was married to him, and Harley, whose real name is Ella, was their daughter."

Teagan's grandma settled into her chair, steepling her hands in front of her mouth. "Why do you think this? Where is this coming from?"

Teagan stood and grabbed Harley's folder. She set in front of her grandma and pulled out the ancestry sheet. "She took one of those family ancestry tests and she found a relative match, an aunt, Robert Thomas's sister. Harley called her this summer. Her name is Sabrina. I spoke to her an hour ago."

Her grandma's hand had gone to her throat. She studied the pages, her face pale. "Could it possibly be true?" she breathed.

"It's true. I know it is. I'm going back over there. I'm going to confront Lisa."

"Confront her?" Her grandma frowned. "Teagan, I don't think that's a good idea."

"I have to know. I need to hear it from her."

Her grandma sighed, rewrapped her sandwich. She picked up both their lunches and put them in the refrigerator. "We'll go together."

50

Lisa had moved from the kitchen to the battered-looking brown couch. The shades were drawn, the room dark, but a cloud of stale smoke hung in the room.

Teagan's grandma sat next to Lisa on the couch and rested a hand on her back. Lisa jumped, her eyes flashing open. "Connie?" she rasped.

"It's me, dear, and Teagan. Can we talk?"

Lisa rubbed her eyes, coughed. "Why? I'm not going to a meeting. Okay? Just forget it."

"It's not about that," Connie said.

"We want to know about Robert Thomas," Teagan blurted.

Her grandma winced, and Lisa drew in a sharp breath. She scratched the armrest of the couch with her bitten-down fingernails.

"I knew she'd tell you," Lisa muttered. "She swore she wouldn't, but of course she did."

"Harley didn't tell me," Teagan retorted. "I found the DNA test she took."

"I don't see why you're bringing him into this. He's dead to me, he's been dead for seventeen years."

"Her dad was a serial killer and you lied about it her whole life. How could you do that?" Teagan demanded.

"Now, Teagan," Connie interjected. "Let's not start placing blame."

"Of course I lied," Lisa roared. "To protect her. Don't you get it? He murdered girls—raped them, stabbed them, dumped them. Do you think I was going to live the rest of my life looking over my shoulder? Driving her up to Marquette for visits with that psychopath?" Lisa slumped forward, fumbled her cigarettes from the table and lit one, pressing it to her lips. "Maybe she's punishing me for lying. Maybe she ran away because I lied to her."

"Harley would never do that," Teagan said. "She isn't punishing you. Something has happened."

"I know that," Lisa snapped. "Do you think I don't know that? You were her friend for ten years. I carried her in my body. I protected her from a monster, from evil. Me. I did that!" Lisa stabbed at her chest.

"When did she find out who her dad was?" Connie asked, pushing a greasy strand of Lisa's hair behind her ear.

An expression of misery clouded Lisa's face. "Over the summer. She confronted me. She was furious. She and Teagan were already enrolled at Husher and you were making plans and... I... I'd blindly, stupidly believed she'd never find out. I begged her not to change her future because of our terrible past. It was behind us.

"That's what they say in AA, 'let go and let God.' When she first wanted to attend Husher, I felt sick, but then... I thought, 'Let go and let God.' Her life is her life. I will not let my dark past cast a shadow on her bright future. I'm the reason she decided to stay the course and go to Husher. She almost backed out after she found out about Robert, said she'd rather go to a community college than attend his alma mater, but I pushed her. I pushed her to not give up on her dream. Husher had the education program she wanted, the sororities she wanted."

"Have you spoken to him? To Robert?" Connie asked.

Fear twisted Lisa's features. "I won't. I can't."

"But he might know something," Teagan yelled. "Harley could have contacted him or, worse... what if he sent someone after her?"

Lisa stood and lurched into the kitchen. Teagan followed, her grandma close behind. Lisa opened a cupboard, took down a bottle of vodka and unscrewed the cap. She emptied her coffee mug and poured vodka into the cup without rinsing. The rim of the bottle clanked against the glass as her hands shook.

Teagan cringed at each clang. "Do you really think that's a good idea?"

Lisa didn't respond. She braced one hand against the counter and tilted the cup to her mouth.

Teagan glanced at her grandma, wondered if she should snatch the bottle from Lisa's hands, but her grandma shook her head no.

Teagan glared at Lisa. "How can you do this to Harley? You're abandoning her. Don't you get it? Every fucking drink is another nail in her coffin."

Lisa spun to face Teagan. The mug slipped from her hand and hit the refrigerator. It cracked and fell to the floor. Lisa held only the handle.

"Not this one," she murmured. "Not my Mother's Day mug."

Teagan stared at the cup broken on the floor. She vaguely remembered it. Harley had bought it at a thrift store. She'd filled it with chocolate-covered pretzels she and Teagan had made themselves and given it to Lisa as a Mother's Day gift.

Now Lisa sobbed over the pieces, gathering them against her chest and rocking as she cried. Teagan's grandma went to her, knelt, and pulled Lisa close.

Two hours later, Teagan's grandma had worked her magic. She'd calmed Lisa down and talked her into returning to their house to eat a sandwich and drink some coffee. They'd also brought Harley's cat Dumbo who sat on the windowsill watching Chowder, who eyed him nervously.

Lisa had taken a shower, put on Connie's light blue robe and sat in a reclining chair, her face drawn, her eyes puffy.

"I met Robert when I was nineteen," she said, picking at the fabric of the robe. "He was twenty-five and real good-lookin'. He had a degree from Husher—had been president of a fraternity. I'd already been in trouble, gotten kicked out of high school, started running with boys who rode motorcycles, did drugs. I'd run off with one of them boys, was livin' in a shack with him and his ma just outside of Husher. One night he and I got into a fight at the bowling alley. Rob stepped in, told my boyfriend he'd kick his ass if he didn't split.

"Rob swept me off my feet. Took me home to his apartment that very night. I'd never dated a boy who'd gone to college. Men like him weren't interested in girls like me. I was pretty enough, but white trash. You know? I kept waitin' for it to be over, for him to kick me to the curb, but I tried real hard to please him. Made dinner every night, kept the apartment clean. He had a job in real estate and he kept everything real separate, you know? I never met his frat buddies, the people he worked with, nobody. But I was just so over the moon that somebody like him wanted somebody like me.

"Later I realized he'd been a farmer's kid, but he pretended he came from money. People thought he was the big man on campus, that he had some rich family out east, but I knew the truth. One single time he took me home to meet his mom and dad. His daddy was religious, stern, miserable. His mother was the real mean one, ruled the family with an iron fist—beat her children, from what Rob said, and maybe her husband too. Rob hated them all, his mother the most. I never did know why he took me there. Maybe he wanted to dump me off on them after he found out I was pregnant.

"In the end, we went back to Husher together and got married, but I was always a secret. His friends didn't know he was married. By then I realized he had girlfriends—at least that's what I thought they were, and I guess there were both, the girls he dated and the girls he killed. Once I was pregnant, he started gettin' mean. Tellin' me how ugly and fat and worthless I was."

"That must have been so terrible for you," Connie murmured. "Was Harley born before he got caught?"

"She was six months old."

"How did they catch him?" Teagan asked.

Lisa looked up, locked eyes with Teagan. "I turned him in."

51

"You did?" Connie asked.

Lisa nodded. "I'd started to suspect Rob after the fourth victim went missin', Laney Dubois. She worked the snack counter at the bowling alley in Husher. We used to go in there sometimes and he'd watch her. Most of the victims had been college girls, but not Laney. It was all over the news. She'd walked into the parking lot after her shift and disappeared without a trace. No signs of a struggle. All the girls went that way, which had the police thinkin' it was probably a normal-seemin' guy, you know, somebody those girls would walk over and talk to, maybe even take a ride with.

"Rob was gone the night Laney went missin'. Said he was meeting one of his frat brothers for a drink, but it was after three in the morning when he got home. There was mud on his shoes the next day and when I went outside to get the mail, I saw a corn husk stuck in the grill of his car and the papers was reportin' how the girls' things had been found by cornfields and three dead girls had been in cornfields.

"I still didn't know nothin' for sure, but then about three months later, another girl disappeared. This one from Husher.

And again, he was gone all night. So I bided my time and one day when he was off showin' houses, I searched his stuff. That's when I found the box."

"The box?"

"It wasn't nothin' special. A Hush Puppies shoebox stuffed way back in his side of the closet. I opened the lid and there was all these girls' things—a little pink pearl earring, a silver and turquoise wrist cuff, a single purple and white striped sock. It was the cuff that did it. It had been Laney's cuff and they hadn't mentioned it on the news, but I'd seen it with my own two eyes when she was handing us sodas or soft pretzels. I'd even told her how pretty it was a couple times. I about threw up when I saw it.

"I went running from the room, scooped up Harley and tore out of the apartment. I'd not even driven a block when it hit me. If I left, he'd get away with it and he'd come after me too. He was real smart, had everybody fooled. So, I went back and found a disposable camera and took pictures of all the"—she wrinkled her nose—"trophies. That's what they called 'em in court later. His trophies. Then I drove to my friend's trailer and called the police. I told them everything I knew and where they could find the box and"—she rubbed her eyes—"that was it."

"They caught him right away?" Connie asked.

"No." Lisa's expression turned bitter. "Course not, because some of 'em knew Rob Thomas. Good ole Rob, who'd sold half of them their houses. He was a real estate guy. He'd sit with those cops and have beers. Everybody loved him.

"They didn't even believe I was married to him, thought I was pulling some stunt because he was my baby daddy, trying to get him in trouble." Spit flew from her lips as she spoke. She'd begun to pick at a spot on the robe, yanking bits of blue thread free.

"How'd you get them to believe you?" Connie asked.

"One of 'em did. Detective Barbero. He was an out-oftowner. Hadn't known Rob the golden boy at Husher. He took the film, got it developed and then things moved real fast. Somebody tipped Rob off, one of them cops probably put a bug in his ear that some psycho ex was trying to frame him for the murder of all those girls. He did a runner. Packed his car and headed north, probably makin' for Canada, but they caught him and that was that."

"Did you have to testify?" Teagan asked.

Lisa nodded. "Yep. For four hours. The longest four hours of my life, him staring me down through my whole testimony, and you've got to understand, I loved him so much and I had a baby at home and..." Lisa started to cry. Connie handed her a tissue and she blew her nose loudly and then balled it up in her fist. "My whole life was over. I didn't trust myself no more after I'd been with him because... how could I have not have known? That's what people said. That's what the papers said."

"Was there ever any talk of an accomplice?" Teagan asked.

Lisa's eyes continued to leak and she wiped her wadded-up Kleenex beneath them. "I don't know. Maybe. Since I was testi-fyin' I wasn't allowed to go to most of the trial, but I wouldn't have anyhow. I had a newborn. I had no money, nothin'. The day after I testified, I packed up my baby and the couple things I owned and I ran away, changed our names, moved back to Jackson where I'd grown up."

Lisa let out a raspy, sad laugh. "I didn't even tell my ma. I moved in with her. She was livin' in a motel, drinkin' herself to death. But it was a roof over our heads."

"Who was Mark Smith?" Teagan asked, thinking of the man she and Harley had believed was her dad—a man who'd gone to prison for armed robbery.

"He was my ticket out of my ma's room and how I ended up here in Baldwin. He had a little trailer and me and Harley moved in. That lasted about two years, then he went up the river for robbin' a couple liquor stores with a gun. He was an easy choice. I knew one day Harley would start askin' about her dad. I sent Mark some money for the commissary in exchange for a couple letters pretendin' to be her dad. He was mean in the letters, made it clear he didn't want any part in her life.

"I thought that was the end of it, and then..." Lisa snapped her fingers. "Poof. Out of nowhere, she spoke the devil's name —Robert Thomas. I about fell over dead. I thought he'd found us, tracked us down and contacted her, but..." Lisa shook her head. "That wasn't how. She'd bought one of them family DNA things, where you send your spit in and they offer up your goddamn ancestors all the way back to the Stone Ages practically. Jesus. Eighteen years ago, such a thing didn't even exist. How was I to know she'd do something like that?"

"And then what? Did she contact him?" Teagan asked.

Lisa returned to plucking at the robe. "I don't know. I begged her not to, begged her to let it all go, the need to know him, but... you know Harley. She's relentless. If she's curious about something she leaves no stone unturned."

"You need to reach out to him, Lisa," Teagan said. "You need to find out if he knows anything."

52

For an hour after her mother left, Blair sat in the sitting room with her sisters at Rho Upsilon Nu listening as they gushed about guys they were into, exams they were dreading and what everyone intended to wear for the Alpha Lambda party on Saturday night.

Now and then she'd catch one of them watching her, eyes curious or even fearful, but they'd quickly look away. When Blair couldn't stand another second sitting in the house, but felt she'd been there long enough to appease the expectation of socializing with her sisters, she claimed she needed to get back to her dorm to study and left.

~

"Are you okay?"

Blair slowed and turned to see Corbin approaching. She wiped at her face, tried to hide the tears, but it was too late.

He hugged her, which only made her cry harder. When it finally subsided, she pulled away, frowning at his shirt. "I got your shirt all gross."

"Nah, it's fine. Come on, let me give you a ride."

"I can walk. It's not far."

"We're not going to your dorm. I'm taking you for a drink."

She sniffled. "I'm not twenty-one."

"I know, but I am. I'll grab us a six-pack and I'll show you my favorite spot to visit when I feel like garbage."

Blair finger-combed her hair, knowing it probably looked terrible. That her face was a mess of splotches and mascara likely trailed from her eyelashes to her chin. "Are you sure? I don't want to upset Sloan."

"Sloan's a big girl. She'll be fine. Come on, join me."

He offered his hand and she took it. As they walked to his car, Blair's eyes drifted to the sorority house. Though she couldn't see through any of the windows, she felt eyes watching them leave.

CORBIN PULLED onto a narrow dirt road that bumped through a ruddy trail and then opened at an abandoned-looking farm. The house was barely standing. Much of the roof and wood siding had fallen away. Behind it stood several, equally dilapidated, barns. He drove down a worn path behind the house and parked near a pond.

"What is this place?" Blair asked, following him out of the car.

He sat the six-pack on the hood, pulled a bottle out and twisted off the cap, handed it to her. "Used to be the Doxon farm. Mostly cornfields, but the guy who owned it donated it to some nature conservancy ages ago, so now it's public use, I guess. Our frat does a few things out here."

"Like what?"

"You know I can't give you secrets from the brotherhood." He winked at her.

Blair stared at the overgrown field, mostly waist-high grass and weeds. A ways out she spotted the distinct shapes of two timeworn scarecrows, their straw stuffing long gone. All that remained were their tattered shirts sagging on their skeletal frames. The property should have seemed serene-but something about the dry grass cracking beneath her feet, the gaping eyes of the windowless house, the swoop of crows in the sky overhead-made Blair uneasy.

Corbin pointed ahead. "There's a path through the woods over here that leads back to a little pond. I've fished it a few times. It's a good place if you need quiet."

Corbin led her through the woods, dark beneath the canopy of leaves. She thought of the missing girls and wondered suddenly if it had been a mistake to go with him.

He stopped at a little bluff that overlooked the pond. A wooden bench carved with dozens of initials and signatures marred the worn wood. She sat beside him , studying the dozens of initials gouged into the wood, tracing her finger along R.T. + P.F. surrounded by a crude heart.

Blair took a sip of her beer. It was dark and heavy, but she didn't mind the flavor. It reminded her a bit of the root beer she'd had at A&W.

"Do you want to talk about what happened yesterday?" he asked.

Blair stared out at the pond, the surface thick with a filmy layer of algae. On the far side several ducks took turns diving beneath the water. "No," she murmured.

From the forest, a bird shrieked and several leaves fell when it took flight.

"I knew your brother, Nolan," Corbin said, taking a sip of his beer and holding the bottle between his hands.

"You did?" Blair asked, surprised.

Corbin nodded. "We pledged together our freshman years. We were pretty close. When I heard..." Corbin frowned. "It's still hard to believe. Do you really think... he did it on purpose?"

Blair tucked her beer between her legs and crossed her arms over her chest, holding tight. "He left a note."

"He did?"

Blair nodded. She'd never read the note. Her mother had forbidden it. It had disappeared after he died.

"Did he say why?"

Blair shook her head. "If he did, my mother never told me."

"What about your dad? He must have read it."

Blair closed her eyes, thought of the way her dad had shut himself away after Nolan's death. He'd never been an affectionate father, more interested in his golf game than reading bedtime stories to his children. But he'd taken a certain pride in Nolan, had loved to show him off, had been grooming him to take over his finance company.

And then one day it had all ended. Their cleaning lady had found Nolan in his bedroom. Pills on the side table, the note beneath. Vomit on the comforter. He'd been dead for hours.

It couldn't have come at a worse time. Blair had been in the hospital. They'd been giving her antipsychotics, but that hadn't made the visions go away. And later she'd blamed herself for Nolan's suicide because he was the only person she'd told about the visitors, the dead people. Except it hadn't been people then. It had been one single girl. A girl who Blair woke to night after night standing beside her bed, hands black with decay as she reached for Blair and screamed silent threats.

"After Nolan died, my mom got rid of everything he owned. She erased him from our lives."

Corbin frowned, looked at her. "That must have been terrible. Why?"

Blair watched a mother duck, with a trail of babies following, ease into the pond. A lone duckling stood on the shore crying out as his family paddled away. "When I was really young, I believed my mom just loved me so much. She put me in pageants and spent hours curling my hair and applying my makeup. She doted on me, obsessed over me even. As I got a little older, like nine or ten, the 'love'"—Blair made air quotes —"started to feel off. I'd see other girls in dance class having a hard time, crying, and their mothers would comfort them, allow them to be upset. My mother absolutely fumed if I ever cried at dance or a pageant. She'd drag me off to some private space and snarl at me to stop crying. She'd pinch me high on my arms." Blair cringed and rubbed the soft flesh above her elbows that still bore the memory of those painful pinches. "She'd tell me I was ruining everything, my makeup, my chances at winning, but most of all I was ruining everything she'd worked so hard for.

"I started to tuck into my shell. That's how I thought of it. I was a turtle and I had this invisible protective shell and anytime my mom was harsh or I was teased at school or my dad was indifferent, I just crawled into my shell and waited for the storm to pass. It was the same with Nolan. If he was performing, scoring touchdowns in football, making good grades, my mother lavished him with praise and gifts and love, but if he failed..." Blair shook her head. "She could go days without so much as looking at him."

"Really?" Corbin seemed surprised. "Your mom has always seemed so nice. She used to come to Alpha Lambda and bring us these big platters of food. She rented us limos one time and got us tickets to a concert in Mount Pleasant. It was awesome."

Blair said nothing. Corbin wasn't the first person to see her mother as the cool mom, the supermom. Blair thought of the Rho girls earlier that day thanking her mom for champagne and pedicures.

"When Nolan came home from school that spring," Blair said, "he was different. Detached, sad. He'd always been such a driven, inspired person. Instead, he seemed... totally lost."

Corbin finished his beer and balanced the bottle on the bench. "He didn't do as well in his spring classes. I remember he was pretty stressed about his grades, but... not enough to... do what he did."

Corbin's phone beeped and he took it from his pocket and sighed. "I've got to get back. We're having a meeting about the Cassie situation tonight."

"The Cassie situation? The other girl who disappeared?"

"Yeah, she's not missing anymore. She showed back up at her parents' house and is making some crazy claims about Alpha Lambda."

"What claims?"

Corbin shrugged. "Beats me, but I guess I'm about to find out."

53

Teagan's grandma pulled her van to a stop in front of Willow Hall. She turned to face Teagan, her eyes still puffy from the emotional conversation with Lisa.

"TT, I think we're in over our heads here. All of us. You, me, Lisa. You're eighteen, a freshman in college. You're not meant to be dealing with this."

"Neither is Harley," Teagan said. "I have to find out what happened to her."

Her grandma sighed, fiddled with the feathers on her charm bracelet. She began to cry and Teagan leaned over, hugged her awkwardly.

"I understand you're trying to protect me, but..." Teagan shook her head. "I can't stop, Grandma. I won't."

"I'm so afraid for you," she whispered.

"Don't be. I dare whoever took Harley to mess with me. I hope they do."

"Don't say that. I can't lose you too. Not you and your mama. It'll kill me."

Teagan pulled back, but held onto her grandma's hands. "I'll be careful. But I'm not going to do what Lisa asked and stay away from Robert Thomas. If she's not going to try to talk to him, then I will."

"Don't do anything, okay? I'll call Drew from AA. His dad was a detective. He might be able to contact the prison for us and get some answers."

Teagan nodded, but didn't answer. She had no intention of waiting for someone else to be a liaison. The clock was ticking.

As Teagan climbed from the car, her grandma blew her a kiss, then turned her face away so Teagan didn't have to watch her cry.

TEAGAN UNLOCKED her dorm room door and walked in. She didn't look at Harley's bed or her shoes or her photos. She walked to Harley's desk and sat down, opened her laptop, and navigated to her email. Harley had sent emails to high school friends, professors at Husher, contacts for volunteer work she did.

But an email she'd sent the previous June immediately caught Teagan's eye.

To: Robert.Thomas.Inmate91821@marquettedepartmentofcorrections.gov

From: Harley Rand

Subject: Visitation

Robert—

You don't know me, but I have recently met your daughter, who now lives under a different name. She has asked me to act as a liaison between you regarding a possible future meeting. If you are open to it, please add me to your visitor list.

Sincerely,

Harley Rand

Teagan read the email a second time, then switched to the inbox and searched for a response. There was none, but an event from that previous summer instantly jumped into Teagan's mind.

It had been late June, and Harley had announced she was taking a Greyhound bus to the Upper Peninsula for a future educator's conference. It had come out of nowhere and Teagan remembered telling her it sounded like a snooze fest.

Teagan hadn't even considered offering to go with Harley. She was working two jobs to save money for school and already had shifts back-to-back for that weekend. She'd been surprised Harley was taking an entire weekend off of work for the conference, but in truth, Teagan hadn't given it much thought.

She tried to remember how Harley had acted when she'd returned. Had she been distant? Agitated? Again, the weeks were a blur. Both of them had been working constantly, and when they weren't, they were thrifting and visiting garage sales in search of stuff for their dorm.

Had Teagan even asked Harley how the conference went? She must have, but only in passing, too absorbed in her own busyness.

But now she understood there'd been no education conference. Harley had taken a Greyhound bus to Marquette and visited her father, and like so much else, she'd hidden it from Teagan.

Just to be sure, Teagan searched Harley's email for any evidence of the education conference. She found nothing. No emails whatsoever about it.

Teagan opened her own email and typed a message to Robert.Thomas.Inmate91821@marquettedepartmentofcorrections.gov. She put the same subject Harley had.

Dear Robert,

I'm a friend of your daughter's and I'd like to speak to you. Please add me to your visitor list.

Teagan ended with her personal information and hit send.

A knock sounded on her door. When Teagan opened it, she found Blair in the hallway.

"Hey," Teagan said. "Are you okay? I tried to call like a hundred times."

"My mom took my phone," Blair explained. She looked tired, eyes red-rimmed, despite the makeup meant to cover it up. "Can I come in?"

Teagan stepped aside and Blair walked into the dorm, sank onto Harley's bean bag and leaned her head back.

"It happened again. The..." She gestured at her head as if that somehow explained it. "I went into a room at Rho that has a bunch of antiques. Things started flying off the walls, curtains blowing, pictures shattered at my feet. It was horrible. Worse than anything that's ever happened before. It was like there was a poltergeist in the room."

"Holy shit." Teagan sat at her desk chair. She had her own 'holy shit' news to share, but suddenly wanted to turn it off, spend the next few minutes pretending Harley's dad wasn't a serial killer—that her best friend hadn't been lying to her for months.

"I couldn't get out," Blair continued. "The door locked. When everyone finally got in, I had to pretend I trashed the room, and go along with my mom saying I was having an episode, but it wasn't me."

"What was it?"

Blair pressed both hands over her eyes. "I don't know."

"Did you have a vision again? Like the one in your dorm room?"

Blair shook her head.

"You sent me that text. What did that mean?"

"I'm not sure what it means. I was suddenly writing 'Peggy' everywhere with lipstick—on the walls, the floor, the furniture." Blair's face flushed, and she covered it with her hands.

Teagan shook her head. "This is not funny and I swear I'm

not laughing at you, but I'd pay money to see the looks on those Rho girls' faces when they walked into that room."

Blair peered at her through her fingers. "I'd pay money to erase it from my mind." Blair tried to sound light, but her voice cracked when she spoke.

Teagan stared at this new friend of hers who was clearly struggling with something Teagan couldn't comprehend. She thought of Harley then. How would she have helped Blair?

"I was about to order a pizza. How's that sound?" It was flimsy therapy, but Teagan could conjure no other offering.

Blair removed her hands from her face, hugged her arms across her chest. "Really?"

"Sure. Why not? We could both use it."

"I'VE ALWAYS FELT FLUID," Blair murmured. "Like I might melt into something. You know? When I feel a really strong connection or become really emotional about something, it's like... I might just become it, cease to exist as myself. The only time I feel normal lately is with you." Blair picked mushrooms off her slice of pizza and stacked them on the edge of her plate.

Teagan gave her a half smile. "Did you expect to feel normal in that brick house of horrors? Or is it whores? Sorry, that was rude."

Blair smiled, let her hair fall over half her face. "No. I didn't, but... I don't know. My mom has been telling stories about Rho Upsilon Nu my entire life. I thought I had to fit in. Like it was in my DNA. She practically said as much."

"I suspect Mommy Dearest is more worried about your resume than your happiness." Teagan took another bite of pizza.

Blair bit her lip and looked like she might cry.

"Hey." Teagan leaned over and rested a hand, greasy with

pizza juice, on Blair's forearm. "I'm sorry. Disregard my bluntness. Harley has always said I deliver the truth like a kick in the teeth, and that's probably not one of my better qualities. I shouldn't talk crap about your mom and your sorority. I just... the people in your life don't strike me as really supportive, genuine people, not even your mom, and maybe I'm wrong about that. If you want me to shut my mouth, just say the word."

Blair shook her head. "You're not wrong. I love my mom. I mean, she's my mom, but..." Blair added another stack of mushrooms next to the first. "Growing up, I sort of felt like her doll, rather than her daughter. She dressed me up and put me on display, but didn't really want me to be a real person, to talk and have opinions and have my own dreams. I feel like I've been more real with you than anyone in my whole life. That's weird, isn't it? But you're so open, so transparent, and you don't judge me."

But I do, Teagan thought. *Because I am Toad, who is judgey and grumpy and pessimistic.*

As she thought of those two little amphibian best friends, whom Teagan and Harley had been reading stories about for years, her eyes came to rest on the framed photo Teagan had given Harley at some long-ago Christmas. A print of the cover of their favorite book—*Frog and Toad are Friends.* It hung next to Harley's dry-erase board. Tears came then and though she tried to stop them, she couldn't. Teagan's eyes filled and spilled over.

Blair jumped from her beanbag and hurried to Teagan. "Oh, gosh. What is it? Did I say something?"

Teagan sniffled, shook her head. "No, it's..." She swiped her face with her sleeve. "I found out today that Harley's dad was Robert Thomas, the Husher Harvester."

"Who?"

"The guy I told you about. The serial killer who was murdering girls at Husher in the late 90s."

"No. Really?"

Teagan nodded, her stomach plunging, her emotions turbulent. Each time she spoke the words, thought the words, heard the words, the truth crashed over her like an avalanche, icy, burying her, destroying the world where Harley had told her everything.

Teagan opened her laptop and typed in Robert Thomas's information. A series of articles about the murders at Husher University populated. Teagan clicked one, jarred once again by the face of the man looking back at her. When she'd first seen his picture with Lex and Nate, something about him struck a chord and now she knew what it was. He had Harley's eyes, or more aptly she had his.

She turned the screen to face Blair, who moved closer to the computer, the color draining from her face.

"Harley told me everything," Teagan said. "Every crush, kiss, stressful exam, everything. But she didn't tell me this. She found out this summer that her dad was a serial killer and she didn't tell me."

Blair put her fingers to her lips, shook her head slowly. "You said her dad was in prison for robbery, right?"

"Her mom made the story up. She changed their names when Harley was a baby. Her real name is Ella. Harley took a DNA test this summer and found out the truth, and she didn't tell me."

Blair sat back on the beanbag. "She must have had a good reason, right? Even best friends hold things back. I mean... maybe she was embarrassed or... what if she decided to stick with her mom's story and pretend she'd never learned any different?"

"Harley visited him. She took a secret trip over the summer to see Robert Thomas in prison. She lied to me and now she's gone and I can't ask her and I don't know if it's connected to her disappearance or just some new irrelevant thread that I'm going to follow to yet another dead end."

Blair shook her head, but continued to stare at the face on the computer screen for a long time. "I don't know," she murmured.

54

The following morning, Teagan woke, determined to find out everything she could about Robert Thomas. When she checked her email, her mouth fell open. She'd received a message from the Marquette Department of Corrections. Robert Thomas had added her to his visitor list.

She called Lex and asked him to bring the file on Thomas back to her dorm.

"I can't. I'm puppy-sitting for my neighbor's dog this morning."

"All right. I'll come to you. Where's your apartment?"

"I didn't invite you over."

She said nothing, biting back her irritated response.

"Fine," he said. "But you need to bring coffee and I expect an apology for how you bailed on me at the dorm. Your track record for getting up and running out on me is starting to damage my ego."

Teagan released an annoyed breath. "Black or with cream?"

"Black. Maybe go for a decaf yourself. I've got enough manic energy with this little yellow lab chewing all my shoes."

TEAGAN ARRIVED at Lex's apartment just after nine.

He opened the door and the puppy—small, golden and wagging its butt so fast it could barely stand—lunged toward Teagan's legs. She thrust the coffee carrier at Lex, knelt and scooped the animal into her arms, allowing him to lick her chin.

"Waffles apparently approves of you," Lex said, stepping aside so she could walk in. "Have you considered you might make a better animal doctor than people doctor?"

Teagan shot Lex a dirty look, then returned her gaze to the dog. "Your name is Waffles?" she asked the little dog, who continued wriggling as she set him back on the floor. "That is not a very distinguished name."

"He's not a very distinguished puppy. Look at my Nikes. He destroyed them." Lex gestured at a pair of tattered tennis shoes next to his couch.

Teagan frowned. "I'm sure you deserved it."

Lex chuckled, pulled a coffee from the carrier and gestured toward the coffee table. "The file is over here." He sat on the couch and flipped the folder open.

"I have to tell you something," Teagan said.

He looked up, raised an eyebrow. "I'm waiting with bated breath."

"Robert Thomas was Harley's dad."

Lex stared at her as if trying to gauge whether she might be joking. "This Robert Thomas?" He tapped the folder.

"Yes. She took a family ancestry test over the summer and found out."

"Whoa. That's... I don't even know what to say to that. Are you sure?"

Teagan nodded. "Her mom confirmed it. She moved away and changed their names after the trial."

He put both hands to his head, shook it slowly. "I'm mind-blown right now. I read about a wife and daughter in some of these articles, but... she didn't know? Harley just found out her dad was a serial killer?"

"Yes. She called Thomas's sister over the summer and she visited him in prison."

"That is disturbing, and it changes everything, right? I mean... doesn't it? What if Harley left because she found that out?"

"No way. She's known since June and honestly, I think she decided to put it behind her. She never even told me."

"Why though? Why would she hide it?"

Teagan slumped onto the couch beside him. "I don't know."

"At the very least, we have to consider the possibility he's involved in her disappearance. Has Harley's mom contacted Robert? Asked him if he knows anything?"

"She won't, which is why I need you."

"Explain."

"You really want to help me?" Teagan asked.

"No. I keep offering to get on your nerves."

"I need a ride to Marquette."

"In the Upper Peninsula? To the prison?"

Teagan nodded.

"That's like five hours away."

"I realize that."

Lex sighed, scratched his chin. "Teagan, if Robert Thomas is connected to all this, he will not admit that to you."

"I have to know. I have to look him in the eyes."

Lex's face looked grim. He clearly wanted to say no.

"Are you going to help me or not?"

He leaned back and stared at the ceiling. "Okay. Sure. Under one condition."

"What?"

"You have to go to all your classes today and hit office hours for every professor and explain what's going on with your friend and assure them you'll be in class every day next week."

"No. No way. I need to stay on top of this."

He crossed his arms over his chest. "Then I guess I can't drive you."

Teagan glared at him. Waffles, as if sensing the tension, stood in front of the table and barked, eyes moving from Lex to Teagan.

Teagan thought of her schedule. She had two classes that day, psychology and math, and she'd missed the previous two sessions of both. It didn't feel important. Nothing except searching for Harley seemed worth her time. "Fine. But we're leaving first thing in the morning."

"Okay," he agreed. "What time is your first class? Waffles and I will walk you."

TEAGAN FELT ODDLY LIGHTER the following morning as she climbed into Lex's car. Despite her guilt the day before about not searching for Harley, it had actually felt good to go to her classes and, amazingly, all of her professors had been understanding about why she'd missed the previous week.

"You're back in good standing with your classes?" Lex asked.

She slid into the passenger seat. "Yes, Professor Lex. I have makeup work and they all said they'd be flexible."

"Good. Don't you feel better?"

She scowled, didn't want to give him the satisfaction of saying yes, but nodded. "Waffles isn't coming on this road trip?" she asked.

"No. Thank God. His mother, the girl who lives across the hall from me, got back from her seminar, but not before he chewed one of my table legs down to a nub."

As they drove, Teagan read aloud from the file Lex had compiled on Robert Thomas.

Thomas had been twenty and a junior at Husher University when he'd committed his first murder. The victim, a Husher freshman, had vanished while walking back to her dorm after a sorority meeting. Over the next six years, he'd commit four more murders, only getting caught when his wife tipped off the police.

Two hours into the drive, Lex pulled into a parking lot outside a whitewashed brick building. A glowing sign stated 'Bertha's Burgers.'

"Where are we going?" Teagan frowned.

"Where does it look like? Lunch."

"Really? Can't we just grab some trail mix from the gas station?"

He wrinkled his nose. "No. Gross. I need brain food."

"I suspect trail mix would be a better option than one of Bertha's burgers."

"If you feel so strongly about it, while I eat my burger you can run over to the Shell station and get yourself a bag," he told her, parking between two pickup trucks.

They sat in a window booth and ordered burgers and fries.

"Have you ever had a boyfriend?" he asked.

She took a bite of her sandwich, a lettuce leaf dangling between her lips until she managed to slurp it in.

Lex grinned.

She chewed and swallowed, shaking her head. "Nope."

"Really?"

Teagan sipped her pop, rolling her eyes. "Don't act so surprised. I'm not exactly a Rho Upsilon Nu."

"To put it mildly." He chuckled. "You must have gone on a couple of dates? At least to prom or whatever."

"Who cares? Are we really talking about this right now?"

He leaned back and blew out an exasperated sigh. "Is it so terrible to do a bit of small talk? I'm stuck in the car with you for another seven hours today. Humor me."

"Fine. I went to my senior prom with Sam Baker, a kid who lived down the block from me and my grandma. It was firmly platonic. Harley went with his twin brother, Stu."

"The two of you went with twins?"

"Yep."

"Identical?"

"Other than the color of their suits."

Lex ate a chip, watching her with interest. "Have there ever been any guys you had feelings for? Any guys you kissed?"

Teagan took another bite, tried to chew with her mouth closed, but it was impossible with the amount of bread and meat she'd crammed between her teeth. She swallowed and nodded. "A few. Nobody I lost sleep over."

"What about Harley? Any boyfriends?"

"Yeah, two who lasted more than a few months. Kurt Monroe our freshman year in high school and Luke Simpson our junior year. Both started during school, fizzled in the summer."

"So, Harley isn't really into guys either."

"She isn't into the drama. We had friends in school who were always losing it because some boy didn't call or he'd gone out with one of her friends. It seemed like such a waste of a weekend sitting around in a car with some dude hoping to make out."

Lex nodded, but his smile told her he'd done it more than a few times. "Don't you want to get married and have kids someday?"

"Good God, where is this conversation going? I don't know, Lex. I'm eighteen. After undergrad and medical school and a residency, maybe I'll be interested in thinking about that stuff. What about you? Did you come to Husher to find a wife?"

He laughed. "Hardly. But there are people who meet their future spouses in college. It's not unheard of."

"Seems like an expensive way to find a date."

He grinned.

Teagan ate fast and stood up the moment she'd popped the last French fry into her mouth. "All right. Thanks for lunch. Let's get back on the road."

Lex eyed the last chunk of his burger, then shoved it in his mouth. He left cash on the table and followed Teagan out the door.

55

Robert Thomas was not what Teagan had expected. He appeared younger than his forty-some years, healthy, with green eyes—Harley's eyes. His hair was dark, cropped close to his head, his jaw square. He smiled at her, an unnerving smile, a wolfish smile.

"To what do I owe the pleasure?" he asked.

"I'm Harley's friend. She came to visit you this summer. She's also friends with your daughter."

"Is she?" He smirked. "Or is she my daughter? Hmm?"

Teagan stared at him, wondered if he was just calling her bluff. She didn't think so. Had Harley admitted to him she was his child? "What makes you think that?" Teagan asked.

"I have my sources."

"Did Harley tell you?"

"You mean did Ella tell me? No. She didn't."

"I'm Harley's best friend."

He raised an eyebrow, but said nothing. "Harley? That's an interesting name—it's got her mother's pedigree all over it. Angie would have named our daughter Kitty or Bambi if it had been left to her."

"Where is she?"

"Who? Angie? You tell me. I haven't heard from her since my trial. Didn't even have the decency to send my money, probably snorted it all up her nose."

"Not Angie. Harley. Where's Harley?"

"Your guess is as good as mine."

"Why did Harley visit you?"

He rubbed his chin, watched her. Teagan saw a tattoo on the back of his wrist. A wolf, head tilted up as if howling. "Ella visited me to meet her father, I suppose. I am her father after all, despite Angie's best efforts to convince her she'd been born from the loins of some piece-of-shit thief."

"Yeah, you're really an upgrade," Teagan snapped.

"Feisty. I like it. Ella lacked the killer instinct. I knew it the instant I laid eyes on her. As innocent as a lamb. Naïve, like her mother. I told her to stay away from Husher. You've got a wolf prowling them grounds, but she wasn't going to listen to me."

"What do you mean, there's a wolf? Do you know who took Harley?"

"Ella," he corrected her again, which made Teagan want to stand up and beat her fists on the bulletproof plexiglass.

"How do you know there's a wolf at Husher?"

Robert leaned close to the divider, dropped his voice. "Because I'm the alpha."

Teagan didn't bother hiding her disgust. "Who is it? Did you have an accomplice when you were killing those girls?"

"What girls? I didn't kill any girls?"

Teagan closed her eyes, tried to settle before she shot out of her chair and started shouting.

"If it wasn't you, who was it?" She had no doubt Thomas had murdered the girls he'd been convicted of killing, and if he hadn't given up the accomplice by now, she doubted he'd suddenly disclose it to her, but she had to try.

He leaned back, smiled, rubbed his hands together. "You've got a lot of questions, little girl."

Teagan glared at him. "Your daughter is missing. She's been abducted. She—"

He held up a hand. "My daughter died the day her trash mom called the police. You think I knew that girl who came in here to see me, all dolled up, trying to tempt me? That's what she wanted to do. She wanted to see the wolf, get a rise out of me, but I've been around a lot longer than her and a lot longer than you. I don't take the bait. I'm the hunter, not the prey."

"Who told you she disappeared?"

"I have eyes and ears everywhere. I'm a legend at Husher. My brothers, sisters—they remember me, idolize me." He chuckled. "I get letters every year from the Alpha Lambda boys. Every single year."

"Why? Why would they idolize you? You're sadistic. You're a murderer."

"They idolize me because I take what I want. I took what they all wanted. I might die here, but in their minds, I'm eternal. I'll live forever."

"You know what happened to her? Don't you? Just tell me!" Teagan's voice rose. She balled her hands into fists.

Robert's eyes widened. He leered at her. She saw in his face that her anger was turning him on.

"Whoever took her must be a sly little fox," he murmured.

"Fuck you," she hissed. She stood and hurried to the door.

Teagan stormed from the prison, gulping air, her anger so raw and powerful she wanted to smash windshields in the parking lot.

Lex walked toward her. "Hey. How'd it go?"

She said nothing, bit her teeth together until they hurt.

"What is it? What can I do?"

"Nothing," she muttered. "You can't do anything."

They said little as Lex drove her back to Husher. When they arrived, Teagan stepped from his car. He followed her out.

"Talk to me. What did he say? How can I help you?"

"Please just... I'll text you tomorrow. I need to be alone." Teagan started away, then turned back. "Thanks for the ride."

TEAGAN UNLOCKED her dorm room door and walked inside. The room smelled of Harley's body spray and when her eyes lifted to Harley's bed, there she was. Her signature pink and yellow polka dot pajamas, her purple bedspread pulled to her waist.

"Harley?" Teagan croaked her name more than spoke it, but as the girl in Harley's bed sat up, another emotion took over Teagan—shock.

Blair, eyes half-lidded, groggy, stared at her as if confused. Several long moments passed and Blair looked down, eyes widening as if seeing her pajamas for the first time.

Teagan, still at a loss for words, said nothing. A frenzy of emotion boiled inside of her.

"I didn't... I'm not..." Blair whispered. She swung her legs off the bed, dropped to the carpet.

Teagan took a step back, and another. The heavy dorm door slid closed, and she stood in the dim hall, lit only by the glowing exit signs at either end.

The door opened and Blair followed her, silhouetted by a light she'd turned on in Teagan's room. "I'm sorry. I... I don't know what happened. I don't remember even coming here."

Teagan studied Blair's face, her eyes, tried to discern if she spoke the truth. The alternative—that Blair had intentionally gone to her dorm room, dressed in Harley's pajamas and crawled into her bed—was too disturbing to consider.

"I'm gonna take a walk," Teagan said, turning away, but Blair reached out and grabbed her arm.

Teagan's first instinct was to jerk it out of her friend's grasp, but Blair released a sound, a sob that seemed to rise from some hollowed-out crater deep within her body.

"Please... please don't go..." Blair begged. She sank to the floor, a puddle, her pale hair fanning across the collar of those familiar pajamas.

"Blair, what's going on?"

Blair didn't move. She cried into the carpet, which Teagan imagined smelled musty and was thick with the dust and the residue of the thousands of girls who'd walked the halls. She wanted to storm away, but Blair had begun to quake and sob on the floor.

"Okay, come on. Get up." Teagan knelt and took hold of Blair's arms, helping her to her feet.

Blair's face was blotchy, her eyes red and tear-filled. She cried as Teagan led her back into the room.

Teagan waited as Blair blotted her face with tissue and sank onto a bean bag. She pulled her knees into her chest, avoiding Teagan's eyes. "It must have happened again. The last thing I remember is sitting in my room and then... nothing."

"I don't get it, Blair. Why would that thing happening cause you to put on Harley's pajamas, get into her bed?"

"Well... umm..." Blair tugged at the collar of the pajamas, cheeks growing red as if remembering anew who they belonged to. "Some strange things have been happening to me for a little while now, kind of since... umm... since Harley disappeared."

Teagan frowned. "Since Harley disappeared?"

Blair's eyes flickered up and back to the floor. She picked at a spot of lint on the beanbag. "I've been seeing Harley."

"What does that mean?"

Blair looked up at her, eyes misty and pleading. "I think it means... that Harley is dead."

The words crossed the gap between them, slithered into Teagan's brain, sank their fangs into her psyche.

Teagan stood, strode across the room, jerked open the door, and ran. She slammed through the exit door so hard it ricocheted off the brick wall and echoed down the stairs. She burst into the night and raced away from the dorm, driven by a need to escape the stifling confines of those brick walls, but more than that a desperation to outrun Blair's words.

WHEN TEAGAN FINALLY STOPPED, slowed by a cramp in her side, her face was wet with tears. Alone in the dark, she collapsed into the grass and cried, allowing the wails to rip free, the fear to take shape at last.

Blair's confession was not confirmation that Harley was dead, but it stirred a dark ember deep in the pit of Teagan's belly, a cinder that had sparked the very first day Harley did not come home. Some part of Teagan had known then that Harley was gone.

"What do I do?" she murmured, the hurt engulfing her, the revelation like quicksand pulling her down.

56

B lair stripped out of Harley's pajamas and put on her clothes, left Teagan's dorm room and hurried upstairs to her room.

Her body was hot with shame and she sat on the edge of her bed, unable to imagine how she could come back from this betrayal. She tried to remember what had happened, how she'd ended up in Harley's pajamas, asleep in Harley's bed.

She'd been sitting in her room sketching and then... nothing. Her notebook lay open on her desk. She moved toward it, afraid to discover what she'd drawn, surprised when her gaze landed on a sketch of a frog and a toad sitting side by side on the banks of a small river. It was a sweet drawing, the kind of image captured in children's books.

She flipped to the page before and froze. The crudely drawn face was a mess of black scribbles and lines, her mouth stretched long and wide, her eyes little more than holes in her charcoal face. Around the image Blair had scrawled *help me* again and again, the writing nearly illegible.

The face was unrecognizable as Harley's and yet it was her.

"What do you want?" Blair whispered.

Her eyes drifted to her desk where the little pouch that held her pills lay. Next to it sat the coin Teagan's grandma had given her. She walked over and picked it up, brushed her fingers over the prayer and then read it out loud. "God, grant me the serenity to accept the things I cannot change, the courage to change the things I can, and the wisdom to know the difference."

Her phone beeped and she looked at the screen, hopeful it was Teagan.

Sloan: *I'm assuming you're on your way? Tonight is Fright Field and all pledges are required to attend!*

Blair stared at her phone, sucked in a shaky breath, tried not to cry. She'd forgotten about the pledge event, which had been described as a competition between the pledges of Rho Upsilon Nu and pledges of Alpha Lambda. The thought of it now made her whole body sandbag-heavy and the tears rushed hot and fast over her cheeks.

THE SORORITY SISTERS loaded into SUVs, five in total, and drove away from the sorority house.

Blair had changed into track pants and a Rho sweatshirt, managed to put on enough makeup to hide her earlier breakdown, but her body felt untethered, as if the effects of whatever had happened earlier when she'd climbed into Harley's pajamas and then her bed had not worn off. She felt both sedated and jittery.

"Any idea what Fright Field is?" Winona whispered to Blair. They sat next to each other in the far back of one of the SUVs, the road humming beneath them.

Blair shook her head.

Paula who sat in front of them, twisted around. She dropped her voice low. "Heather wouldn't give me details, but she said she peed herself freshman year when she did it. I made sure to hit the bathroom before we left."

Blair exchanged a troubled look with Winona, who turned to stare out the window. Dark fields flashed by on their right.

Suddenly the SUV in front of them turned and they followed, bumping down a weedy trail that led alongside a cornfield. The SUV stopped and Ginger, who was driving, called out.

"It's go time, pledges. Pile out."

The girls climbed from of the truck. Save the SUV driven by Sloan, which also included Heather and several other senior Rho Upsilon Nus, the rest of the sorority sisters had continued down the road rather than turning off into the field.

Sloan and the other sisters exited their SUV. Sloan held up a handful of ropes. Blair noted another sister carried strips of burlap fabric.

"Welcome to Fright Field," Sloan said. "The ultimate test as to whether or not you can hack it as a future Rho. The rules are simple. A Rho pledge on one side of a corn row, an Alpha pledge on the other. The first to get to the scarecrow in the middle and grab the flag from his shirt wins."

"It's a foot race?" Winona asked. "I mean, isn't that unfair? The boys will be faster."

"It's not just a foot race. I'm going to tie your hands behind your back. Heather will blindfold you. Then we'll guide you to your row." She pointed to the dark rows between the towering stalks of corn. "The boys are also tied, blindfolded, and you girls get a one-minute head start."

"Blindfolded with our hands tied?" Jocelyn, usually the most enthusiastic of the pledges, looked anxious.

"This isn't about speed, ladies," Sloan said. "It's about fortitude, grit. Can you take the pressure? The instant you're set free, you start moving, but you can also try to get your hands loose and your blindfold off. The quicker you do those things, the faster you can run."

Blair's stomach squirmed. She was afraid she'd be sick and suddenly her bladder was heavy, her body too warm. Sweat slipped between her shoulder blades.

"The winner, so you know what's at stake," Sloan went on, "doesn't just get bragging rights. If we win, the Alpha Lambda boys are our slaves for an entire week. They'll carry our books to class, massage our feet, cook us breakfast, the works. Which means if they win, *we'll* be the slaves, and I think we all know what they'll be expecting us to do."

Paula giggled nervously.

"Don't look so scared, girls!" Heather said. "When it's over we're doing a mega-bonfire and Ginger brought bourbon apple cider. We're going to celebrate til the cows come home."

"If we win, that is," Sloan added, her steely gaze settling on Blair. "Turn around, pledges. It's time."

BLAIR FORCED her breath to slow, her body to stop trembling as she was guided, blindfolded, hands secured behind her, toward the cornfield. Sloan stopped and jerked Blair back a pace. "Don't move until you hear the shot. Got it?"

Blair nodded, the shaking growing more intense. Sloan obviously felt it, but said nothing.

Somewhere far off, Blair heard someone shout. "Ready, set..." And then the blast echoed, and Sloan released her.

Blair pitched forward, stumbled, nearly lost her footing. She managed to stabilize. She didn't want to run, was sure if she tried she'd fall or veer the wrong direction and end up lost in the cornfield, but the thought of being the last to the scarecrow, the looks of disappointment and irritation on the other Rhos' faces, urged her into the darkness.

Sharp leaves raked her cheeks and arms as she ran. She sucked in snatches of breath. Hands slick, she picked at the ropes with her fingers and wiggled her wrists trying to get free. Her foot hit a rock and she fell, managed to keep her knees under her and not pitch face-first into the soil.

Grunting, she struggled back to her feet and continued, favoring her right leg, the knee sore from where it struck the ground. She could hear little above her own ragged breaths, wondered how close the other pledges were.

"Right beside me," she murmured, needing to believe it, to expel the sense that she alone ran through that dark field.

Something cracked nearby, a cornstalk in the next row, she thought. The pattering of feet beside her, behind her.

Whispers surrounded her, filled her head. Two names repeated, almost merging together: *Blair-Peggy-Blair-Peggy-Blair-Peggy.*

The blindfold slipped down and she could see through one eye. It was dark, but not the black she'd been looking at moments before. She could make out the stalks around her, their leaves glossy and silver in the moonlight.

Again, that swish as someone moved through the leaves. Stumbling on, wrists grinding raw against the rope, Blair glanced sideways, expected to see one of her sorority sisters. Instead, the figure keeping pace had stringy blonde hair matted with blood and dirt. The dead girl moved stiffly, her head too far in front of her body, her spine poking through the back of her once-pink dress.

It's happening again.

57

Blair forced her eyes ahead, struggled harder against the ropes binding her hands.

"She's not real. She's not real." But even as Blair whispered the words, she felt the dead girl had turned and was staring at her now, watching her as she loped forward, preparing to take hold of Blair and keep her in the cornfield forever.

Blair caught snatches of movement deeper in the rows. Other dead girls trapped here, girls who didn't want to be alone anymore.

Blair ran harder, breath wheezing. She tried to imagine the door Ramona described, to slam it shut on these spectral figures, but there was something behind her now, giving chase. They could smell Blair's fear. They were gaining on her.

Her vision blurred. Black fuzzy edges crept in, and she wanted to rub her eyes, but could do nothing with her wrists bound. She knew what was happening-one of the dead girls was slithering into her psyche.

At any moment, Blair's mind would get wrenched out of the cornfield and dropped into the memory of someone who'd died-been murdered. Blair's sorority sisters would find her curled in the dirt crying. They'd all stand over her and laugh. Her mother would come and they'd take Blair away.

Moaning, fighting the pull of the spirit trying to steal into her consciousness, Blair felt the rope surrounding her right wrist loosen. She gasped and ripped her hand free, which allowed space to tear her other arm from its knot.

She tore the blindfold from her face and shot forward-ran harder than she ever had in her life. Tears and sweat streamed into her eyes. The muscles in her legs burned, trembled. Behind her the thing gained. She could smell it now, that rotted flesh smell, putrid, making her stomach seize.

The whisper of fingers in her hair. Blair screamed. Ahead of her she saw the scarecrow, not far beyond it an Alpha Lambda, still blindfolded, struggling with his arms bound behind him.

Blair bypassed the scarecrow and ran into the Alpha Lambda pledge full speed, knocking them both to the ground. He grunted, startled. She ripped his mask down, needed him to see what stalked them in the cornfield.

He blinked at her, winced. "Shit... my hands. I've got to get these ropes off."

Blair scrambled off of him as he rolled to the side. She looked behind her. The long row she'd just struggled down lay empty except for the scarecrow, its head tilted, its eyes two black x's in its burlap face.

"Can you help?" he asked, lying sideways in the dirt, craning to look back over his shoulder at her.

The tremor in her hands made it almost impossible to free him, but after a minute she managed. He climbed to his feet, helped Blair to hers.

He grinned, brushed a lock of sweaty brown hair from his forehead. "That was insane! You definitely bested me." He hugged her, picking her up off the ground. "Grab the flag and let's find this bonfire."

BLAIR SAT on an overturned stump near the enormous bonfire. She nursed a can of beer and watched the flames. Her heart had finally slowed to a reasonable pace, but her legs continued to tremble and she had to force her knees together to steady them.

The Rho Upsilon Nu girls had won Fright Field three to two, and Sloan and Heather were making the Alpha Lambda pledges do a striptease on the opposite side of the fire.

"Hey." Corbin appeared beside her. Like the other Alpha Lambdas, he wore a red flannel shirt and jeans. He pulled a stump close and sat down. "You okay? When you walked out of that field, I thought you and Jay might have had a near-fight to the death at the scarecrow."

Blair shook her head, took another sip of beer, then pressed the cold can against her knee. "No. Jay was good. I just... I fell once and hurt my knee."

"Here, let me see." Corbin pulled her beer aside and lifted her track pants. His fingers were warm, gentle as he felt around her knee. "No bones sticking out." He grinned. "Probably just bruised it. I'll get you some ice."

"You don't have to do that," she told him.

He stood. "Actually, I do. I'm a slave for this next week, so your wish is my command."

Blair watched him walk away. The other Rho pledges stood with Heather and Sloan hooting as the Alpha Lambda pledges paraded around in their underwear. Blair caught the eye of Jay, the Alpha Lambda she'd plowed into in her race to the scarecrow, and he winked at her. She smiled at him.

It had been terrible and yet in the afterglow, having made it through-not lost her mind, not failed-the horrors of those minutes in the cornfield almost seemed worth it.

Blair caught sight of Sloan who stared past her at Corbin as he returned with a bandana filled with ice. He pressed it against Blair's knee. Blair quickly looked away from Sloan.

"Oh, damn, looks like your hand is bleeding too." Corbin lifted her hand, still bandaged where she'd gotten stitches days before. Splotches of red showed through the white gauze.

"It's okay. It's fine, I'm sure."

Corbin frowned, pulled off his flannel, which left him in a plain white t-shirt. He wrapped the flannel around her hand.

"Thanks," she said, eyes searching again for Sloan, who'd disappeared from the opposite side of the fire. "Did you do this when you pledged Alpha Lambda?" Blair asked.

"Fright Field? Oh, yeah. And it was bizarrely cold and wet that year, so we froze our asses off. Not to mention about five steps into my row, I faceplanted in the mud."

"Were you scared?"

He studied her, shook his head. "Nah. I mean, I was scared to lose." He chuckled. "And at one point my shoe came off while I was running and I ended up having a blister the size of Mount Rushmore on my heel."

"Why the cornfield and the scarecrow stuff?"

"I don't know exactly when it started, but the whole thing was weirdly inspired by a guy who used to be an Alpha Lambda."

"Robert Thomas," Blair murmured.

Corbin appeared surprised. "You've heard of him?"

"The Husher Harvester."

Corbin nodded. "Yeah. He's the one. It's morbid, right? But I guess that's where it came from. I don't know the specifics, but one year someone suggested a pledge event in a cornfield with senior members dressed in the Harvester's costume of choice— the creepy scarecrow face. They thought it'd be scary. Then the Rho sisters got in on it. It kind of stuck after that."

"But... it's like paying homage to a serial killer."

Corbin moved the ice to a different spot. "I think it's more about how groups claim their most notorious members. You know? Obviously, none of us knew Thomas, but he's infamous in Alpha Lambda and the whole idea of a serial killer stalking our campus, bringing girls out to these cornfields, is... well, it's terrifying, right? And who doesn't love to be a little terrified now and then?"

"Me."

He laughed. "Don't worry, I'll protect you if the Harvester comes out of that field."

Blair looked back toward the dark, seemingly endless rows of corn. It wasn't the Harvester she was afraid of.

58

Teagan saw Blair sitting alone in the cafeteria. She looked tired, her hair pulled down so it hid most of her face. Teagan added eggs, sausage and a cinnamon roll to her plate and walked to Blair's table, sat beside her.

Blair looked up and her face flushed. "Oh, umm... hi. I was going to call you last night, but I ended up at this nightmare pledge thing and—"

"No. It's okay. I'm sorry I freaked out. I know it's not your fault and whatever's happening is beyond your control. Hearing you say what you said... I couldn't handle it."

Blair nodded, tucked her hair behind her ears. "I could be wrong, Teagan. It's a mystery to me too, and I shouldn't have said that about Harley because I don't really know—"

"She's been missing for more than a week. I don't want to believe she's truly gone, but I think in my heart... I'm afraid she is. I just don't understand, if it is her... spirit contacting you, why it's happening. I mean, you didn't even know her."

Blair nodded. "Ramona sort of explained it to me. She said a lot of times spirits can't get through to the people they had strong emotional bonds with, almost like they get too scattered because of the intensity of their desire to make the connection, so they reach for someone more detached. In my case, I also happen to have this... ability. Ramona called it a skill. It doesn't feel like a skill. It feels like a disease, a virus that takes over my body. I'm sorry, Teagan. I don't want it to happen and I really have no memory of even going into your room, let alone putting on her clothes. I'm so embarrassed I did that."

"Don't be. Okay? Maybe... maybe if you let Harley in, she can tell you something about what happened."

"Maybe," Blair murmured.

"But you don't think so?"

Blair swirled her spoon in her oatmeal, expression troubled. "It's never been very clear what they're trying to tell me, or if they're trying to tell me anything at all."

"What was the nightmare pledge thing?"

Blair bit her lip. "Honestly, I feel really weird talking about it considering..."

Teagan waited.

"It's called Fright Field. They do it every year. It's kind of a race through a cornfield. Rho pledges against Alpha Lambda pledges."

"Through a cornfield?"

"Yeah. And it's all inspired by the Husher Harvester."

"Are you serious?" Teagan stared at her, disgusted.

"Yeah. I felt the same way. Why would they have based this game—scary game, I might add—on this horrible person who killed girls at this school?"

"Why did they?"

"I don't really know. I mean, Corbin, one of the Alpha Lambda guys, said Robert Thomas sort of had this notoriety, this legendary quality for the fraternity. They set it up to scare the pledges and Rho embraced it too, so..."

"More evidence that fraternities and sororities are demented."

"I wish I could disagree, but last night was definitely demented."

"You should report them, Blair. That's hazing."

Blair's eyes went wide. "No. God, no. I could never do that."

"Why?"

"I told you. My mom loves Rho. Loves them. She'd never forgive me. Please don't tell anyone about the Fright Field thing. Okay? Please?"

Teagan scowled. "I won't. But I really think you should consider whether you want to be a part of all that."

TEAGAN ATTENDED her classes all day. She struggled to focus, thought repeatedly of Blair's horrifying tale of running blindfolded, hands tied, through a cornfield at night. If Harley hadn't vanished, she too would likely have gone through the horrifying ordeal, and yet even that would have been better than the unknown.

Despite what felt like an exhaustive search, no sign of Harley had emerged. It was as if a hole had opened in the sidewalk and she'd disappeared forever.

Just after five, Teagan got a text from Lex asking her to meet him and Nate at the newspaper.

She stopped back at her dorm and grabbed Harley's laptop.

SEVERAL STAFF MEMBERS stood hunched over desks when Teagan arrived. She found Nate and Lex in the lounge room both reading printed articles. They had arranged additional articles about Robert Thomas on the large coffee table.

Teagan stared at the black and white picture of the victims, who were all young and pretty and blonde. They all looked like Harley.

"Did a tip come into the paper?" Teagan asked.

"No tip," Nate said, "But we found an interesting name here in an interview after Robert Thomas's trial."

"Who?"

"Jamie Ackerman," Lex said.

Teagan shook her head. "Doesn't ring a bell."

"It's the professor I'm a teaching assistant for. He testified at Robert's trial. He was an Alpha Lambda and apparently a close friend of Robert's."

"No way."

"Yes way. He's meeting us here," Lex said.

"Okay, well, what are we hoping to get out of him?"

"He was close to Rob. He might know about a potential accomplice," Nate said. "Lex mentioned that Thomas told you there was a wolf at Husher, right? I mean, that implies he knows someone is stalking women and I'd hazard to say he knows who it is, which makes us both think there might have been a second person involved in those murders."

"What's the laptop for?" Lex asked.

"It's Harley's. I've searched it, but I'm not a computer whiz. I thought maybe one of you could look at it or might know someone who could dig around, see if there's anything about Robert Thomas, or really anything at all that might help us find her."

"The police haven't taken it?" Nate asked.

Teagan scowled. "The campus police told me her case has been transferred to the Husher Police Department. They haven't called me a single time. No one has searched our room, taken a statement from me. Nothing."

Nate and Lex exchanged a look.

"What?" Teagan asked.

"One of our staff reporters here at the paper has an uncle

with the Husher police. They're convinced she took off. Supposedly someone called in anonymously saying they've been in contact with Harley and she wants to be left alone."

"What? Who?"

"That's the problem with anonymous tips."

"Why would the police believe it? It's not true."

"Until they have evidence that proves otherwise, they're probably not going to do much. And Cassie showing back up has only added to their theory that Harley did the same thing and just hasn't resurfaced."

"Why did Cassie take off? Was the rumor about her being assaulted true?" Teagan asked.

Lex nodded. "It seems that way. Yeah. But a bunch of lawyers are involved now. Cassie's parents pulled her out of school. I'm guessing they're going to settle with the Alpha Lambdas, which means what happened won't go public."

"That's bullshit!" Teagan snapped, nearly dropping Harley's computer.

"Let me check this out," Nate said, taking the laptop. "I'm far from an expert. But I'll look."

"It is bullshit," Lex agreed. "When the time is right, I'll ask Corbin and see if I can find out what actually happened." Lex's cell phone beeped. "Professor Ackerman's here," Lex announced. "I'm going to meet him out front."

everal minutes later Lex returned with a tall, wiry man who had a reddish goatee and hair tied at the nape of his neck. He wore a rumpled suit and smelled of cigarette smoke.

"Professor Ackerman, this is Teagan Kelso and Nate Dryden."

"I know Nate," Ackerman said, slapping him on the back. "Had him in class last year, kept me on my toes. Teagan"—he extended his hand—"good to meet you."

"You too." Teagan watched the professor sit and cross his legs. His gaze drifted to the newspaper clippings and he visibly recoiled. His eyes darted to Lex.

"I thought you said this was an interview about freedom of speech?"

"My friend is missing. Her name is Harley Rand," Teagan said.

Ackerman nodded slowly. "I've seen the emails and the fliers."

"She was Robert Thomas's daughter."

Ackerman steepled his fingers beneath his chin, frowning. "His daughter?"

"Yes," Lex interjected. "She took an ancestry test and found out over the summer. Your name is in a transcript from Robert's trial. You testified against him."

"Well... hold on now. I was a witness for the prosecution, but I wouldn't say I testified against him. I had no idea what he was up to. None of us at Alpha Lambda did. We would have turned him in in a second."

"We just want to know more about him. Anything you can tell us." Lex turned on a tape recorder, which clearly unnerved Ackerman.

"Lex, I respect whatever you all are up to here, but that was almost twenty years ago and, truth be told, I don't want my name linked to the man. I worked hard to become a professor at this school and—"

"We're not publishing anything you say," Nate said, still focused on Harley's computer.

"We're trying to find out if he might be involved in Harley's disappearance," Teagan said.

"Involved?"

Lex nodded. "It's a theory, but please, just anything you can tell us. Who was Rob? What was he like during school?"

Ackerman blew out a breath, shot another wary look at the tape recorder and then spoke. "Off the record?"

"Off the record," Lex agreed.

"All right. Huh, where do I even begin? Robert was kind of the class clown of the Alpha Lambda brothers, always playing practical jokes. One of his go-to jokes was to dress up in this super creepy scarecrow mask and jump-scare the Rho girls when they came over for parties. Obviously later when we found out he was the Husher Harvester that made those antics pretty disturbing, but... other than the practical jokes, he was a pretty dedicated guy. Pulled good grades, charismatic. He seemed like the rest of us.

"That spring when Rob and I graduated, two girls had already been killed. Zoe was a freshman at Husher who was rushing sororities when she vanished. Then there was Maddison, a junior, who went missing after some beauty pageant on campus. Police dropped the ball with Zoe. They did the usual 'she took off' business, but then bodies started turning up.

"They actually found Maddison's body first, about two weeks after she disappeared, in a cornfield out at Doxon's farm. Zoe's body wouldn't be found for another few months in the spring, when the snow had melted, also in a cornfield. Both were strangled, stabbed, and sexually assaulted. It was horrendous.

"After graduation, I stayed at Husher and started grad school and the tension around here was thick. All the girls were scared.

"Rob got into a real estate office, started making bank right away. He'd always been a good salesman. We stayed friends, we all did. Had beers every Thursday night at Lucky's Pub. It's gone now. There's a Chinese restaurant in there."

"Did you know Lisa?" Teagan asked.

"Lisa?"

"Angie. Her name was Angie. Robert's wife."

"Oh, Angie, uh, no. I didn't know her. I saw her once riding in Rob's car, but when I asked him later, he said it was his pregnant sister who was crashing at his place for a while. I never even questioned it. He had a pretty serious girlfriend when we were at Husher. They'd been dating on and off during our last two years and we all figured he'd marry her. She ended up having a baby right after we graduated and marrying some older guy who was rollin' in the money, apparently, but we all knew Rob still harbored serious feelings for her.

"We all stayed close after graduation, those of us in the area anyway. I knew Rob got around. He'd always been a ladies man. Then we learned during the trial he was married and had a newborn. I think if that hadn't come out, I would have really struggled to believe Rob was the killer. Finding out he'd been lying to all of us for months about having a wife and kid really showed me this guy was not who he pretended to be."

"By the end of the trial, you believed he was guilty?" Lex asked.

"Oh, he was guilty all right. He had a shoebox full of their stuff—the victims' stuff. And that was the tip of the iceberg. Blood in his trunk. Corn stalks stuck up underneath the frame of his car. His tire treads matched tire marks at the scenes where the bodies were found. He had newspaper clippings on all of the girls stashed in his desk at the real estate office. Once the police started looking, the evidence of his guilt was undeniable."

"Did anything about an accomplice come up during the trial?" Lex asked.

Ackerman leaned forward, stared at several of the articles, nodded slowly. "His defense launched some theory about a Ken and Barbie type killing, sort of inspired by that couple out of Canada from the early 90s. Know who I'm talking about? I can't remember their names offhand, but the press dubbed them the Ken and Barbie murderers because a bunch of teenage girls ended up dead and that blue-eyed, blonde-haired couple had murdered them. Rob's lawyer floated a similar scenario, but claimed Barbie was the mastermind. Basically, his lawyer said Robert was a pawn in the hands of his devious girlfriend."

"Not Lisa?"

"No. Not the wife, the girlfriend who'd been at Husher with us. The defense said this girl had lost some beauty competition to Maddie and had killed her to get revenge or to get even..." He shook his head. "It was a half-cocked theory and nobody bought it. By the time, Rob went to trial, his ex-girlfriend was married with a toddler and a newborn, and they were livin' in suburbia or whatever. Good luck convincing people she'd helped Rob stalk girls through a cornfield big and pregnant. It was a bizarre theory. Her husband kept her name out of the papers. She did testify, but had some deal with the judge to keep the court closed. I don't know how it all worked exactly, but it was plain as day who the killer was—Robert Thomas."

"Do you think there's any chance he did have an accomplice?" Teagan asked.

"Huh..." He scratched his goatee. "I find it hard to believe anyone knew what he was up to. I've read a thing or two about serial killers. They usually work alone, but if I had to say someone had an inkling about what was going on, I'd lean toward the defense's theory. Rob and his girlfriend were real tight and she had his same kind of dark sense of humor and I think they were still off and on when the first two murders were committed. That being said, at most, I'd think she had knowledge, not that she was directly involved.

"Still, I remember seeing her a few times after he'd been caught. I expected her to be a wreck, heartbroken, shocked like the rest of us, but..." He shook his head. "Nope. Cool as a cucumber."

"What was her name?" Lex asked.

"Peggy," Ackerman said. "Leggy Peggy, we called her at Alpha Lambda. She was a bombshell."

Teagan sat up straighter. "Peggy?"

"Peggy..." Lex echoed.

"Do you have any idea what her full name was?" Teagan asked.

"Hmmm... what was her maiden name? Let's see, I want to say Fairfield. Peggy Fairfield. That sounds right. You know, what's funny is she's back. I just ran into her other day."

"Wait, what? She still lives in the area?" Lex asked.

"I don't know about that, but she has a kid going to school

here. I saw her on campus. Looks as beautiful as she did when we were in college. Still has that edge though. Looks at ya like she's seein' right through ya."

Teagan's mind reeled. She exchanged a look with Lex, who appeared equally confounded by this news.

"Who's her kid?" Lex asked.

Ackerman shook his head. "Now that I can't tell you, but I can tell you whoever it is, they're a Rho. I ran into Peggy at the t-shirt shop picking up a whole stack of pink and gold Rho Upsilon Nu t-shirts for her daughter."

After Ackerman left, Teagan, Lex and Nate talked about the likelihood of a Rho Upsilon Nu mother being connected to Harley's disappearance.

"It seems unlikely," Lex murmured. "A forty- or fifty-something year old woman abducting university coeds?"

"What about a copycat killer?" Nate asked. "Maybe even a copycat couple? Anybody from Rho or Alpha Lambda who'd fit the bill?"

Teagan looked to Lex, who knew far more about the fraternity and sorority than she did.

He stared at the series of articles, his forehead creased. "Jeez, I don't know. What an insane thing to ponder."

"What about Sloan?" Teagan demanded.

"The president of Rho Upsilon Nu? She can be a little frosty, but I'd struggle to rank her among the Lizzie Bordens of the world."

"Does she have a boyfriend?" Nate asked.

"Kind of. She and Corbin are always on-again, off-again."

"That's exactly how Ackerman described Robert and Peggy. Plus, Corbin is the one who installed our lofts at the dorm," Teagan said.

Lex brushed both hands through his hair. "I hate to say it, but I feel like we're grasping at straws."

"What else do we have to grasp at?" Teagan demanded.

60

Teagan knocked on Blair's door first thing the following morning.

Blair opened her door, still clad in pajamas.

"There's someone at Rho whose mother's name is Peggy. Who is it?"

Blair blinked at her, rubbed her eyes. "Huh?"

"Peggy. One of the sorority sisters at Rho has a mom named Peggy."

"Peggy? Like the text I sent you?"

"Yes. Who has a mom named Peggy?"

Blair frowned. "No one that I can think of. Sloan's mom is named Paige, which kind of sounds like Peggy. I don't know the names of all the mothers."

"I need you to find out."

"It's not even eight in the morning," Blair said. "Why? Who is she?"

"She was Robert Thomas's girlfriend when he was committing the murders."

"But wait, I thought he was married to Harley's mom."

"He was, but he was cheating on her."

Blair looked at her watch. "I have to get ready for class, but, umm... I have sorority meeting later and then I think we're going to a movie on campus. I could try to ask around then."

"The whole sorority is going to the movie?"

"I think so. Yeah."

"I need you to get me into Rho Upsilon Nu."

An expression of terror washed over Blair's face. "That's not a good idea, Teagan. I'll just ask around and—"

"No. There's something going on there. I want inside."

BLAIR OPENED the back door at Rho Upsilon Nu, and Teagan slipped into the hall. Blair held her finger to her lips.

"We're leaving now," she whispered. "Hide in the laundry closet. You have to be gone by ten."

Teagan nodded and crept into the closet, crouching behind a tall hamper.

She waited for ten minutes after the voices had faded, then crept from the closet and followed Blair's directions to the second and then the third floor.

The single door at the top led through the room Blair had described as the ritual room. Maroon robes hung from hooks along the wall. A wooden table held a large black cauldron surrounded by globs of melted red candlewax. Another door led off the room—a room Blair suspected was where the records were kept—but when Teagan tried the knob, she found it locked.

"Shit..." Teagan wiggled the knob back and forth. The knob was old and antique-looking, with a skeleton-type hole for the key. She doubted she could pick it.

She retreated from the room and walked down to the second floor, hurrying along the hallway, reading the names on doors until she found the one labelled Sloan-the likely keyholder.

She eased open Sloan's door. It was dark and she didn't dare turn on the light for fear someone outside might see it. Teagan took out her cell phone and slid open her flashlight app. She slipped into the room, closing the door behind her.

Her light skittered over Sloan's full bed, her desk neatly arranged. Teagan thought of her conversation with Lex and Nate, the idea of a copycat Ken and Barbie killer. Teagan opened desk drawers, peered in the closet. If Sloan had been involved in Harley's disappearance, what would she have kept, if anything, and where would she have stashed it?

Nothing stood out, and Teagan knew she could waste an hour hunting in Sloan's room for something that wasn't there. She had to focus on finding the key.

A coat hung on the back of Sloan's chair. Teagan checked the pockets, but found only a tube of lip gloss. She moved to the desk and searched drawers—no keys.

"Where is the key?" she whispered, standing and moving her light from space to space. Something dark on the windowsill caught her eye. She moved closer. A single skeleton key rested on the white ledge.

Teagan grabbed it, slid from the room and hurried back to the third floor. She pushed the key into the lock and heard it click. When it swung in, she held her breath, had a momentary fear of seeing Harley dead, rolled into a carpet or stuffed into a wooden box. No such horrors greeted her. The room was an office with a large desk overlooking a small window. Two file cabinets occupied one wall. A squat safe sat beneath the center of the desk.

Teagan went to the file cabinet and opened it. Files with girls' names were stuffed so tight, Teagan could barely sift through them. Still, she scanned quickly, searching for the name 'Peggy,' though doubtful she'd find it. Peggy would have been a Rho nearly two decades before. Even if she'd once been in the cabinet, her file had likely been taken out years before.

The second file cabinet was equally packed. Teagan moved to a little closet and risked turning on the hanging bulb. She jumped, startled, when a hideous-looking scarecrow gazed at her from the darkness.

Teagan held her light closer and realized it was a mask and cloak displayed on a wire hanger. Teagan thought instantly of Ackerman's story about Robert Thomas scaring the girls in a creepy scarecrow mask.

"What the fuck?" Teagan muttered. She lifted her phone, turned on the flash and took a picture of the mask.

Beneath the costume stood another, shorter, file cabinet. On top sat a small black tape recorder. Teagan opened the cabinet. No names were labeled on the files in this cabinet. Instead, they were labeled with dates. Teagan's eyes flicked over the dates. Several had been recent and she paused when she saw the date that Harley had vanished.

She opened the file and looked inside where a small cassette tape sat.

She picked it up. This too held no label.

Teagan eyed the cassette player. Without it, she wasn't sure she could play the tape. From somewhere outside, Teagan heard voices. Blood pumping, she dashed to the window in time to see four girls climb out of a dark car. They were Rho girls and they were walking toward the house.

Teagan didn't think. She bolted into the closet, snatched the tape recorder and made for the door. There were two staircases that led to the second floor. Teagan hoped if the girls were coming upstairs, they would take the stairs at the front of the house. She slipped down the back stairs, snuck through the door and ran.

～

TEAGAN SAT on the floor in her dorm room, placed the tape recorder in front of her, and tried not to think of what would happen when Sloan realized it was gone. Maybe she wouldn't. If there was nothing relevant in the tape, Teagan could slip the recorder, the tape and the key all back to Blair and everything could get replaced with no one the wiser.

Teagan slid the tape into the deck and hit play.

The reel turned, but no sound emerged. Teagan turned up the volume and after a moment, a burst of static came through.

And then a voice—Blair's voice.

"This is Blair Davenport. This is my Scream Sister rush tape." She said the date-the same date Harley had disappeared.

There were more sounds, the rustling of clothes, heavy breath, footsteps.

The sounds grew a little louder, the breathing heavier, and then a voice.

"What do you want?"

Teagan froze, stared at the recorder.

The voice came again. "Leave me alone!" Louder, scared.

Harley's voice.

More rustling, footsteps running, and then Harley's scream, long and loud, shrilled from the recorder.

TEAGAN'S EARS RANG. The recorder had stopped, the little reel no longer turning, but the scream echoed in Teagan's head.

She stood and lurched from the room and froze. Blair was halfway down the hall, hurrying toward her, face hopeful. Their eyes locked and Blair slowed, stopped. Her half smile fell away.

"Teagan?" she asked, her voice small.

"It was you. You chased her," Teagan said.

The color vanished from Blair's face. Her eyes welled with tears and spilled over.

"Okay..." Blair nodded. She swiped at her wet cheeks. "Okay. It's true. It was me. I... umm..." She tugged at her hair. "It's part of the initiation at Rho Upsilon Nu. They call themselves the Scream Sisters and you have to dress up in this black robe and put on a mask and... umm... you follow a girl. They pick the girl. They slip a letter under your door with the name of the student you have to follow and where they'll be at a particular time. So, I went to that stretch of woods and you can only do it if no one is around. You lose points if... um... anyone else sees you in the costume. And they give you a voice recorder and you have to record the scream of the girl and then they rate them."

Teagan could not move, speak, even blink.

"I followed Harley and she got scared and then she suddenly turned and ran into the street and flagged down a car. She got in and just... They drove away."

Teagan sagged against the wall, struggled to stand. "How could you? You've known all this time. You pretended to be my friend?"

"No. I swear. I am your friend. You're my only friend. Please." Blair reached for Teagan, but a black rage suddenly filled Teagan's head.

Teagan shot forward, grabbed Blair hard by both arms, pushed her against the wall. "It's your fault. You chased her. You scared her!" Teagan roared.

Down the hall a door opened and a girl peered out. Beyond that another door swung in. The R.A. walked into the hall.

"What's going on?" she asked, eyes narrowing at Teagan and Blair.

Teagan released Blair's arms and stepped away.

"It's okay," Blair called meekly. "We're fine."

"Teagan?" the R.A. asked.

"Yeah. Everything's fine."

"Should we go into your room?" Blair asked.

Teagan's jaw tightened, but she pushed through the door and left it open for Blair to follow.

Once inside, Blair's eyes trailed down to the tape recorder on the floor.

Teagan paced away from her, struggled to keep her fury at bay. She wanted to rip things from the walls. She wanted to hurt Blair, make her pay for what she'd done. "I've been losing my mind and you hid this from me. Don't you understand what you've done? Whoever picked her up... they... they..."

"Maybe not. I mean... she might have—"

Teagan turned on her. "What?" she spat. "She might have what?"

"I'm sorry. I'm so sorry." Blair cried harder, her face a puffy mass of streaming makeup. Her shoulders hunched forward and she buried her face in her hands.

"What did the car look like?" Teagan demanded.

Blair looked up, eyes filled with desperation. "Umm... it was four doors, maybe like a dark green or blue color."

"That's not good enough! What else? Think."

Blair nodded slowly. "There was a bumper sticker. Not words but like a picture. It was a dog with three heads."

"Cerberus," Teagan muttered.

Teagan said nothing else to Blair. She turned and strode from the room.

61

B lair opened her dorm room door to her mother, whom she'd called just after her confrontation with Teagan.

Margo watched her suspiciously as she walked into Blair's room. "What is it? What on earth is the matter? I was afraid on the phone you'd had another of your episodes."

"Umm..." Blair hiccupped, wiped her streaming eyes. "I did something... something bad."

Margo, impatient, grabbed a wad of Kleenex and wiped at Blair's face. "I'm buying you new mascara. This is running everywhere. You look like a clown. Get on with it then. What did you do?"

"The girl who went missing. Harley Rand. I... umm..."

"Don't say 'umm,'" her mother snapped.

"I chased her. It's part of the rush process. They call it the Scream Sisters and..."

"I know what it is, Blair. I was a Rho long before you were. What's the point?"

"Did you do it, Mom? As a Rho?"

Margo rolled her eyes. "It was harmless, Blair. It is harmless.

And to be brutally honest, it's the type of experience you grow from. That kind of fear is motivating, empowering."

"But I followed Harley and she got into a car and now she's missing. She's probably dead. Someone murdered her because of me."

"You don't know that. And don't let me ever hear those words come out of your mouth again. You deny everything. Do you understand me? Everything. Your sisters will stand behind you."

Blair stared at her mother, appalled, sick in her stomach. She didn't care that Harley was missing and likely dead.

"This is going to ruin my life," Blair said. "The chapter will be shut down. The university will never allow it to continue when they find out."

The slap was so shocking, so out of nowhere, that it toppled Blair off balance and she sprawled sideways, landing hard on the floor. Her cheek throbbed.

Instead of apologizing, begging Blair's forgiveness, Margo stood and glared down at her daughter. "You swore an oath and you will take your secrets to the grave. You will not ruin your life or the lives of those other girls. Do you understand me?"

Blair nodded meekly. She pressed cool fingers against her burning cheek.

"Now go to bed. I can't stand to look at you for another minute."

62

Teagan pounded on Lex's door. When he opened it, he was shirtless, wearing only flannel pants, a textbook clutched in his hand.

"Hey. You all right?"

She pushed into his apartment. "Blair chased Harley the night she disappeared. It was part of some sadistic fucking Rho Upsilon Nu initiation. She was dressed up in a mask and she followed Harley, and Harley ran into the road and got into a car."

Lex frowned, set his book on his coffee table already stacked high with textbooks. "Your friend, Blair?"

"Yes. I broke into the Rho sorority house and they had this closet upstairs and it had a scarecrow costume, and underneath it this file cabinet full of tapes and a tape recorder and I stole the recorder and the tape marked with the date Harley disappeared. And when I listened to it..." She trailed off, suddenly sick. "Oh, God. I left it in my dorm. I forgot it and Blair was in there and she'll take it and destroy it and we have to go get it. Right now. We have to go."

"Slow down. Okay? Take a breath."

"No. I need you to drive me. Please."

"Okay. One minute." Lex walked into the kitchen and returned with a glass of water. "Sit. Drink some water. I'll get dressed."

Teagan took the water, but didn't sit. She paced around the living room, pausing to stare at the spread of newspaper articles on his coffee table. They were printouts of the Husher Harvester case. In one corner sat Harley's missing poster and next to it the missing poster for Jesscia Meyers.

Teagan picked it up and considered the pretty blonde wearing a Portland t-shirt. Three smaller photos occupied the lower third of the page labelled: *distinctive accessories and clothing worn the night Jesscia vanished.*

The first image showed a pair of purple and yellow tennis shoes. The second depicted a zip-up black and white checkered hoodie.

When Teagan scanned the third photo, she froze.

A Minnie Mouse watch with a red band filled the square.

"What?" Lex asked. He'd changed into jeans, a green t-shirt and flip flops.

"This watch was in the basement at Rho Upsilon Nu. Blair found it."

He walked over, gazed down at the picture. "Are you sure?"

"Yes." She thought of Blair in her dorm room, eyes glassy, body as still as a statue as she recalled running, terrified, through a field.

"They killed her. Someone at that sorority was involved in Jesscia's murder. It has to be what Nate said-Ken and Barbie murders. Someone from Alpha Lambda and someone from Rho Upsilon Nu are doing this together."

Lex stared grimly at the missing poster. "Where's the watch now?"

"Blair has it."

He rubbed his forehead, shook his head slowly.

"It doesn't matter right now. Our priority is the recorder. Let's go."

～

WHEN THEY ARRIVED at Willow Hall, Lex didn't attempt to accompany her in. The dorm had strict rules about boys coming in after nine o'clock.

"Are you sure it's safe?" he asked, brows drawn together as he stared at the building.

"She wouldn't hurt me."

"You don't know that. I told you what they said happened at Rho. I think she might be unbalanced. Don't confront her."

"I'm not going to. The recorder was in my room."

"What if she's still in your room?"

Teagan thought of Blair wearing Harley's pajamas, the story Colette had told her about gruesome disturbing pictures in Blair's notebook, the stream of lies. All of it pointed to an unhinged person, a person capable of anything, and yet...

Teagan shook her head. "She won't hurt me. Don't ask me how I know, but I do."

"Okay." He sighed. "But keep your phone on you and be quick."

～

TEN MINUTES LATER, Teagan climbed back into Lex's car. She held up the recorder triumphantly.

"Wow. She didn't take it," he said.

"No. It was right where I left it."

"Did you see her?"

"No."

Back at Lex's apartment, Teagan stared at the recorder

sitting on a stack of his books. "I can't listen to it again," she said.

"You don't need to. The important thing is you have it. You have to go to the police. You have to tell Blair to go to the police," Lex said.

Teagan shook her head. "Not yet. No. The moment the police get involved, Blair's mom will hire a lawyer. Every person in Rho and Alpha Lambda will have lawyers by dinner. Blair told me the car had a Cerberus bumper sticker on it. It's the Alpha Lambda mascot. One of them picked Harley up and whatever evidence is still lying around will be destroyed the minute they know the police are involved. Their parents will go into those houses and wipe everything clean."

Lex sighed, clearly troubled by her theory, but not arguing with her either.

"You know it's true," she said.

"No. I don't. But I also don't think it's impossible. What do you want to do then?"

"I want to find the car."

LEX PARKED on the street a block away from the Alpha Lambda fraternity. "Why don't I go? If they see you lurking around, they'll get suspicious."

"No." Teagan shook her head. "I want to do it." She didn't wait for him to argue. She slid from the passenger seat and hurried down the street.

It was nearly midnight, but lights still blazed in several of the Alpha Lambda fraternity windows. Teagan crept to the large driveway and moved closer to the cars, peering at bumpers. A lot of them had bumper stickers, many with the Greek letters for the fraternity, a few others for Husher University or sports teams.

Her eyes drifted over a four-door navy blue Toyota. There on the back bumper was the faded sticker—a three headed dog, its faces tilted up, sharp teeth exposed: Cerberus.

Teagan walked to the driver's side door, muscles taut, eyes flicking back to the house, alert for any movement. She touched the handle, then pulled, cringing at the creak as the door opened. She slipped inside and eased the door closed, leaned to the passenger side and opened the glove box.

From the house, a door slammed and voices moved toward her.

"Oh, fuck," she muttered, grabbed the seat lever and laid the driver's seat flat. She stared at the ceiling, listened as the voices of two men grew closer. They were coming to this car. They'd see her and then what?

Nearby doors opened and slammed; another car started up. She listened, blood thrumming in her ears, until the engine had faded.

Moving quickly, she returned the seat to upright and snatched paperwork from the glove box—an owner's manual, a stack of mechanic receipts and finally a small square slip of paper. The car's registration. She searched for the name and found it.

Owner: Brody Edwards.

She blinked at it, remembered the frat boy who'd taken her upstairs, who'd likely roofied her the night she'd gone to the house in search of information. Of course it had been him. He'd had a thing for Harley the very first night they'd gone to Alpha Lambda. And Harley would likely have trusted him if he offered her a ride.

Teagan shoved the papers back into the glovebox, jumped from the car and ran back to Lex.

～

"DID YOU FIND IT?" Lex asked.

"It was Brody."

"Brody Edwards?"

Teagan nodded.

Lex whistled through his teeth. "His dad's a big defense attorney. Shit."

"He'll never admit to it. He's an arrogant bastard. I need to get into his room or—"

"Whoa, hold on." Lex started the car and pulled down the street. "If you're right and he picked up Harley and did something to her, you cannot break into his room. Not only will that compromise a future investigation, if he catches you, he's liable to do whatever it takes to silence you. He's going to Stanford next year to law school. He's already been accepted."

Teagan slapped her hands against the dashboard so hard it stung. "Fuck Stanford. Fuck Brody. I'll kill him. I'll kill him if he hurt her."

Lex said nothing. His lips were pursed in a thin line. "I don't know him well, but... I see him around a lot. I feel like... if he were behind this, if he hurt her, he'd be acting off. You know? He's not. He's totally normal."

"Because he's a psychopath."

"You don't know that."

"He picked Harley up and she's never been seen again."

Lex slowed and pulled to the curb. He turned to face Teagan. "Teagan, you need to take all this information to the police. The tape, the information about the watch at Rho. If Blair still has it, the police can get access to her dorm. It's physical evidence and probably the best shot you have-"

"No. Not yet. I need more."

"Would Harley want you to risk your life trying to play the hero, or would she want you to take the evidence you have and go to the police?"

Teagan glared at him. Harley would want her to go to the

police because Harley would have trusted them to do the right thing. The problem, of course, was they hadn't done the right thing.

"You still don't get it, do you?" Teagan jerked her arm from his grasp, grabbed her backpack and fled from the car.

63

Throughout the following day, Teagan's phone rang and rang. She ignored it, speaking only to her grandma, who she told little of what she'd discovered. Like Lex, her grandma would insist she take the information and go to the police.

Several times people knocked on her door. She suspected Lex, possibly Blair, but she didn't answer.

The rest of the previous sleepless night she'd ruminated on the tape. Blair, directed by Sloan, had worn a mask and frightened Harley so badly she'd fled into the street and climbed into a passing car. How many of the Rho Upsilon Nu girls and Alpha Lambda boys knew and hadn't said a word? How many of them were in on what had happened to Harley after that fateful ride?

All day Teagan contemplated how to confront Brody, how to force him to talk, and she came to the conclusion that nothing short of a direct attack would work. She laid out dark clothes, a black hooded sweatshirt, a can of pepper spray and most importantly her Glock pellet gun.

Teagan held it up in front of the mirror, pointed it. It looked real. That was why her grandma had originally bought it after a string of burglaries in their neighborhood.

Teagan had been the one who enjoyed using the air gun, shooting targets in the backyard, and ultimately it had become hers. A discerning eye might notice it was plastic rather than steel, but it looked real enough, she thought, real enough to scare someone.

Gun tucked into her backpack, Teagan walked down the stairs at Willow Hall.

"Be careful out there," a girl from her floor called. "Tornado warnings. One touched down in Ludington. They said it's headed this way."

"Thanks," Teagan told her.

When she opened the door, the wind gusted so hard it nearly ripped the door from her hand. Teagan shoved it closed, pulled her hood up, and headed for Greek Row.

Unsurprisingly, the lawns were all filled with students. Thursday through Saturday nights seemed to be a non-stop party on the street that housed the fraternities and sororities. The potential tornado seemed only to have amplified the celebratory energy.

Teagan walked into Alpha Lambda and searched for Brody.

After scanning the crowded downstairs and backyard, she hurried to the second floor and paused outside his bedroom door. She opened her phone, clicked on the voice recorder and tucked it into her back pocket. She pushed in his door and walked inside.

Brody looked up from his desk, startled. He appeared different than the previous times she'd seen him. He wore glasses that had dropped toward the end of his nose as he leaned over a notebook, furiously scribbling with one hand as he paged through a textbook with the other. He glanced at her, then returned his eyes to his work. "I'll be down in a few minutes. I have to finish these notes."

Teagan stepped into the room, slid the door closed behind her.

Brody looked up again, pulled off his glasses, then set his pencil down and leaned back. "Okay then. If you're looking for E, I'm fresh out. I might be able to track some down for a little striptease."

"I know you picked her up," Teagan said.

Brody's smile faltered. He seemed unsure whether she was joking and, after a moment more, he realized she was not. "Oh, shit. You're that chick who hangs with Blair. I wouldn't let that psycho in my car if she was unconscious. Didn't you hear what she did at Rho? Trashed the place. She's completely nuts. I tried to give her the benefit of the doubt because Nolan was one of my best friends, but shit... some girls are just crazy."

Teagan stared at him. "What do you mean because Nolan was one of your best friends? What does he have to do with Blair?"

"He was her brother. Duh. Everyone knows that."

"Her bother..." Teagan breathed, unsure what to make of the revelation.

"Yeah. Nolan Davenport, Blair Davenport. It doesn't take a genius to put two and two together."

"You said he *was* her brother?"

Brody let his head fall back, his mouth flopping open as if she were the dumbest girl on the planet. "He's dead. Are you for real right now? Aren't you friends with her? Maybe you're not, huh? I don't blame you. That's the kind of girl you'll wake up to standing above your bed with a butcher knife in her hand. Mark my words-total freak-and not the good kind."

Teagan shook her head, had to think straight, get back to why she'd come.

"Harley," Teagan said. "You picked up Harley."

He screwed up his eyes. "The girl who took off? I can assure you I didn't."

"Blair saw you that night." Teagan heard a door slam down the hallway, the sounds of two guys talking. "Harley ran into the street scared and got into your car."

"I don't have time for this." He stood and moved toward her, tried to nudge her aside, but Teagan, hand already on the gun in her bag, drew it out and pointed it at him.

"Back up," she hissed.

Brody froze, lifted his hands and shuffled backwards, his face a mixture of incredulity and contempt. "You realize you're going to go to jail for this, right?"

"Not me. You. You're going to jail because you picked up Harley and you... you..." She couldn't finish, couldn't speak the words, bitter in the back of her throat.

"I DID NOT PICK UP YOUR FRIEND!" he yelled at Teagan, gesturing with his hands as if doing exaggerated sign language. "Do you have cotton in your ears? Are you a slow learner? She was never in my car."

"Blair saw her get into your car the night she disappeared. It had your Cerberus bumper sticker on the back fender."

Brody sighed, eyes flicking to the gun. She saw something in his face, an expression that said he might rush her. She took a step back and adjusted the gun so it pointed squarely at his face.

"We share my car here at the frat," he said. "The key hangs on the hook by the front door. A dozen guys who live here drive it. I'm not saying it happened, but if it did, I wasn't the guy behind the wheel."

Teagan didn't drop the gun. It could be a lie. He might say anything to escape the room, but what could she do? Shoot him with a pellet? She didn't think it was even loaded. She took another step back, stared at him, searched for that knowing deep in her body, the crack where the truth would spill out. She felt nothing. "It was a Wednesday the thirteenth, a week and half ago. Who would have been driving that night?"

He scowled at her, blew out an angry breath. "The thirteenth," he muttered. "I'm here on Wednesday nights. A group of us who are in pre-law have a study group." His eyes darted to the gun and a bead of sweat rolled from his hairline down the side of his face. "Corbin or Mark. They have evening classes on Wednesday."

"The police will be able to check your story. They'll know," she said.

"Go to the police. I'd happily deal with them over you. Better yet, I'll have my dad reach out to them. He's a defense attorney, probably knows every single one of them."

"Swear it," she said. "Swear to me that you didn't pick up Harley. That you didn't hurt her."

"I don't even know who Harley is. If I hadn't seen her face plastered on every telephone pole on campus, I wouldn't know she existed."

"You hit on her at a party here during welcome week."

He sputtered, then laughed. "Jesus! You're a real piece of work. It'd be easier to single out who I *didn't* hit on during welcome week."

Teagan didn't know if she believed him, but the conversation had not gone as she'd imagined. He'd made no confession, no threats, no incriminating comments.

The seconds stretched and his eyes were now trained on her air gun and she suspected he'd begun to recognize the fake.

Outside a sudden and furious gust of wind rocked the house and through the window something exploded. There was a flash of light and the room went dark.

64

"It's mascot night on Greek Row!" Ginger shouted, dancing through the two lines of girls who'd all put on their Rho Upsilon Nu bracelets, pink with a gold fox wearing a crown. "And I for one am ready to par-tay!"

The other Rhos cheered and clapped.

Blair glanced at Sloan, who she'd been trying to get alone for the last hour. As the groups of girls trickled through the front door headed for the Alpha Lambda house, Blair grabbed Sloan's hand.

Sloan jerked her hand away and glared at Blair. "What?" she demanded.

"Can we talk alone, please? It's important."

Sloan released an irritated sigh, but followed Blair into the living room. Wind pushed against the window panes.

"Teagan found out about the Scream Sister thing. About my chasing Harley," Blair blurted.

Sloan stared at her, face impassive. "And how did she find out exactly?"

Blair had begun to sweat. Her legs were little more than stilts. Her mother had told her to say nothing, to tell no one.

She could not reveal how Teagan had gotten the tape without admitting the part she'd played.

"Blair, let me give it to you straight. Okay? Your sisters have grown wary of you. The Alpha Lambda's think you're certifiable and honestly, I'm sick to death of all your drama. Whatever Teagan thinks she knows will get buried beneath our denials. Understand?"

"But the tape-"

Sloan held up a hand. "Shut up," she fumed through slitted teeth. "Don't you ever mention it again."

Outside a deafening boom exploded in the night and the lights in Rho Upsilon Nu went black.

BLAIR FOLLOWED the mass of girls making their way toward Alpha Lambda. She'd lost Sloan in the crowd and didn't bother trying to find her. Wind whipped the trees and blew debris across the yards. A beach towel hit Blair in the face and she clawed it away, watched it tangle in the branches of a tree.

A guy on the sidewalk yelled, "A transformer blew. Power on the whole block is out."

Blair blinked into the darkness, stopped when she reached the lawn at Alpha Lambda where, despite the sudden commotion, the party continued.

Around her, people began turning on their camera flashlights and holding their phones high as if at a concert.

"Blair!" Corbin made his way to her through the crowd, eyes wide. "How crazy is this?" He had to yell to be heard over the wind.

"Very," she yelled back, wishing she hadn't left her dorm that night, had stayed hidden in her room beneath her heap of blankets.

Corbin peered at her. "Are you okay?"

Blair swallowed, nodded, but tears filled her eyes.

Corbin slipped his arm through hers. "I have candles in my room. Want to go upstairs?"

"Yeah," she murmured.

~

"WHY ARE you being so nice to me?" Blair asked softly, watching Corbin move around his room lighting candles.

He glanced back at her. "Why wouldn't I be nice to you?"

Blair thought of Sloan's words-'the Alpha Lambda's think you're certifiable.' But it wasn't only Sloan. Teagan hated her now too. Her own mother hated her.

And she deserved it.

She thought of Harley's last known night. Blair had stalked her, hidden like a coward beneath the hideous scarecrow mask. And for what? The approval of Rho Upsilon Nu? And now Harley was dead and Blair had chased her into the path of a murderer.

Corbin was the only person who didn't look at her and see someone broken.

Blair touched her bandaged hand. He knew what had happened at the Rho Upsilon Nu house. All the Alpha Lambdas knew. She'd seen it in their faces at the bonfire. Only Corbin continued to look her in the eye, to smile at her, speak to her. The others watched her with a sort of curious repulsion, as if she were a loose cannon. She'd seen the expressions before on people in high school. They wondered how someone so pretty, so normal in appearance, could be so unhinged.

"Everyone screws up, acts out sometimes. We've all been there, even if our fellow Lambdas and Rhos like to pretend we're all perfect. We're not. I'm not, they're not, you're not."

"I find it hard to believe you've ever screwed anything up."

"I have, believe me." He pulled a chair toward the bed and sat right in front of her, their faces inches apart. "You're so beautiful," Corbin murmured.

She stared at him, wanted to believe him, wanted to believe someone in the world existed who could see past everything that was wrong with her.

He played with the ends of her pale hair and then he leaned forward and kissed her. He tasted like beer, smelled like some kind of earthy cologne.

Blair said nothing as he slipped the straps of her dress down, kissed her shoulder.

He stood and gently pressed her back on the bed. He pulled off his shirt and climbed on top of her, pushing her dress up around her hips.

BLAIR STUDIED Corbin's naked body, the rise and fall of his chest. She traced her fingers along his collarbone.

"Tell me," she murmured. "How have you screwed up?"

He turned and gazed at her, reached to wipe a bead of sweat from her temple.

"Where do I begin. In second grade I peed my pants on the jungle gym in front of my whole class. In fifth grade, I lost the school spelling bee on the word recruit." He hooked his index and middle fingers together. "Twisted up the i and u. Who does that? My junior year I got so drunk after prom I threw up in the limo all over my date who was wearing a yellow dress."

Blair smiled. "While all of those sound terrible, I thought there might be something a little more serious. If the worst you've ever done is puke in a limo, I'd almost call you a saint."

He stared at her and some of the color seeped from his face. He blew out a breath and pinched the bridge of his nose.

"Is there something else? Believe me I am the last person who will judge you."

He gazed at her for several more seconds, his eyes troubled as if he couldn't decide whether or not to spill his secrets.

"You can tell me," she whispered.

He closed his eyes, took her hand and held it on his chest. His heart beat softly beneath her palm.

"Your mom helped me a lot my sophomore year. Me and Nolan both. We got into some trouble with a girl. You might have heard of her—Jessica Meyers."

Blair grew still, watched Corbin's eyes shift to the ceiling, felt the thrum of his heart grow faster.

"It wasn't that big of a deal. Everyone does it. It's part of the pledging process and it's not like she was a virgin. But Nolan gave her the drug and when she woke up, she knew something had happened, that she'd been... you know, that a bunch of guys slept with her."

Blair's eyesight grew fuzzy. The candlelight flickered and cast weird shadows on Corbin's face, made it look longer, pointed. She blinked, forced the image away.

"Your mom made the problem go away. She set the whole thing up. Sloan did the scare and when Jessica ran, I picked her up and drove her to where your mom was waiting."

"What did my mom do?" Her voice came out as little more than a whisper. She slowly pulled her hand from Corbin's chest.

Corbin turned, eyes getting big. He sat up. "Blair? Why do you have that look on your face? She didn't hurt her. She scared her off. Gave her some money and a plane ticket and sent her back out west. She was all too happy to take it. Jessica didn't like Husher, didn't fit in."

"But she's still missing. She never made it home."

He shook his head. "That's what she wants people to think, Blair. Your mom's still in contact with her. Jessica sends her a postcard once a year from some other country. She started a new life."

Across the room one of the candles flickered and puffed out. A gust of wind rocked the house and branches scratched the window.

Black spots popped at the corners of Blair's vision and the sound of the storm outside grew muffled.

As fluid as a dream, Blair slipped away, found herself standing in front of the white door that led to the basement at Rho Upsilon Nu.

She twisted the knob, pulled open the door, stepped onto the narrow wooden stairs.

Blair-merely a witness-a voyeur tucked behind the girl's eyes knew what lay ahead, wanted to reach through space and time and shout 'look out!' But it was too late. Two years too late.

The shove came from behind, sent her teetering and then plummeting toward the concrete floor. Pain exploded through her hands and wrists, which had struck with such impact her Minnie Mouse watch snapped and skittered across the floor.

Pain radiated up her arms-surely her right wrist was broken. Stunned, she twisted around and stared at the woman marching toward her.

Blair straddled two worlds. The girl's, whose mind was unspooling-the trauma to her body-the shock of the attack-rendered her incapable of action. And Blair's-who watched her mother whose eyes were as dull as an unpolished black stone and who carried something small and black and sparking.

The vision dissolved and a new one replaced it. The girl came to as the back door of the woman's SUV lifted open. She lay in the fetal position, her broken wrists bound behind her. Blair's mother gripped the girl and dragged her out, forced her to stand.

The girl blinked into the night and stared at a stretch of high grass and corn, a ragged field with no lights, no voices. Except the woman who'd attacked her-she was utterly alone.

"Please," she murmured, *tears rolling down her cheeks. "I swear I won't tell anyone."*

"Shut up and walk," the woman snarled, *prodding her on the back.*

The girl took a step, another and then she ran, bolting for the field.

"Blair? Blair?" Corbin's voice seemed to reach from the dark sky overhead, but already Blair was slipping back, returning to herself.

She stared at him, her skin clammy, body shivering.

"That's why Nolan killed himself," she whispered, rewinding back two years to the first night she'd awoken to the dead girl at her bedside. A dead girl she now realized was Jesscia Meyers. Days before Blair's first visit from the girl, Nolan had called their mother and asked her to come to Husher University. Blair never learned what had compelled him to reach out, but now she understood. He'd had a problem and their mother had taken care of it.

She felt sticky suddenly, not with sweat and semen, but with blood. It shimmered on Corbin's skin and on her own, dripped from his brow line, down his neck.

Corbin sat up taller, ran his hands through his damp hair. "You don't know that's why he did it. He'd been taking those pills, way too many, and drinking. I'm sure he didn't mean to—"

"I told you there was a note," she said sharply, standing from the bed. Had Nolan known what their mother did? Had the guilt led him into his bedroom with a fistful of pills and a bottle of vodka?

Blair snatched her dress from the floor, slid it over her head.

Corbin frowned, as if unsure what had caused her sudden change in mood.

She yanked open the door and then stopped, turning back. "Did you pick up Harley?"

He blinked at her. Another candle flame flickered and went out. "I... Your mom said—"

"Was it you? Did you pick her up that night?"

"She's fine, okay? Your mom helped her. She knows Harley's dad and they set the whole thing up."

For a moment, Blair imagined believing him, believing her mother like he did now. Her mother was a fixer. She'd fixed things, but not the way he thought.

"Harley is dead and Jessica Meyers is dead."

Something twitched near his right eye. Another candle flickered out.

Blair ran from the room, hadn't even bothered finding her shoes. She raced down the stairs and out the front door.

BLAIR WAS NOT EVEN HALFWAY BACK to campus when the stupidity of her choice to run barefoot from the Alpha Lambda house became painfully apparent. Her feet ached. Blisters had formed on the pads of both her feet and every pebble stabbed into the soft center of her foot like a razorblade.

Rain had begun to fall, a warm heavy downpour so hard and fast, Blair had to cup her hands above her eyes to see. She limped along, slowing when a car pulled to the curb beside her. The door flung open and Lex jumped out.

"Blair? You're getting soaked, and where are your shoes?"

Blair gestured feebly back toward Greek Row.

"Come on, get in. I'll give you a ride."

Blair moaned when she slid into the passenger seat and rested her feet on the dry, carpeted floor.

"Where's Teagan? I've been driving for like an hour hoping I'd spot her."

"I don't know. I was with Corbin and..." She almost said the words, revealed what he'd told her, the sickening truth, but it got lodged in her throat.

"Did you know?" Lex asked.

Blair blinked at him, thought suddenly he'd discovered what her mother had done.

He took out his cell phone, clicked an image, and handed the phone to Blair.

65

Teagan wove through the bodies downstairs at Alpha Lambda. They'd begun to turn on their flashlights.

Outside the lawn was filled with students and when she turned toward Rho Upsilon Nu, she saw most of the girls were headed for Alpha Lambda. The Rho house was deserted when Teagan reached it.

She thought of the cabinet of tapes. Was there another one from the night Jessica Meyers had disappeared?

Teagan breezed through the front door, unlocked, no one guarding it. She ran up the stairs to the third floor, found those rooms too still unlocked. Teagan doubted anyone had even noticed she'd opened them.

She hurried through the ritual room, casting a disgusted glance at the cauldron by the window, and slipped into the office, paused at the file cabinet in the closet.

Her phone buzzed.

Teagan looked at it—Lex.

She ignored the call. A text immediately appeared.

Lex: *Check your email. It's important.*

Teagan frowned, turned her attention back to the cabinet and started rifling through folders, searching for the tapes from two years before.

Another message lit up on her phone.

Lex: *URGENT! Stop whatever you are doing and check your email!*

Teagan scowled, closed her message app and opened her email. At the top of her emails, she saw a message from Nate with Lex cc'd.

Subject: Harley's Family Tree

Teagan and Lex,

I found something on Harley's computer. Before she disappeared, she was in contact with a woman named Celeste Cleary—a genetic genealogist who helped Harley build out her family tree. What she found was pretty shocking. See for yourself.

Best,

Nate

Teagan clicked a link and an image started to populate the screen. A basic family tree appeared with boxes labelled for Harley as well as her parents, Robert Thomas and Lisa Rand.

Another line appeared next to Robert's name and beneath it two additional boxes with an arrow, which read 'half siblings.'

"Half-siblings?" Teagan murmured, waiting impatiently for the names to appear on the screen. "Who were they?" Even as she asked the question the names materialized, as did the name of their mother.

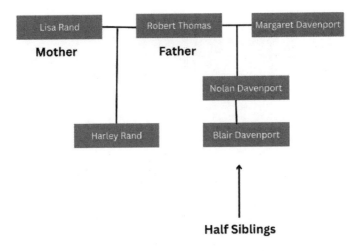

Half Siblings

Across the room, the door swung open.

66

Teagan darkened her phone and tucked herself into the corner of the closet, holding perfectly still. Footsteps moved through the ritual room and paused at the open doorway of the office. She held her breath, imagined Sloan or maybe the Rho Upsilon Nu house mother out there, wondering why the office door was not only unlocked but standing open.

After a moment the door pulled closed and silence resumed.

Teagan sighed, pressed a hand against her heart thumping behind her ribs, and stepped from the closet.

Across the room a figure stood inside the door. In the dark, Teagan could see only their silhouette, and yet she knew she gazed at Blair's mother—Margo Davenport.

"I know everything," Teagan blurted. "I know you're Peggy —Robert Thomas's college girlfriend—and that your children are Robert's biological kids and that." But what did she know? Not that Margo was involved in Harley's disappearance. Or Jessica's.

Something sparked blue in Margo's hand. Teagan started,

tried to make sense of it and then realized Margo held a stun gun.

"It was you," Teagan said, eyes fixed on the stun gun. "You did something to Harley."

The woman didn't speak, and Teagan braced herself. She sensed Margo would soon rush her, and if she tased her and got her unconscious she'd likely never wake up. She'd go to the same place Harley had gone and Jessica before her.

"Why?" Teagan demanded.

Margo said nothing. Her breath came out low and deep, animal-like. Teagan fixed her eyes on the door beside her, knew she'd never get to it. She glanced toward the window, that high third-story window with no balcony, no feasible roof to crawl onto, nothing but a forty-foot drop to the ground.

"It's because she confronted you, isn't it?" Teagan asked. "Harley told you she knew that Blair and Nolan were Robert Thomas's kids-her half siblings."

Teagan's eyes stayed locked on the stun gun, but her mind tripped over the links. It didn't make sense. Had Harley threatened to expose the truth or was Margo just that cold hearted? Had she killed Harley to ensure no one ever knew. Or was it something else that made her kill, the same something that caused her to be implicated In Thomas's murders.

Teagan risked a look at Margos' face and even in the dark, she saw the white of her teeth. Margo was smiling. She wasn't afraid-wasn't filled with horror. Like Robert as he'd leered at Teagan through the bullet proof glass-this woman, this wolf, was reveling in having cornered her prey.

"You're sick," Teagan muttered. "You're sick and you'll never get away-"

Before she could utter the words, Margo darted forward, arm outstretched, stun gun releasing little blue sparks.

Teagan screamed and dove to the side, kicking out a leg. She connected with Margo's arm, but not the one that held the stun gun, and the woman had already turned, twisted toward her.

"Mom! No!" The scream ripped through the room and suddenly Blair was there, barreling into her mother, who shrieked and bared her teeth and tried to whip the stun gun toward Blair's face.

Teagan crawled forward, grabbed one of Margo's ankles and pulled her back, prevented her from reaching her daughter, who'd fallen backwards and landed with a crack that Teagan suspected meant a fractured bone.

BLAIR GASPED as her elbow connected with the wood floor. The pain, unlike anything she'd ever experienced, sent a bolt of searing red light into the center of her skull. Maybe she screamed. She didn't know.

Suddenly her vision was fuzzy, her consciousness liquid, and the door into the room was no longer a plain brown wood. It was a brilliant scarlet and it pulsed and groaned as if something large and angry wanted to break through. Dazed, Blair stared at the throbbing door, the pain a distant memory, the sounds in the room fading.

Margo jerked her ankle from Teagan's grasp and lunged toward Blair.

The scarlet door burst open and shadows poured into the room. Blair watched as they took shape. Girls. Once-pretty girls with long blonde hair whose skin had gone gray or fallen away filled the room, screaming and sobbing.

Margo, who'd been reaching for Blair, inches from shoving the stun gun into her face, faltered as if she too could see the dead girls, hear them, or perhaps, like her daughter, both.

"Peggy," they whispered, their voices sandpaper. "Peggy..."

The door to the room slammed closed. The file cabin

drawers crashed open and shut. Papers burst into the room and filled the air. A picture above the desk fell and shattered.

Blair didn't move, couldn't move.

Someone pounded on the door.

Margo, her eyes void of feeling, turned back to Blair. She bolted forward and pressed the stun gun against Blair's neck. The jolt moved through Blair, fire in her veins. Her body went rigid, her teeth clamped shut and her bladder released.

Teagan screamed and stood, tried to intervene, but the huge wood desk slid across the room and trapped her against the wall.

Margo tased Blair a second time, a third. Spit flew from her lips. She was growling and screaming. "Ungrateful... ungrateful!" she shrieked.

Blair was no longer in her body. She was above watching as the windows exploded, as the papers rained down, as the scarecrow mask flung from the closet and struck Margo in the face.

The swirl of gray-faced girls slipped into Blair's unconscious body. Blair watched herself stand, though she had no control of her limbs, was little more than a whisper in the howling room.

Margo cried out and shrank away from her daughter, who snatched the stun gun from her hand and forced it against Margo's chest.

Teagan sat on the curb. Lex had wrapped a blanket around her shoulders and held her near to him. He'd called the police and the block swarmed with emergency vehicles, lights flashing.

They'd set up spotlights, as the power still hadn't come back on. The lawns, streets and sidewalk were filled with students, their faces turned toward Rho Upsilon Nu.

Both Blair and her mother were gone, rushed away in ambulances.

"I tried to get in," Lex said again. "But the door..."

Teagan nodded. She knew he'd tried, had heard him outside pounding, screaming. She also knew that no one was getting in that room until the girls, those wisps of light and dark, a roiling energy of life stolen, had had their chance at Margo.

∼

WHEN TEAGAN'S grandma arrived her face was ashen, her shoulders slumped.

"It's okay," Teagan told her. "I'm okay."

But her grandma didn't perk up and Teagan waited for the words she sensed were coming.

"Lisa called me on my way here," her grandma said. "This afternoon the Husher Police received an anonymous tip. The caller said they knew the location of Harley's body."

Teagan closed her eyes, felt Lex's arm pull tighter as if she might run.

"They think they found her, but... Lisa can't identify her, so I said I would."

Teagan opened her eyes. They were full, spilling over. "I have to do it. I need to see her."

HOLDING tight to her grandma's hand, Teagan walked down the long dim hallway and stood at the glass that peered into the cold, steel room where the person she'd loved most in the world lay obscured beneath a white sheet.

When the coroner pulled the sheet back, there was Harley.

Teagan's breath hitched as she stared at her friend, who, even in death, was as familiar to Teagan as her own face in the mirror. Harley's eyes were closed, and if Teagan tried really hard she could almost imagine her friend was merely asleep.

"Goodbye, Frog," Teagan murmured as her grandma sobbed quietly beside her. Teagan's own tears rolled like ocean waves down her face and her body shook as if she were adrift on a turbulent sea.

When they emerged from the room, Lisa, Buzz beside her, crumpled to the floor. Teagan went to her, knelt and gathered Harley's mother in her arms.

EPILOGUE

T*hree Weeks Later*

"Do you think Robert knew all along?" Lex asked Teagan.

They sat in A&W drinking root beer floats and talking about all the horrible things that had come to light since Margo's arrest—an arrest largely attributed to Robert Thomas.

Robert had called the Husher police tip line anonymously, but it had been easily traced back to the Marquette Department of Corrections. Robert told investigators he suspected Harley Rand and any other girls who'd gone missing from Husher might be located in an old root cellar on the Doxon farm.

He'd also turned over letters to police-letters that had been going on for years between him and Margo Davenport and though she never confessed to him what she'd done, the innuendos were there. In her most recent letter, which had been dated the day after Harley vanished, Margo had written: 'The wolf took another sheep last night. No matter how hard she tries to be good, the wild in her must be satisfied.'

Teagan remembered her meeting with Robert Thomas, his cold, measuring eyes. Had he already known what Margo had done? Had he encouraged her to do it?

"I don't know. He must have had that letter for days before he called the police."

"There she is," Lex said.

Teagan turned as Blair walked into the restaurant. She'd cut her long blonde hair short and dyed it brown. Teagan barely recognized her.

Blair offered them a nervous smile and walked over.

Lex stood and hugged her. "You look good, Blair," he said. "I'm going to get some curly fries. Give you two some time to talk."

Blair sat across from Teagan. When their eyes met, Blair's filled with tears. "Thank you for the flowers and card in the hospital."

"I was worried," Teagan admitted. "I was really afraid you might not..."

"Wake up?"

Teagan nodded.

"There was a time when I was unconscious when I didn't want to," Blair admitted. "It was so peaceful. I didn't want to come back, but... this is going to sound weird and I hope it doesn't freak you out, but I saw Harley. She said I had to come back."

Teagan slipped back to those long, strange minutes on the third floor of the Rho Upsilon Nu house. The swarm of girls, a glimpse of one who looked like Harley, green eyes and long wheat hair, there and then gone.

"I'm glad she sent you back," Teagan whispered, her own tears breaking loose.

Blair reached into her bookbag, pulled out a notebook and

flipped it open to a face that resembled Jessica Meyers, though in Blair's depiction, the girl's eyes were black, her mouth a yawning hole.

"I was a junior in High School when I started drawing her. Nolan was a freshman here at Husher. I didn't know who she was, but night after night I woke up to her next to my bed— bloody, crying out with no voice.

"One day at school, I was standing in the cafeteria. I'd just gotten my food, and I realize now somebody had called out 'Jessica,' to a girl in my class. And it's like someone shouting her name summoned this Jessica and suddenly she was right in front of me, clawing at me. I screamed and threw my tray at her, except it wasn't her. I hit Miss Rayner, the art teacher. I broke her nose. Blood exploded everywhere.

"It was so terrible and Jessica, the ghost Jessica who'd always been silent, started screaming, and I couldn't hear anything except her screaming and everyone in the lunchroom panicked. I lay on the floor, covered my ears. They ended up calling the police, an ambulance. I spent three weeks in a mental hospital. After that I was 'that girl,' weird, creepy, unstable.

"I'd always had the... visions, visits, whatever you want to call them, but Jessica was the beginning of the really dark stuff —the scary stuff.

"I didn't realize who she was until Corbin told me what he and Nolan and the other Alpha Lambdas had done. And then I understood. Jessica wasn't trying to reach me. I was just the doorway. She wanted Nolan and my mother. They were the ones who hurt her."

"Why didn't you tell me about your brother?" Teagan asked.

Blair sighed, closed her notebook. "My mother erased him and... I let her. It was easier that way, easier not to remember him. There were so many things she asked me to do that I just accepted."

"Since that night at Rho, have you seen any more of the... ghosts?"

"No. I believe, honestly, it's because they were found, Harley and Jessica. They weren't lost anymore."

Lex returned, slid a root beer float in front of Blair and left a basket of curly fries. "Just dropping these off," he said, winking at Teagan.

"Thank you," Blair told him. She pulled the float close, took a drink.

"What about your mom?" Teagan asked. "Has she confessed or-"

"My dad says she's taking a plea deal, whatever that means. Even if she does, the prosecutors might go after her for the murders back in the nineties. At the time, they didn't believe she could have been involved, but now they're giving it a second look."

"What about Robert Thomas? He's still not giving her up?"

Blair shook her head. "He won't talk about the murders he was convicted of. My dad says he operated alone-that my mom couldn't have been involved, but... he's never seen her for what she is."

"He's still defending her after this? She murdered Harley and Jesscia. She tried to kill you. Not to mention she was obviously not faithful to him. Both you and your brother are Robert Thomas's kids."

Blair rubbed her eyes. "I think my mom is telling him she was a victim of Robert. That he'd abused her and even after she married my dad, he'd show up when my dad was at work and force her to..." Blair trailed off. "I don't want to think about it. It's a lie. Everything she says is a lie."

"Have you seen her?"

Blair wrapped her arms across her chest. "I'm going to visit her tomorrow. I'm dreading it."

"I can't even imagine what this is like for you," Teagan murmured.

"Yeah, me neither most days. My dad has been oddly more present, which is especially strange considering he discovered that he's not my biological father. I almost think... maybe he suspected all this time, and now that he has an answer, he can be more open, more himself."

"Harley was your half-sister," Teagan said, still unnerved by that news.

Blair nodded. "Teagan, I am so sorry I chased her that night. If I could change places with her, if it could all be different..."

Teagan wiped her eyes, shook her head. "It can't be."

"Yeah." Blair sighed.

"Blair, do you have any idea why Sloan visited Harley at Curly's the last night she was seen alive?"

Blair fingered her hair, tried to pull a strand long, but let it fall as if realizing yet again she'd cut it short. "I think she went there to confirm Harley intended to walk straight back to her dorm that night. Sloan had lined everything up, I'm assuming at the request of my mother though she never told me that. I was set-up to scare Harley. Corbin was in place to pick her up, and my mom must have been waiting..."

"To kill her," Teagan muttered. "If only Harley had run into the woods, turned the other way. Anything." But Teagan doubted such a maneuver would have saved Harley's life. Margo had made a decision that Harley had to die and would likely have tried again if the first attempt failed.

"Teagan, I'd do anything to turn back time-"

"It's all right," Teagan told her. "I know you never intended for any of this to happen."

"But I shouldn't have lied. If I'd have gone to the police or told you right away..." Blair trailed off.

For a while Teagan said nothing. She wasn't sure she'd completely forgiven Blair for her silence, didn't know if she ever

would, but when she looked at the girl across the table, she saw
flickers of her former best friend and knew she could not turn
her back on her.

"So... ummm... how are you?" Blair asked.

Teagan peered out the window, stared at the outline of
Husher University buildings in the distance, felt that deep ache
that lived with her all the time now. "I'm really sad, but I don't
feel as angry anymore. I'm not sure what that means."

Blair offered a half smile, reached across the table and held
her hand.

BLAIR SAT across from her mother in the county jail. Margo's
face appeared sallow, her hair frizzy.

"Why?" Blair asked.

Margo scoffed, smoothed back her hair, and when she
caught sight of her orange prison jumpsuit, she looked like she
might be sick.

"I did it for you—for you and Nolan. When I was young my
mother was very dramatic. 'Oh, you'll be the death of me,' she'd
yell anytime me and my siblings displeased her. And only
when you and your brother came into the world did I understand. Even in the womb, children drain their mothers. Like
little vampires you both were, taking, taking until there was
nothing left, and what did I do? I kept giving, of course.
Married a man I didn't love to ensure a decent life for you.

"When Nolan got into trouble with that girl, I took care of it.
Me." She jabbed a finger at her chest. "And how did he repay
me? He committed the ultimate act of betrayal. The ultimate
humiliation for me. He took his own life. What do you think
people said? I'll tell you what they said. That I was a terrible
mother. That I failed him."

"Did he know? That you killed Jessica?"

"It was an accident," Margo snapped, glancing toward the cameras and then twisting around to give the guard near the door a dirty look. "He made his choice, and I would not let him ruin our lives, mine and yours. I picked up the pieces, and I moved on." She released a hysterical laugh. "I moved on for my beautiful insane daughter. Because that's what people said about you, Blair. That you belonged in an institution. That you saw things that weren't there. But do you think I listened to them? No. I was determined to give you a great life, an extraordinary life." She steepled her hands together in front of her, caught sight of her chipped fingernail polish, and grimaced.

"You murdered two people to give Nolan and I great lives? You're the one who's insane, Mother."

"I did not murder anyone!" Her eyes again darted toward the cameras. "Harley had an accident, and yes, I concealed her body to protect you."

"You killed her because she found out that Robert Thomas was our biological father. You were afraid Dad would leave you if he knew."

"Is that what you think? I feared your father would leave me? Think again little girl. No one leaves me. No one."

Blair stared at her mother, at the woman whose control she'd lived under for so long, who even now treated her as little more than a possession.

"That's where you're wrong," Blair said. "Goodbye, Mother." Blair stood and walked to the guard by the door. She stepped from the room without looking back.

THEY SAT TOGETHER, Teagan, Blair, Lex and Nate, in the lounge room at the *Husher Student Newspaper* watching on television the mass exodus from the houses of Rho Upsilon Nu and Alpha

Lambda. The sorority sisters and fraternity brothers carried their suitcases and totes out of the houses. Some of them were crying, others looked shocked. At Rho, Sloan was absent, as was her mother. At Alpha Lambda, there was no sign of Corbin.

The police didn't yet know how much the sorority and the fraternity knew about what had happened to Jessica Meyers and Harley Rand. The police interviews with the students had begun weeks before and would continue for months. Not only were police considering the possibility both Greek houses had been aware of, or played a part in, the murders, there were mounting sexual assault allegations against Alpha Lambda and accusations that sisters at Rho Upsilon Nu had assisted the fraternity in drugging victims and covering up the assaults.

Margo's sentencing date hadn't been set, and although she'd pleaded guilty to second-degree murder, there would be other trials.

Old blood spatter had been found in the basement at Rho Upsilon Nu in the area where Blair had discovered Jessica Meyers' watch. Police suspected Margo had killed her there, though how she'd managed to commit the murder and get her out of the house without help and without anyone in the sorority knowing was unclear.

The campus was rife with rumors about who at Rho Upsilon Nu might have assisted in the cover-up, a murder apparently committed for the sole purpose of preventing Jessica Meyers from going to the police about the sexual assault at Alpha Lambda. For all the brothers and sisters of Alpha Lambda and Rho Upsilon Nu, the future looked bleak.

"I better get going," Blair said, eyes lingering for another moment on the television. "I joined that sculpture group and we're meeting in a half hour."

"I have to go, too," Teagan agreed. "My shift at the library starts in twenty minutes."

Lex stood, pulled Teagan against him, and kissed her

goodbye.

"Don't get all mushy on me," she said. "I'll see you in a few hours."

"I like getting all mushy on you." He nuzzled his face into her neck.

"Eight o'clock at the Den for dinner?" Blair asked.

"We'll be there," Lex said, squeezing Teagan closer.

"I have to get tomorrow's paper ready to go out," Nate explained. "And then I'll walk over. I might be a few minutes late. There's a lot to cover in this issue."

On the television, the image changed to one of a reporter running up behind a red SUV. The reporter caught Sloan off guard as she was climbing from the passenger seat of her mother's car.

"How much did Rho Upsilon Nu know about the murders of Jessica Meyers and Harley Rand? And what do you have to say about documents outlining extensive hazing rituals inspired by the serial killer Robert Thomas and approved by you, the president of Rho Upsilon Nu?" the reporter asked, shoving a microphone in Sloan's face.

Sloan stared with dark, unfeeling eyes at the reporter, then shifted her gaze to the camera. "No comment."

She turned on her heel and followed her mother into the attorney's office.

IT HAD BEEN an emotional day for Teagan as she, along with Lisa and her grandma, packed up Harley's things and moved them out of the dorm. The picture of Frog and Toad stayed, the shot glasses, and a few of Harley's clothes that Teagan couldn't bear to part with.

After Lisa and her grandma left, Teagan sat alone in the room. She was drained and needed to shower and get ready for dinner with Lex. He was taking her out to a restaurant he insisted had the best tacos in Michigan.

She opened the closet and searched for Harley's Husher University sweatshirt, which she'd kept. She found it on a hanger in the far back and realized they'd missed a vintage canvas bag Harley had bought at a thrift store years before. Teagan pulled it out. It smelled of the little lavender satchels Harley used to sneak into drawers that suffered from the musty odor of age.

As she carried it into the room, something crumpled inside. Teagan opened the bag and peered in to see several letters. She sat and pulled them out. The first two were addressed to Ella Thomas and had been sent to a P.O. Box in Baldwin. The return address was the Marquette Department of Corrections.

Teagan held the letters for a long time, her fingers growing clammy on the paper. Finally, she pulled one out and started to read.

Dear Ella,

Thank for you for writing. I suspected when you visited you were not who you claimed to be, but I understand the desire for anonymity. As I'm sure you're aware, I too wore many masks.

As for staying the course and attending Husher, I respect your choice, though I should warn you. There are people there who will not have your best interests at heart. Perhaps you won't trust this advice coming from a man such as myself, but you'd do well to heed it.

If you do attend Husher and rush a sorority as you mentioned you intend to do, might I recommend Chi Omega or Delta Gamma? Remember, I know the Greek community at Husher and, having met you, I suspect you will be better placed in a sorority that is nurturing rather than punishing.

I'll say no more. As you yourself mentioned, you'd made it eigh-

teen years without my advice and can't imagine needing it now.

I hope you don't.

Please consider writing again. I have enjoyed our correspondence.

Sincerely,

Robert

TEAGAN FROWNED AT THE LETTER. It did not sound like the man she'd met, who'd been so vile and mean. She opened the next envelope and withdrew the letter.

DEAR ELLA,

I was elated you wrote me again until I realized you had discovered news of your half-siblings. I do not know these children anymore than I know you, but I'm aware of their existence. Their mother is my twin flame. For better or worse, we are bound in ways you cannot begin to comprehend. I hope you never find yourself in such an ill-fated coupling.

I am not one to plead, but I will humble myself for your benefit. DO NOT CONTACT HER OR HER CHILD. There is only one child who remains. The other took his own life.

She is a wolf and she will devour you. Do not take this warning lightly. There are predators and prey in this world. I have been intimately acquainted with both, and though this will insult you, it is not meant as an affront. There were many times I longed to be a more feeling soul. Sadly, I am not and neither is she. She is a huntress and if she becomes aware of your knowledge, you will become the hunted.

I can imagine you reading this letter, disregarding my counsel, believing perhaps I want only to lead you astray.

Evil is closer than you think. Tread carefully.

Sincerely,

Robert

. . .

THERE WAS one final letter addressed to the Marquette Correctional Center from Harley. It was stamped, but she hadn't sent it.

DEAR ROBERT,

As I'm sure you can understand, it is difficult for me to believe you. I've spent these last months reading about your crimes, learning about all the horrors you committed when you were not much older than me. It's almost incomprehensible.

Even during the hardest parts of my life, and there have been plenty, I have always rested in the belief that good triumphs over evil. Despite the terrible things you did, I still believe there is good in you.

I know in my heart that someday I will die still believing that. You might be telling me the truth about your so-called 'twin flame,' but I believe there is good in her too.

I recently met my half-sister. How strange to look into eyes so like my own and not be able to share the secret that connects us. We belong in each other's lives. Our serendipitous meeting proves it. But I don't want to ruin the marriage between her parents. I am the product of a broken and dysfunctional home. I would never wish that on another person.

Which is why I will first speak to her mother, and if she insists I say nothing, I will consider her reasons for demanding the lie live on.

I'm tired of all the lies. I've told my own these last months and they haunt me. But soon the truth will come to light because that is how we extinguish the dark.

Perhaps the next time I visit, if there is a next time, my sister will join me.

Peace be with you,
Harley

THE TRUE STORY THAT INSPIRED THE SCREAM SISTERS

In 1987, the paths of Paul Bernardo, a handsome and seemingly successful man from Canada, and Karla Homolka, an attractive teenage girl, crossed. Despite their outward appearances, the couple would later become infamous as the "Ken and Barbie Killers." Bernardo, initially a popular figure in Toronto, harbored dark fantasies of rape and torture. Homolka not only accepted but actively encouraged these violent inclinations.

Their crimes escalated when, in 1990, they plotted to sexually assault Homolka's 14-year-old sister, Tammy, who tragically died during the assault. The couple continued their spree, kidnapping and murdering Leslie Mahaffy in 1991 and Kristen French in 1992. The details of these crimes were gruesome, involving rape, torture, and murder.

Homolka, after confessing to her family, struck a plea deal, testifying against Bernardo in exchange for a reduced sentence. Bernardo was convicted of multiple rapes and two murders, while Homolka served a shortened sentence for manslaughter. Her release in 2005 sparked public outrage in Canada.

The case continues to raise ethical questions about justice, punishment, and the lasting impact of notorious crimes on a community.

For a more in depth look at the 'Ken and Barbie Killings,' visit my website jrericksonauthor.com

ALSO BY J.R. ERICKSON

Dark River Inn
Helme House
Darkness Stirring
Ashwood's Girls
Still Falling
Flowers in Her Bones
Black Hollow Hideaway
Grave Devotion
After She Fled
The Scream Sisters

Or dive into the completed eight-book stand-alone
paranormal series:
The Northern Michigan Asylum Series

ACKNOWLEDGMENTS

Many thanks to the people who made this book possible. Thank you to Team Miblart for the beautiful cover. Thank you to RJ Locksley for copy editing The Scream Sisters. Many thanks to Will St. John for beta reading the original manuscript, and to Emily H. And Saundra W. for finding those final pesky typos that slip in. Thank you to Jessica Meyers for offering up her name as a character in this novel. Thank you to my amazing Advanced Reader Team. Lastly, and most of all, thank you to my family and friends for always supporting and encouraging me on this journey.

ABOUT THE AUTHOR

J.R. Erickson, also known as Jacki Riegle, is an indie author who writes ghost stories. She is the author of the Troubled Spirits Series, which blends true crime with paranormal murder mysteries. Her Northern Michigan Asylum Series are stand-alone paranormal novels inspired by a real former asylum in Traverse City.

These days, Jacki passes the time in the Traverse City area with her excavator husband, her wild little boy, and her three kitties.

To find out more about J.R. Erickson, visit her website at www.jrericksonauthor.com.